Mean to Meaningful

Mean to Meaningful

Edward B. Wile

Second Edition

ISBN: 1539873439
ISBN 13: 9781539873433
Library of Congress Control Number: 2016918351
CreateSpace Independent Publishing Platform
North Charleston, South Carolina

Author Endorsements And Comments

Football is a contact sport which was easy and natural to Ed. However, he was short on social graces and southern etiquette. As best man in his wedding to his elegant and beautiful wife, Vickey Key, I quickly learned that direct is best with Ed—I told him to quit bitching and just do what you're told. I personally saw him transform from an angry young man to a successful business leader, caring husband, father, and community leader. Ed Wile's story is an inspiration for anyone who has obstacles to overcome.—**Jerry Richardson, Founder and Principal Owner, Carolina Panther**

Edward Wile is the greatest man I know. He leads by example and had an impact over thousands of people, some of whom he will never know. His humble beginnings molded his character, and his chance encounters in Spartanburg, South Carolina, shaped his life. His life is a testament to never giving up despite the odds, learning from your mistakes, and always wanting to do your best for the benefit of others. Everyone has a hero, someone they aspire to be; for me, that's Edward Wile, and lucky for me, I get to call him "Dad."—**Chip Wile, President, Daytona International Speedway**

Ed is the toughest nice guy I have ever met, with a wife that can smooth over anything. If I ever had an issue to ponder, his voice was the one I wanted to hear. Ed's life story should be required reading for anyone facing adversity.—**Albert Harris, Private Investor, Inventor and Entrepreneur**

This is more than an autobiographical rags to riches story. It is a story of a young Great Gatsby who goes from Ohio poverty to Mount Kilimanjaro; it is the critical shaping influence of a southern belle and complicated family crisis; it is football and NASCAR; it is business management and entrepreneurship, manufacturing and sales; it is leadership. Primarily it is a lifelong story of personal growth enabled by self-criticism and the impact of lives of other human beings, big and small. This story has multiple levels of insight for a wide range of readers.—**Joe Lesesne, Retired President, Wofford College**

Ed Wile has been my friend, brother in law, and golf partner for almost thirty years. His memoir is a riveting story of human perseverance and the successful ability to rise above life's obstacles. It is simultaneously inspirational and educational and a must read from my perspective.— **Tommy Millner, Chief Executive Officer and Director, Cabela's Inc.**

Ed Wile is a winner and the ultimate competitor. Whether it is on the athletic field or boardroom or in family life, he can show you how to get it done. He was a joy for me to coach, and his leadership and outstanding play led Wofford College to some of its most successful seasons in its football history. Give me a team of Ed Wiles, and we will whip anybody. You will enjoy reading how his successful life draws on his experiences from the gridiron, in everyday business and personal challenges in everyday family life. This is really a great read that will inspire you to be successful in all phases of your life even though the odds don't seem great. The people and their influence in Ed's life deserve a lot of credit, and you will enjoy getting to know them. This book is Ed's way of giving back and can show you how you can be a success in all areas of responsibility in your life. Ed Wile is a winner, and from this book you can learn what it takes to be one.—**Fisher DeBerry, Retired Head Football Coach, Air Force Academy**

Inspiration comes in many forms. Sometimes from where you least expect it. That is the life story of Ed Wile, and he tells it beautifully in this must read autobiography. With a multitude of reasons for failure and few for success, Ed's story is one of perseverance and determination. And one that provides hope and inspiration for all.—**Danny Morrison, President, Carolina Panthers**

This book is vintage Ed Wile. From the candor and reality of his incredible journey through life to his descriptions of those people around him to whom he gives all the credit, always others. Through this book, you become familiar with the man, a remarkably caring man, a man of purposeful living, a man of unique and significant talents and accomplishments. Many of us have modeled our lives after Ed and, importantly, Vickey. For me and my wife, and I suspect many others, that is probably the most significant lesson herein: love without limits, care without the expectation of credit. His, for sure, has been a life abundantly lived for the greater good.—**Harold Chandler, Chairman, Milliken & Company**

I have walked the journey with Ed for over thirty years as we entered and matured in the financial services industry together. I have appreciated his friendship and sense of humor through our many challenges of global investing. Ed's unique desire to help others through a lifetime of experiences, his compassion for the underdog, his competitive spirit, and his wisdom have benefited me and many others in our firm. This book is a reflection of his life's work.—**Allen Wright, Senior Vice President, UBS**

Firing him was the best thing I did for his career.—**Ernest D. Key Jr., Retired Chairman, Atlanta Belting Company**

I am humbled to write an endorsement for Ed Wile. I met Ed in 1990 and have watched with great appreciation his ability to balance a career, business, and family. He serves as a mentor in my life. His story is the quintessential example of the life changing opportunity that college athletics provides for young people. His story also offers great insight into redemption, the power of unconditional love, and, most importantly, family.—**Charlie Cobb, Director of Athletics, Georgia State University**

Ed and I have been friends for over forty-five years. He is a man who has great talents that required much time to develop and mature. His persistence and hard work are character traits he learned long ago, and they have served him well. He made two great decisions early on. The first was his decision to attend Wofford College, and the second was marrying the perfect woman to nurture his possibilities.—**William S. Ervin III, MD, Practicing Physician**

Ed and I met at Kiawah Island after he retired from UBS. My instincts told me that his journeys in life run deep. He is a unique person with a subtle but edgy confidence. From our many golf outings, I discovered that he was a gracious and intense competitor. It was clear that he was a great teammate. Through our discussions, it was obvious that he has a serious passion and love for his friends, wife, and family. After wading in the shallow waters of his journey, I cannot wait to read the book and jump into the deep water.—**Don Ashbaugh, Retired Area President, NVR Inc.**

Ed was my first leader in business. He proved to me that with great perseverance and hard work you can reach your highest goals. His rise from the streets to a successful business executive is a true life miracle. He learned during his business success that family emotions are a powerful motivator.—**Karl Cone, Regional Branch Manager, Ram Tool & Construction Supply**

This is an extraordinary story of catharsis and redemption, of a life transformed. It is an inspiring lesson of the value of living life not by the constraint of pain and anger, but rather by the power of paying forward kindness. —**Nayef Samhat, President, Wofford College**

A remarkable American story of personal growth and success...the transformation of a troubled youth into a caring husband and father and an executive whose success benefited many...from the homeless to the institution he attended. An inspiring story.—**Edmund W. Jones, DDS, Retired Oral Surgeon**

Ed's story should be an example for all of us. His life is one of tenacity, determination, successes, but most of all, it is a life about love. Although Ed's achievements are many, I will always know him best for the love and care he has for others. Though a leader in an industry that seemed to face one crisis after another, Ed was never too busy to lend a helping hand, mentor a peer, and, most importantly, make time for his beloved family. He may have been known by many as a tough and driven businessman, but those who knew him best understood what really mattered most to him, and that is what is so inspirational about Ed's life.—**Jerry Johnson, Managing Director, UBS**

Working with Ed for over eight years, I observed his exceptional drive, tenacity, and relentless commitment to achieve his clients' financial goals. Ed Wile exemplifies the phrase "His word is his bond."—**Larry D. Radford, Retired Managing Director, UBS**

Eddie has always been a brother whom I greatly admired. Watching him grow up through the years has been amazing. He always had a chip on his shoulder, but you would have never known it after all he has accomplished. He is a good husband, father, and businessman. I know that Grandma is smiling down on him. His adventures and accomplishments prove that dreams really can come true.—**Diana Montgomery, Retired United States Air Force**

Having witnessed the business successes and personal trials shared in this book firsthand, I can attest that this story should be required reading for anyone who needs an example of overcoming the reality and harshness of life. The nuggets of wisdom shared through Ed's stories, his "God winks," are inspirational and educational. For those who need an example to follow, a path to leadership and success, your road map can be found inside the pages of this book.—**Harris Gignilliat, Senior Vice President, UBS**

Ed Wile's story is one of perseverance, passion, and inspiration. I have had the honor to share and witness Ed's amazing life journey for over forty years.—**Mackie Horton, Chief Operating Officer, ELI Inc.**

Everyone is tested time and time again throughout life. Ed Wile shows us all that, regardless of what the circumstances are, with the affection of a few good people and some real determination, you can make it to the top. If you don't believe that behind every good man stands a good woman, read this book.—**Joe Taylor, Former Secretary of Commerce of South Carolina**

Ed Wile has stood side by side with our coaches and professors to help Wofford students become the best they can possibly be. Students need role models and inspiration—they need to understand that anything is possible with hard work, dedication, commitment, and the right educational foundation. Ed serves as this inspiration to countless student athletes...plus more than a few adults. His love for Wofford and our mission is unprecedented, and his story inspires our students to *reach higher*.—**Richard Johnson, Athletic Director, Wofford College**

An amazing man's story of change, growth, determination, and perseverance. Insight into his life story of hard beginnings to incredible "God wink" moments along the way to becoming a leader and mentor in his industry and to the people around him. You will gain much wisdom and knowledge as well as respect for the man.—**Laura Wellon, Senior Vice President, UBS**

Mean to Meaningful is today's *Angela's Ashes*—a true story of despair that becomes hope, and hope that finally brings inward peace and success. It is the journey of a tough kid who fights his way from the streets to the boardroom and into the hearts of readers who can embrace this book.**—Gregory L. Vistica, Founder, Chairman, and CEO, Washington Media Group**

Growing from a need to fight for his life and any future, to a life where he would become a fighter for his marriage, family, and others in need, this is an inspiring story of how God places people and circumstances in life not just to change their lives, but to give them the chance to truly impact the lives of others.**—Jim Reese, President and CEO, Atlanta Mission**

This is the true life story of a friend who has been up and down the hills of life. He has proved that perseverance, hard work, and the ability to follow his star toward its true light will bring success and happiness. This book, so honestly written, will inspire readers to face their own challenges with new insight and the determination to get up and keep going— and then, like Ed Wile, to turn and give back to others.**— Harriet Sessoms, Devoted Wife, Mother and Grandmother**

An honest, gritty account of a troubled youth who escapes a bleak future and his own demons through sports opportunities, the love of the right woman, and the encouragement of adults who believed in his potential. Ed's inspiring journey ultimately provided success and valuable life lessons, as he learned to be a devoted husband, proud father, business mentor, and supporter of his community and those less fortunate—truly a transformational story.**—Walter McClelland, Founding Partner, Mabry and McClelland**

Ed Wile looks back from the perspective of a life well lived from boyhood in the streets of the postindustrial Midwest to adulthood in the elegant New South, from the gridiron to the boardrooms of business, nonprofits, and academia. In an era lacking in personal responsibility, Ed lays out the eternal truth of self-reliance. Giving full credit to those who helped him on his journey and acknowledging his mentors, he clearly asserts that ultimately one must depend on oneself. This not a business memoir of the "how to succeed" variety. Rather, it is an extremely frank dissection of one man's life and one couple's marriage, with the realization that no one, irrespective of apparent outward success, gets out of life free. Joy is almost invariably accompanied by pain and suffering. However, ultimately the message is optimistic: character is paramount and provides the inner strength to overcome the many obstacles in our lives.—**George S. Tyson, MD, Retired Cardiovascular Surgeon**

I first met Ed Wile in 1969 during Wofford College summer football practice. He was a very angry young man from Wooster, Ohio. Ed stayed angry for most of the years we shared at Wofford. Fifteen years after we graduated, our paths crossed again as business professionals. Time had changed Ed. He had become a polished investment consultant, and the anger had subsided. Today he is one of my closest friends and a fellow trustee of Wofford College. His life story is an amazing testimony of how "God winks" change our lives.—**Mike James, Retired Founder and General Partner, Wedge Capital Management**

Ed has been a dear and close friend for over thirty years. His ability to overcome his humble beginnings and struggles to get where he is today is truly a rags to riches story. To understand Ed's successes and accomplishments is to appreciate the compassion, determination, and focus he brings to whatever he undertakes. Having Vickey by his side to share in the highs and the lows of the journey has made him the person that he is today.—**Chel Tanger, Retired Partner, PWC**

I know that I have always been Ed's favorite uncle. He had many obstacles to overcome as a child, but with the loving guidance of a grandmother and the fact that he excelled in sports, which was a big factor in his life, he survived and eventually thrived. As I watched him grow up, I always felt that there was something special in Eddie, and I knew it was up to us to bring it out. He left for college with his high school football coach, which was a good choice. Later in life, Ed told me that he realized how much his coach, Jack Peterson, had done for him. When he met Vickey, his wife to be, she became his number one encourager. When he excelled in business, his two children and seven grandchildren came right along with him, and today his family is a big part of his life. I am proud to be considered his favorite uncle, but behind all of this I'm sure that there was a much higher power at work.—**Virgil Nelson, Retired Production Manager,** *Daily Record*

Readers of this book will come to know and love Ed Wile. He tells his life story with emotion and honesty. It is a story of replacing frustration with achievement and anger with gratitude. We became friends at Wofford College, where I was a member of the faculty and he was a student in my classes. His football coach, Jack Peterson, knew the person Ed could become, and he encouraged him to attend Wofford. Ed's motivation at the time was to escape from poverty and an unpromising future. But he accomplished much more than that. He brought spirit, energy, and intelligence; he learned how to achieve; and he moved into the world with confidence. He conquered personal and professional challenges. The results are a loving family, financial success, and leadership in boardrooms, and community. Today he is at peace, his heart is filled with appreciation, and his joy is in empowering others to create productive lives. His story will change you. You will not forget Ed Wile.—**Dan B. Maultsby, Retired Professor, Senior Vice President for Academic Affairs and Dean, Wofford College**

Ed Wile has been climbing mountains his whole life; he just did not know it. Long before Kilimanjaro, he had conquered many of life's mountains: poverty, anger, fear, and doubt. By the grace of God and the strong love of a lady named Vickey and the sport of football, he was able to discover the really important things in life. His motto of "Just show me the way" has served him well, and the journey has been blessed. This story is about helping others climb their mountains. I have known Ed for over two decades, and I cherish our friendship. I wish him and Vickey and their family God's continued blessings. Keep climbing.—**Mike Ayers, Head Football Coach, Wofford College**

Preface

This is a story about a little boy born under a dark cloud in a sleepy town. The thrill of sports eventually awakens the child, but a mean streak emerges resulting in a reckless, angry, insecure, confusing, and challenging childhood. Absent the care, influence and guidance of a few special coaches this story probably ends in a graveyard.

During college, a caring young woman enters the picture and battles to reset his faulty compass. They marry, and her impact is nothing short of a miracle. This autobiographical account candidly shares a lifetime of unlikely experiences, obstacles, and challenges that reveal many meaningful personal, parental, and business discoveries.

You might appreciate this book as a rags to riches story, or you could use the meaningful content as a user's guide for chasing greatness. Regardless of your agenda, there is something here for you. As my friend Jerry Richardson said, "This story is an inspiration for anyone who has obstacles to overcome."

However, let it be perfectly clear that I am writing this book for my children and grandchildren. The purpose is to share living mistakes, learning experiences, and precious wisdom from the school of hard knocks to educate, inspire, and engage them to be better citizens of the world. I want them to understand how important it is to challenge themselves to do and to be their best.

This is my first book, and you will quickly discover that I am a simple man with a small vocabulary and unsophisticated writing skills. In spite of these limitations, I hope that you will enjoy the journey.

One

CURIOUS

Uncertainty is the refuge of hope.

—Henri-Frédéric Amiel

We arrived at the Dik Lodge shortly after lunch to make our final preparations. We met with Vendelin Tarimo, who would be our senior guide. He was a tall, thin, well-educated man who spoke fluent English. Right away, you knew he was different. We would discover from the other guides and porters along the way that he was among the best on the mountain. We spent an hour or so reviewing the checklist and discussing expectations. As we concluded our meeting, I said, "I feel like we are well equipped for this journey, but it is clear to me that our personal safety and the trip's success rest squarely on your shoulders. I must ask, can we depend on you to take care of us and to show us the way?"

He smiled broadly, said yes, and shook his head to affirm his response. He then told us that breakfast would be available starting at five in the morning, that we should be in the lobby with our gear ready to go at six, and that the drive to the mountain would take about two hours.

After the meeting, Vickey and I had a nice dinner and retired to our room. We went to bed early but slept very little and were both up early. After breakfast, we anxiously boarded the bus with our twenty-three porters and two guides, and before we knew it, we were on our way to the mountain.

On the drive, the porters joked with each other in their local Swahili tongue. We had no idea what they were saying, but from their interactions it appeared they enjoyed being together. We would learn that the mountain was where they socialized, as they rarely saw one another at home in their crowded villages. Most of them climbed at least twice a month, and knowing that they were seasoned professionals went a long way toward easing our anxieties. When we arrived at the mountain, our guides went to the park ranger's office to authenticate our climbing credentials while the porters unloaded the camping gear and food. We were witnessing a well-oiled machine in action, and it was clear that this was not their first rodeo.

It was Sunday evening, July 20, 2014. We had been hiking, climbing, and camping for a week when we reached the base camp. We were exhausted from the long, grueling days of hiking from dawn to dusk. As we climbed into our sleeping bags, we hugged and agreed that we would abandon the climb if either of us was unable to continue. We were not quitters, but this was a bucket list adventure, and we wanted to complete the experience together or not at all. Vickey reminded me that prior to this trip we had never slept in a sleeping bag or camped in a tent.

During the next twenty-four hours, we would face the most difficult challenges of the trip. We would get a few hours of sleep and then begin our hike to the top of the mountain, which should take about eight hours. We would have to climb four thousand feet in elevation and hike over five miles. If we were able to reach the summit, we would have a snack, enjoy a brief celebration, take some pictures, and then hike back down to our next camp. Depending on the weather and our physical stamina, it would take another six hours.

At eleven o'clock, in the middle of the night, we crawled out of our sleeping bags, dressed in our warmest clothes, and emerged from the small two person pup tent that had been our home for the past week. We had a quick snack, filled our water bottles, and strapped on our headlights and backpacks. I felt the freezing cold on my face and saw that our tent was covered in ice. The guides pointed us to the trail leading to Uhuru Peak, the top of Mount Kilimanjaro. With an elevation of 19,341 feet, this peak is known as the "Roof of Africa" and is the tallest freestanding mountain in the world. With great anticipation and against all odds, we forged ahead.

The trip had taken a heavy toll on my aging body. As we began the ascent, I knew from the start that I would be challenged to complete the climb. Up until then, I had believed I was bulletproof and could do anything. I had casually prepared for the hike and was in relatively good physical condition, but the difficulty of the climb was much more than expected, and I struggled. To make things even worse, I lost my appetite and rarely got more than a few hours of sleep each night due to the high altitudes.

Vickey, on the other hand, was in top physical condition. She diligently worked out every day and had hiked the local mountains in Georgia to prepare for this adventure. She was clearly more prepared than me. I never said anything to her because I knew she would worry. I just put on a smile and headed up the steep, dark trail into the stars.

Our guides told us that few people completed this grueling journey, and on day two, we were quite surprised to discover that we were the oldest climbers on the mountain. On day four, we learned that one of the young climbers in a group from Russia had died during the night, further evidence of the danger and difficulty of this bold bucket list experience.

During the week, we hiked from the bottom of a majestic mountain through a beautiful rain forest, weaved our way through arctic deserts, and learned the art of rock scrambling. The journey challenged our physical conditioning and mental endurance. We slept each night in a small tent under an enchanting canopy of stars and rose each day to a majestic sunrise with Mother Nature's magic all around us. We trusted others to lead us while braving the rocks, sand, altitude, cliffs, rain, ice, and cold.

I was exhausted and ached all over when I suddenly realized that, in so many ways, this climb symbolized my life's journey. I pushed on and was comforted to know that this experience and it's once in a lifetime memories would belong to us regardless of the final outcome.

I was born on a cold, snowy morning in Wooster, Ohio, a small town in northeastern Ohio. I grew up on North Street, a modest neighborhood, where most of the neighbors worked in the local factories.

My biological parents had to get married. They were just youngsters who, I imagine, still suffered from the dreaded perils of acne. One thing that they had in common was uncontrollable teenage hormones. Unfortunately, a reckless moment of passion drastically changed their destinies.

When I was born, my parents were living with Grandma at her home on McDonald Street. My father, Wilbur Edison Wile, was the middle child with an older sister and a younger brother. He was a small, thin man with black hair who worked as an auto mechanic at the local Chevrolet dealer. My mom, Joan Elizabeth Little was a petite woman, the youngest of three girls. At the time she worked as a waitress at the Farm Dairy restaurant, a popular local diner.

Mom lost her father to a tragic accident at the age of five and was raised by her mother. Apparently, Mom struggled as a child. She had a minor speech impediment, which caused her to believe she was dumb. It showed up in her personal behavior. She was—and still is—a quiet and shy person. The truth is that she is actually a very smart woman and sometimes "slow plays" situations to make a point or to get her way.

According to Mom, marriage was not what she expected. "There was seldom a happy time. Your dad was enrolled in the National Guard, and shortly after we married, his unit was called up. He went to boot camp in Louisiana and got sick. He had trouble breathing, and it was so severe that he was transported to Denver, Colorado, to the veterans' hospital, where they removed a portion of his lung. He was medically disabled and honorably discharged. During that time, I had no car nor any means of transportation. I was making a monthly car payment with my waitressing tips, but the car was sitting in his parents' garage. I was very pregnant and walked back and forth to work. It was wrong, and I was angry, but had no voice in the matter. As it turned out, I never had a voice in anything because his parents, especially his mother, made all of our decisions. She treated me like I was stupid, and I resented her condescending behavior."

Shortly after I was born, my parents left Grandma's house and moved into a small apartment and then another and another and another. Mom said, "As a married couple and parents, I thought that it was time to get our own place. It seemed like a good idea, but the apartments were dreadful, and we never lived anywhere more than two or three months. When Wilbur finally moved out, your sister Diana was a newborn, and you were still in diapers. It was a shitty time—no pun intended."

Because of the circumstances, I got to spend a lot of time with Grandma. She was the built in babysitter, teacher, caretaker, and general support system. She would not allow us to sleep in the streets or go hungry on her watch. This was a blessing. She loved and cared for my mother very much, but over the years I often heard them trade many harsh words. Grandma was quick to administer tough love, but regardless of the situation or circumstances, she was always present.

My grandmother's name was Laura Elizabeth Little. She was a well-regarded lady with distinctive, long red hair, and I remember she always smelled good. She was a seamstress, and she could make just about anything. She was well known for her beautiful quilts. She always wore a dress and had a pleasant but firm demeanor. Some of my fondest memories as a young child were with her. When we spent the night at her house, she would make it a point to come into the bedroom and tuck me in. We would say our prayers together—you know, the "Now I lay me down to sleep, I pray the lord my soul to keep" one. As I look back, it was amazing how she brought happiness and stability to those difficult times of uncertainty.

I would later learn that Grandma's life was no walk in the park. She faced some of life's most tragic and difficult challenges. I imagine that she was quite a catch when she married John Little. From old pictures, I would describe my grandfather as a tall, handsome, rugged man. Later in life, I asked grandma to tell me about my grandfather, and it went something like this: "Your grandfather was a good electrician and a hard worker. However, he had his share of weaknesses and was not perfect, but I still loved him very much." Reflecting back on Grandma's ambiguous description of the man she loved, the father of her children and her only husband, I should have asked a lot more questions.

The accident was sudden and tragic. My grandfather worked for the power company as a lineman. He kissed my grandmother good bye one morning and went to work just like every other day. As the story is told, he was working on high tension power lines with limited protection when he brushed up against a high voltage line and was electrocuted. He fell from the telephone pole to his death. This left Grandma to raise three young girls as a single mother: mom was five, Mary was seven, and Margaret was nine.

I can only guess that these strenuous circumstances and her deep faith made her a stronger person and a better mother. When my grandfather died, they were living in a run-down rooming house on the corner of South Market and Henry Street. The place was infested with rodents, and the area was among the worst in town. It had to be a very difficult time filled with constant financial and parenting challenges.

There was a small settlement, which Grandma used to build a modest cottage on McDonald Street. It was the first house on the street, an attractive three bedroom cottage with a detached one car garage. Grandma said, "It was a very sad time for us. I lost my husband, and the girls lost their father. The truth is that the death settlement wasn't a lot of money, but it was all there was. We had to get out of that apartment, so I used the money to build us a place to live, and then went to work. I cleaned homes, cooked, and sewed for other families during the day, and cleaned offices at night."

As I got older, I was curious and known to ask a lot of questions. I remember that she loved to visit with me and was always available and eager to answer questions. Her answers were not always what I expected, and she worked hard to engage me in conversations. She was a shrewd lady, and I vividly remember that she constantly encouraged me to always do my best. I can hear her today: "You have to do your best to be your best." That message was brilliantly woven into virtually every conversation.

As a teenager I was surprised to learn that Grandma never had a driver's license. She walked everywhere even though later in life she suffered from crippling arthritis. When I got my driver's license, I bought a motorcycle and would often take her to and from her office cleaning jobs downtown. That was quite a sight: a crazy teenage boy with long hair on a motorcycle with a gray haired lady in tow, her lovely long dress blowing in the wind.

Mean to Meaningful

Thank goodness Grandma was in the picture because the situation with my parents was deteriorating rapidly. Their relationship and marriage was limping along, just waiting to die and be buried. I was still in diapers when Diana was born. Mom struggled to care for two babies while Dad was up to no good running around town in his fancy new car with other women.

Mom said, "I was devastated and hated your father for what he was doing. It was humiliating, and I finally got up the courage to confront him. We had an argument, and said many unkind things to each other. The next day, your father packed his things, and left for good. I learned that he moved back in with his parents, which was fine with me because the marriage was over."

With two babies, no money, no car, and no job, mom found herself in a deep hole frantically digging. She was lucky that Grandma, as a seasoned single parent and mother, finally took the shovel.

Mom went back to work as a waitress at Isaly's, another local diner. The owners knew Grandma and really liked Mom. They had known her since she was a little girl. She was a hard worker and a good waitress, but back then she worked for tips only—a meager existence. The owners knew Mom had two young children to feed, so at night they often allowed her to take home the leftovers from the steam table buffet. We had no money, but we usually ate well.

According to the records, my parents were finally divorced when I was around two years old. I am told that the judge looked at my mother as he was awarding her forty-five dollars a month in child support payments and said, "You are an attractive, healthy young woman, and you are capable of more than just waitressing. I would suggest that you find a better paying job, because you are going to need it to take care of your children." Mom received a call the next morning from Frito Lay with a job offer, which she took. It was a good factory job and she worked on their potato chip line for almost a decade.

According to mom, Dad went about his life as if we did not exist. I have no recollection of those times, and have no memories of my father— only stories. Even though he lived in the same town, just a few miles away, we would have to wait to make his formal acquaintance.

Mom was now alone and on her own, and as a divorced single parent, she struggled to provide for us. Not knowing exactly what would be required made it a scary time for her. She told me that we continued to move around after Dad left and that we lived in several local flophouses. I was not familiar with the term *flophouse*, so I asked what they were like, and after hearing her detailed description of the places and tenants, I will just refer to them as homeless shelters without supervision.

Mom was determined to prove that she could take care of herself and her children. As a child, I cannot remember a time that Mom was not working. She worked extra shifts, overtime, and holidays whenever possible. There was never time for us to visit, play, or talk. I was lonely and often questioned whether Mom really cared about us. I wondered if she really loved us or if we were the unfortunate consequences of a failed marriage—maybe just excess baggage to be dealt with at some later date. I was confused and wondered why Mom chose to work when she could be at home with us.

I eventually asked her why she worked all the time, and she told me, "I have to in order to pay the bills. I believe hard work will make things better and we need the money to survive. I know that your grandmother is disappointed in me. I was rebellious and struggled as a child, and I have to do better. I just want mom to be as proud of me as she is of Mary and Margaret."

Mom lived in the past and allowed her history to haunt her. It is true that she made some bad choices, but she acted as though she did not deserve to be happy. Little, if any, energy was spent on living in the present. As a result, she was willing to settle for less. It was a sad existence and so much less than she deserved.

Grandma, on the other hand, lived in the present and loved people. She was always with a crowd and looked for opportunities to help. She never turned her back on anyone. It just wasn't in her DNA. She was a masterful teacher and a good listener. She always asked a lot of questions. It was not always a question to which she was seeking an answer; it could be an important question that she wanted you to figure out. I remember when I was a little boy, she insisted we go with her to church. I did not like to go, but she came by the house to pick us up every Sunday morning, rain or shine, with Uncle Virgil, Aunt Mary, and their children, John, Jim, and Carol. We really had no choice. We had to go. We all crammed into Uncle Virgil's little car like sardines. Church services and Sunday school were boring. I now realize that Grandma's intent was not all about church or God, although she was a deeply religious woman; her real purpose was to consciously expose us to the good people in the congregation—folks with integrity and character. Yes, she had a plan; I just didn't know it. She was a strong force in my life right up until the day she died and even some after that.

Grandma and Mom were both inspiring women who were forced into combat duty and learned their survival skills on the job. As an open book and virtual sponge, I was able to learn much about people and the world around me as I watched them interact and live their lives with completely different agendas, styles, and goals. It is obvious that, without them, I would never have made it out of the neighborhood. As it turns out, I would need everything they had to offer and more.

After the divorce, we eventually ended up in a three room apartment on North Street. This is the first place of which I have any memories of my own. The rent was forty dollars a month, and Mom rented out the bedroom. I asked Mom why other people had to live with us, and she said we needed their rent money in order to make ends meet. Mom; my baby sister, Diana; and I slept in the living room on the sofa and the floor. One of the very first renters was a single, young mother and her son, Rodney. We were about the same age and played together. We seemed to have a lot in common because he did not have a dad either. We became friends, but they moved on after several months.

One Saturday morning, Mom woke us up, visibly upset, and said to Diana and me, "Get dressed and packed. Your father called last night and told me that he is coming today to get you and Diana for the weekend, but since he never does what he promises, do not get your hopes up. When we divorced, I got custody, and your dad was awarded monthly visitation privileges. That means he is allowed to get you and Diana one weekend every month. He is not dependable and never keeps his promises. This is a perfect example of what I mean. This is his first scheduled visit since the divorce. I will be surprised if he even shows up." This was a harsh message coming from Mom, because she rarely mentioned our dad. In the past, she had treated the subject of our father and Dad himself as though they did not exist. She was upset, and it was obvious that Dad's sudden reappearance had opened painful wounds.

We met our father later that day. Dad and his wife, Marie, picked Diana and me up for our first weekend visitation. Dad had divorced Mom and married Marie, so it was a little awkward when they arrived. As I recall, Dad was driving a brand new car. We would discover that he was a car guy and that he always had distinctive cars. Diana and I did not know what to expect, but we were naturally excited to finally meet our dad; however, we were understandably anxious and somewhat confused about how to act. When Dad came to the front door, things did not start off well. Mom and Dad were disrespectful to each other, using some bad words, some of which I had never heard before. When we finally made our formal introductions and left the apartment, Dad pointed to the car and told Diana and me, in his deep, raspy voice, "Get in the car. We are going to my house for the weekend. My place is more fun and much nicer than this dump." When we returned from that first visit, Mom sat us down and queried us about every detail.

Mom was correct. Dad's visits turned out to be once or sometimes twice a year. Although Dad had revealed himself, he was still not present. He remained the absentee father that we had come to know. Diana and I discussed our feelings and determined that Dad was a busy man with a lot of other things going on. His message came through loud and clear: we were just not that important. We would not see Dad again that year until Christmas. Future weekend visits were few and far between. It did not matter to us. We were conditioned to have low expectations. And we were very happy with scraps.

Mom met Phil Jewell at the diner where she worked. She made sure that she waited on him whenever he came in. According to Mom, he was a handsome man and a very good tipper. They married and he moved in with us.

Later in life I would learn that Phil had his own baggage: being abandoned at birth, spending many years in an orphanage as a throwaway child, and then doing hard time in jail, all before the age of twenty one. He was different, but he helped our mother put a roof over our heads and food on the table.

Even though Phil came into the house as our stepfather, we never established a meaningful relationship. His habits, actions, and behaviors confused me and it bothered me that he did not treat Mom with the respect and dignity that she so deserved. He never called Mom by her name. She was always "woman" or "broad," never "Joan" or "honey" or "sweetheart."

Mom and Phil had two daughters. Although we lived in the same house, I never got to know either of them very well. We rarely did anything as a family. There was minimal guidance, communication, interaction or supervision. The existence felt more like a boarding house than a home. As a result, we remained virtual strangers and more or less just passed in the night.

North Street was a one way cobblestone street that ran through a neighborhood of older apartment houses and single family homes. There were few garages, and most people parked their cars on the street. The neighbors were all hardworking people. The houses were modest by today's standards, but there was plenty of outdoor space, and it was common to see folks cooking dinner on the grill, a father throwing a baseball or football with a child in the yard, or people working in their gardens.

We lived in several different places on North Street. Coincidentally, they were all on the same block. The first place was 365, a three room apartment, one of the older properties on the street. The wallpaper was peeling, and the faded yellow floor linoleum was original. The exterior siding was brick imprinted asphalt shingles, which provided minimal insulation. On cold winter nights we had to go into the damp dark basement and shovel coal into the furnace because that was our only source of heat. We eventually moved next door to 369. It was larger, newer and fortunately had an electric furnace. After several years, we moved across the alley to 375, a larger single family home. It was one of the nicer houses on the street, with a detached two car garage and a small workshop. The property was larger than most, with a generous grassy side yard that Diana and I used regularly for football and baseball games.

I found another exciting world when I started kindergarten at the Walnut Street School. It was an architecturally beautiful, traditional building with a wonderful playground, swings, sandboxes, slides, and monkey bars in the front and a small baseball diamond, football field, and basketball court in the back. It was conveniently located just a few blocks from our house on North Street.

When I discovered sports, I wanted to spend every waking hour on the school playground. I made excuses and often lied so that I could go to school early and stay late in order to play baseball, basketball, and football. I loved the competition and was a tough player. I was a good student and made excellent grades, but one moment I could be hugging a teacher, and then a few minutes later, I was on the playground hosting a bloody fight.

When you looked under the hood, you could detect serious problems brewing. I was emotionally immature with an ugly Irish temper. The anger often turned into rage. When it occurred, it was overwhelming and uncontrollable. Those fight or flight emotions would eventually cause significant personal challenges. That was the bad news. The good news was that sports would keep me occupied and out of trouble. What I did not realize was the amazing influence that sports and a few special coaches would have on my future.

I sought independence at an early age. I was a loner with little guidance or supervision at home and I quickly discovered that the only person who was going to take care of me was me. Fending for myself forced me to be resourceful. I wanted a new baseball glove and a bike. There was just one problem: I had no money. So I got a job.

At seven years old, I applied for a paper route. Uncle Virgil, who was married to mom's middle sister, Mary, was an executive at the *Daily Record*, the local newspaper. He vouched for me, and I was quickly awarded a small paper route in the neighborhoods around the Walnut Street School. As a young paper route executive, I learned how to manage a small business.

Mean to Meaningful

Uncle Virgil was a thoughtful man, and I admired his kindness and willingness to help. He turned out to be a positive influence and a distant role model. He made it a point to spend time with me at family outings and made sure that I always felt included. He somehow knew that I was always going to be an outsider, but he stood up for me whenever possible, and I would always do my best to please him. I was dependable and never missed a paper delivery, even in the most severe weather conditions—and believe me, it snowed a lot in Ohio.

To this day, I question why our stepfather was so different from Uncle Virgil. Was it bloodlines, genes, or was it plain and simple intellectual capabilities and curiosities? Was there really any way to know? I knew that they both had spent significant time in orphanages. They both had difficult and challenging childhood circumstances. They were both smart, but I knew that neither graduated from high school. But that is where the obvious similarities ended. Phil was quiet and somewhat reclusive with a bad temper. Uncle Virgil was an extrovert who loved to talk. He never met a stranger and seemed to know something about practically everything. Phil worked in a local factory, lacked authentic emotion, and was not engaged as a father. Uncle Virgil ran the local newspaper, cherished his wife, and was actively engaged in his children's lives. They had polar opposite opinions and attitudes toward people, politics, and life. The question as to why these men were so different remains unanswered; however, I often wondered what it would have been like to have Uncle Virgil as a father.

I ran with a fast crowd of less popular kids at school and was socially awkward and unsophisticated. I was ashamed of who I was, but I did not know how to change, so I kept charging full speed ahead.

There were few rules at the house which created lots of opportunity for bad outcomes. Because I was mean, determined, independent and stubborn, I would aggressively pursue them all.

Two

HOPE

How you coach them is how they are going to play.

—Stefan Fatsis

Sports led me to coaches who served as invaluable mentors. They taught the fundamentals of the game and provided knowledge, discipline, structure, and inspiration. Although I did not realize it at the time, they were meaningful role models and the first of many outside forces that would nourish the values and character that would shape my future.

When I was eight years old, I played on the Walnut Street School flag football team coached by Ron Baus. He had a nice family and was a handsome, well built, highly organized local businessman. I assumed that he was in the construction business because he drove a large pickup truck. From his physical appearance, you had to believe that he was a former jock. His wife, Lucy, was a tall, attractive woman. She was a successful real estate agent, and their beautiful daughter Linda was my first puppy love.

Coach Baus always got to practices and games early. He was a serious man, dressed well, carried a clipboard, and always appeared to be over prepared. I learned from him to be early and come ready to play. When I joined the team he pulled me aside and said, "We are going to let you play end. You are fast and have soft hands. If you practice and work hard you will do well." He patted me on the back and made me believe that I was special. He had a way about him and was able to make everyone believe that they were talented. He encouraged and never criticized, a valuable practice that would eventually yield a lifetime of dividends for me. He made us believe we were talented beyond our abilities and then showed us how to win. We lived up to his expectations by winning city championships almost every season.

Coach Baus taught me to love football, and his encouraging style would have a profound impact on me. He was a great teacher, and I secretly aspired to be like him when I grew up. It is possible that absent his influence, I might have never gone on to become a Hall of Fame football player at Wofford College.

I first learned to play baseball in pick-up softball games on the grade school playground. I loved baseball and wanted to play all the time. After a few years, I discovered that I might be able to play on an organized Little League team. To play you had to try out and be selected so I decided to try out.

It was pouring buckets of rain that morning, and I doubt that Babe Ruth or Mickey Mantle would have battled that weather. I had no aspirations of becoming a New York Yankee, nor did I know they would come calling later. I just wanted to play baseball, so I prayed for the rain to stop. That was unusual because although I went to church with Grandma every Sunday, I rarely prayed. I rode my bike through the driving rain to the tryouts. God was surely smiling on me that day, because the rain stopped, and the sun came out a few minutes before the scheduled tryouts.

When I arrived, there were many serious looking men standing around with clipboards. I had never attended a tryout, so I anxiously watched their every move and concluded that they were coaches who were here to evaluate the players. I was told that the draft would take place that night, in which those same coaches would attempt to draft their favorite players.

I used some money from the paper route to buy a new Rawlings baseball glove. I was prepared and took advantage of every opportunity to showcase my skills. As I remember, we were organized into several large groups in the outfield. The coaches took turns hitting balls to each group as the others watched. I successfully fielded every ball hit in my direction. I selfishly hogged the field and did not allow the other players a chance. I was not showing off—I was just trying to get noticed.

The next day, I learned that I had been drafted by the Wooster City Police team, coached by Don Sigler and Milo Messmore. I later discovered that the Wooster City Police was a team of eleven and twelve year olds. I was confused because I was just nine. I was told that I would be playing up. I did not know what that meant, nor did I care.

Milo was the assistant coach and took care of the balls, bats, and equipment. He was an older man with thinning gray hair and was definitely nonathletic. When he walked, I remember that it was more like a duck waddle. He lived across from the high school in a modest house. I was curious why he was willing to spend so much time coaching when he had no children on the team and nothing to gain.

We played our games at Miller Field. The land, field and facilities had been donated by an older wealthy gentleman in town. It was a beautiful, state of the art baseball complex with two large lighted baseball fields and nice dugouts. I rode my bike across town to the games. After the first night game, Milo told me to load my bike in the back of his truck. He said, "I cannot allow you to ride home in the dark. You might have an accident and get hurt. That would not be good, and your mother would never forgive me. Get in the truck, and I will take you home." As the season progressed, he suggested that I ride my bike to his house and that we ride together.

Don Sigler, the head coach, was competitive and had a reputation for winning. He was a short, muscular man in his thirties. He was quiet and serious and rarely smiled. He was highly disciplined, and I was deathly afraid of him. I did not want to disappoint or cross him. I thought that he worked for the police department because they were the team sponsor, and I believed that he was capable of killing you, if necessary. As a young boy, this actually worked well, because I needed strict discipline and structure to mitigate the anger and personal insecurities. Coach Sigler made it clear at the first practice that he expected our best and anything less would earn us a seat on the bench. His coaching style focused on hard work, and I was fortunate to play for him for four years.

During those formative childhood years, I needed Coaches Baus, Messmore, and Sigler. They were authentically interested in my personal growth and well-being. They were invested in my future, and I practiced tirelessly, sometimes late into the night, because I wanted to please them and did everything possible to make them proud of me. The collateral benefit was that there was little time for anything else.

I am eternally grateful to these special men for their encouragement, kindness, discipline, care, and guidance. They were present and firmly pointed me in the right direction when necessary…which was almost always.

As I grew older and became more aware of the world around me, I hated being without a responsible everyday father. Although Dad made an occasional appearance, I still considered him missing in action, and Phil made it clear that he had no interest.

When I was ten, the Soap Box Derby brought Dad and me together. He was active in the local race scene, and his brother and sister had sons competing. I believe that Dad was eager to compete, but back then, the derby was limited to boys, so he needed me, as his only son, to get into the game.

The telephone rang, and Mom answered. She frowned and handed me the receiver and said, "It is your father, and he wants to talk with you."

Dad had never called me before, but he acted as if we talked all the time. He told me all about the Soap Box Derby and eventually asked if I wanted to build a car and race. It sounded exciting, but I knew that I would need Mom's permission, so I said, "I will ask mom and let you know."

When I got off the phone, I talked with Mom. As I recall, the request greatly upset her, and she responded accordingly. "Who does he think he is? We are struggling each day for survival, and he wants to build race cars. There is no way that you are going to spend more time with him as long as he is behind on his child support payments."

Over the years I had overheard a lot of ugly telephone conversations regarding those important child support payments. Dad was always behind, while Mom was doing everything in her power to keep a roof over our heads and put food on the table. I knew that she was killing herself to make ends meet. She needed the child support money, and I knew that Dad could pay, but didn't. Even so, I still begged Mom to let me go. They eventually talked and reached an agreement, and we were off to the races.

Dad lived in a new three bedroom home in an upscale subdivision on the edge of town. On the first visit, I was amazed at how spacious and nice the house was, and I was intrigued by the wide selection of tools in his workshop. I assumed that it was equipped with everything we needed to build a winning race car.

The best thing about the Soap Box Derby days was that I got to spend every Tuesday and Thursday night with Dad. He picked me up at Mom's house on North Street at six. We had a quick dinner together and then went down to the workshop. During those Soap Box Derby years, I learned much about woodworking, construction, and mechanics...but not that much about Dad.

I did learn that Dad had been a car mechanic before he went back to school and became an accountant. He loved cars and was good with his hands, and it was obvious that he knew how to use the tools. I was curious about his experience, so I asked him, "Where did you learn to use these tools?"

"I grew up in the garage with my dad," he said. "Your grandfather runs the new car department for the Chevrolet dealer, and he is one of the best mechanics in town. We had a stock car racing team when I was younger. We raced every Friday night. I drove the car, and Dad was the mechanic, tire changer, gasman, and crew chief. We won some races, but it cost more to race than you could win back in those days. It was long before the big NASCAR purses. We loved it for as long as we could afford it, which was about two seasons."

I quickly discovered that Dad was a smart man, and he would learn that I was a curious child. I would ask a lot of questions about life and the world around us, and he delighted in the opportunity to provide answers. His answers led to a much better understanding of the world, which ultimately led to more questions. I valued our time together. I saw and heard a lot of things that I liked, but I was disappointed in some of my discoveries.

One night, the subject of divorce came up. I asked Dad, "Why do people get divorced?"

After an obviously uncomfortable explanation that was filled with useless information, I was still quietly waiting for an answer. Dad finally looked at me in frustration and screamed, "What is your real question? This is a waste of time. What do you really want to know?"

I sheepishly responded, "I am trying to understand why you and Mom did not stay married. I am curious why you divorced."

He offered further explanation that led to more questions. When I kept following his every answer with more questions, he eventually stopped me. It was obvious that he was upset with my curiosities, and he finally responded with the simple, unadulterated truth: "Your mom and I were not meant for each other. We were young with our whole lives ahead of us, and we were not happy together. I could give you a lot more, but it is just that simple."

"That makes sense. OK, but I am curious—how do you get a divorce?" I asked.

"In our case, we got an attorney and filed the legal divorce papers with the court. As I recall, there was a waiting period, and we eventually went to court and appeared before a judge, and he granted us the divorce. The judge then ordered me to make a monthly child support payment to your mother. As you know, I am required to send her a check every month. You know that child support is the screw you get for the screw you got." We laughed together, and at the time I thought that was pretty funny.

The first Soap Box Derby car was clunky and primitive. We lost our first heat. The next year the car was a little better. We won one heat. By the third year, we had discovered many engineering improvements. We had a sleek car, won three heats, and made it to the quarterfinals. The day after the race, Dad and I went back to the drawing board to design our final car. When we started the construction, I was thirteen. The car was sleek, and the cockpit was purposefully small. We had no idea how much I would grow in twelve months. When the car was finished, it fit like a tight glove. It took a while to force my body into the cockpit. Dad said, "It is important for you to get low in the car to avoid all potential wind drag." Unfortunately, my feet had grown too, which made it difficult to reach the small braking pedal in the nose of the car.

The car stood out in a crowd. We incorporated everything we had learned from the earlier races and other competitors, including a sleek finish, a smooth brake opening, a special steering system, shoulder guards, and a low height and width design for minimal wind resistance. It was beautiful and an engineering work of art—except for one thing.

Fought Signs was my car's sponsor. They were a respected local sign company and painted all the sponsor signs on the derby cars. Their own signage was most attractive. It was a painting palette with delicate long handled paintbrushes. Unlike other signs, it covered the entire side of the car and was colorfully distinctive.

The Saturday night before the race, there was a big party and open house at the local armory; all the cars were on display. They were roped off so no one could touch them, and they would be impounded immediately after the event and transported by truck to the racetrack. The local armory was a large brick building that was rarely used for public events. Helicopters, tanks, and other war relics dotted the front lawn at the entrance to the building. That night, the building was filled with Soap Box Derby race cars, and everyone in town was there to support the derby and preview the race cars. Even though this was dad's event, I came with Mom and Grandma, who were there to support me. I think that they wanted to see my car, too. Most car designs had been kept top secret until that night. The Fought Signs owner got his first look at our car when we brought it in to have the sign painted. He was so enamored with the car that he and his wife decided to attend the open house that night for the first time ever. They spent most of the evening standing proudly near their car, visiting with the many admirers.

It was a tradition of the event to present the Best Constructed Car award. As the evening wound down, the crowd gathered around the awards podium. There was specific interest because in the past, this award had usually been a good indicator of the derby winner. The sleek blue and white Fought Signs–sponsored car with my name painted prominently on the side definitely stood out as one of the favorites. When the time came, the crowd was silent in anticipation. When the winner was announced, I calmly walked up to the podium to accept the award and scanned the room for my father. When I found him in the crowd, I saw that he was smiling ear to ear and shaking hands around the room. The prize was a metal toolbox with a complete set of tools, which I still have and use today.

Winning the award was huge for Dad. In an interesting way, it made him the big man on campus and certainly validated him. The night could not have turned out any better. Before we went home, Dad and I sat down in a quiet corner and went through the checklist of things we had to do the next day in order to win.

The race day weather was perfect. There was not a cloud in the sky as the drivers prepared for the two car elimination races. When the time came, I got into the car and forced my growing body into the cockpit. When the nose of the car was placed at the starting line, I was ready. The heavy starting gates dropped with a loud clang, and we were on our way. We picked up speed quickly, and I guided the car down the center line, just as Dad had instructed. I never left the center line, and posted what turned out to be the fastest time of the race.

The teenage growth factor was the only overlooked detail. Unfortunately, from the tight driving position, I was unable to apply the brakes and crashed into the hay bales at the end of the track. We attempted to make repairs between heats, but the damage was severe. We lost the next race and were done. After the race, our father son relationship quickly cooled—no, it actually turned to ice. Once again it was like I had never existed. I was confused, and as the summer progressed, there were no calls and no word from Dad. The radio silence was not a surprise. It is what I had come to expect.

I considered giving up the paper route and getting more involved at school, but after serious thought, I decided to keep the route because it was my only source of income and security. It was the only sure thing I had going on in life. Every day after school, I went to the Annex store to pick up, prepare, and deliver the newspapers. The route had grown, and Diana often helped me. She was a sweet girl and a great partner, and she knew every customer by name. I continued with the paper route, but when I finished eighth grade, I decided it was time to move on, and I received permission from the *Daily Record* and Uncle Virgil to transition ownership of the route to Diana.

I had become a loner and saw myself as nothing more than poor white trash. I grew up on the wrong side of town in a working class neighborhood. I had only a handful of friends and my self-esteem was at an all-time low. Most of this was my own fault because, as my granddaughter Parks says, I never learned how to "let my light shine."

I was mean, but never a bully. Even so, my Irish temper was well documented, and my reputation was set. I was crazy mean...someone you didn't want to cross under any circumstances.

I resisted any and all types of authority; however, I was a smart kid and established myself as a good student. I enjoyed learning but was never academically motivated. I think I did well only because I did not want to be considered one of the dumb ones.

In the ninth grade, I tried out for the freshman football team. As a small, skinny blond headed kid weighing ninety-eight pounds, I was not really built for contact football, and the tryouts were far different than I had expected. The players were big, the gear was heavy, and the drills were difficult. When I arrived, I discovered that there were sixty boys trying out for a forty man roster. It was another valuable life lesson. You had to earn your place, and only the most qualified and determined would make the team. When the names were finally posted on the coach's door, I discovered both good and bad news. The good news was that I made the team. The bad news was that I was the smallest player.

I wanted to fit in, and was determined to do whatever it took to play. As a small player, I knew it would be difficult. The coaches told me that my size would probably limit my opportunities. They were obviously concerned about my physical safety. I worked hard and earned a starting role as the offensive center. Those physical blocking duties made me a tough and durable player. The largest player on the team was Bob Adair, who weighed 190 pounds. He played middle guard, and I had the opportunity to block him on every play, every day during every practice.

He was a very good player, and I credit him for teaching me how to effectively block the big boys.

The next season, I played flanker back, a position that was better suited to my size. As in grade school, I was fast with soft hands, and I loved catching the football. I had gained some weight, but there would be no more assignments blocking big, mean defensive linemen for survival.

Bob Fravel was the junior varsity quarterback. He was a popular leader and a star pitcher on the baseball team. His father was a well-respected roofing contractor. I frequently spent the night at his home. We had grown up together, we were friends, and I considered him one of the good guys.

Coincidently, Bob was the quarterback on Coach Baus's championship teams, so we had played together for years. He threw me thousands of passes during our time together. Thanks to Bob, I caught a lot of passes that season. Our successful junior varsity performances earned us both the opportunity to dress out for several varsity games toward the end of the season. It was quite an honor because there were no other sophomores on the team. We only played a handful of plays, but the staff, including the head football coach, Jack Peterson, knew we would be back.

Meanwhile, I struggled, and not a week passed without a fight. I suffered several disciplinary suspensions and regularly sported black eyes and bruises, which, at the time, I considered badges of courage. Fighting was intoxicating, and I came to love the sight of blood—especially when it wasn't mine. I was willing to do whatever it took to win—right or wrong. As a result, my friend Jon Viar, our fullback and team captain, started calling me "Mean Wile." The name was uniquely suited, and it stuck. Truth be known, I liked being recognized as a mean guy who was a few cards short of a full deck.

Outside forces were my primary support system. Coaches and friends turned out to be all I had as role models and advisors. Dad was nowhere to be found, and mom was working day and night just to make ends meet. Our stepfather was absent and did his best to avoid me. Out of desperation, I learned to take care of myself.

As a sixteen year old, I had my own car, and was independent in almost every way. There were few rules or supervision. I was required to be in the house by midnight, but everything else was wide open. I worked at the corner market every night until ten and then cruised around town looking for fun until midnight. That was where I first learned that the trouble with trouble is that it always starts out as fun.

Late that summer before my senior year, Phil and I had an irreparable event. I had returned home from work and on the way to my bedroom, I saw my precious thirteen year old sister in her nightshirt with our stepfather standing over her with belt in hand lashing at her legs. He was a bully, and the belt was his weapon of choice. From experience, I was well versed on how it worked.

She was defenseless, and I could see the welts on her legs. I was pretty sure there was nothing she could have done to deserve such a beating. It was cruel and brutal punishment, and she was a good girl. Punishment like this happened far too often and most times without good reason. I felt like sometimes the reason for punishment was that the belt just needed a good workout. The next few seconds would ensure that tonight would be the belt's final performance.

When I saw what was happening, I screamed for him to stop. He ignored me, so I stood him straight up and then hit him. The angry blow landed solidly below his left eye. His knees buckled and he fell to the floor. When he realized what had happened, he looked up at me in shock. He eventually got up, stumbled into the hallway, and fell down a flight of steps. As he struggled to his feet, he looked up at me and yelled, "Get the hell out of my house!"

I knew my sister was now safe, and so I snapped back without a moment's hesitation, "No problem! I am on my way."

I immediately packed my belongings into a duffel bag and left. It took the better part of five minutes. I spent the night with Jim Underwood. His house was friendly and one that I would eventually come to know well.

The next day, I was surprised when Dad reached out to me. He somehow heard about the incident and invited me to move in with him. I was desperate, had no place to live, and saw little downside to his offer, so I accepted.

Even with the soap box derby experience we never developed a traditional father son bond. We were more strangers than family. We never learned to trust or respect each other. Our everyday communications were strained and often confrontational. In the best of times, our relationship was awkward and fragile.

I had to wonder. Would this time with him be any different?

Three

*Treat a person as he is, and he will remain as he is. Treat him
as what he could be, and he will become what he should be.*

—*Jimmy Johnson*

In the fall of 1968, our high school football team won the Cardinal
Conference Championship. Much of the season's credit was given to our
tenacious defense, which shut out five teams and gave up only fifty
points the entire season. At the end of the season, eight players,
including me, were selected for the All Cardinal Conference Team.

The head coach, Jack Peterson, arrived at Wooster High School in
the fall of 1966. He was a highly regarded coach from Canfield High
School, where he had successfully coached and taught for five years.
Jack was a fit man, and he and his wife, Marge, had three young
children: two sons and an older daughter. He had a firm and confident
but private personality. He appeared to be a happy guy who smiled all
the time. I often wondered if he was one of those guys who was only
smiling on the outside. I would discover that he was fiercely competitive
and was wound as tight as a tick.

When I was in high school, I always thought of Jack as a big man,
and I remember that he always dressed like a professional coach. He
wore a collared gold or white golf shirt, gray or black coaching shorts,
and white knee high socks with black coach's shoes. He was very neat,
and his clothes were always freshly starched and pressed. I am sure
Marge made sure that he always looked put together. Jack inspired me,

26

and I respected him. He showed me the discipline that I lacked in my home life. During our years together, he was a strong father figure, but he was more demanding than most real fathers, as he modeled and encouraged us to *reach higher*, an expectation that I eagerly embraced.

Jack grew up in Ohio and was the youngest of six children. He had a brother and four sisters. His brother, Bill, was the oldest, and Jack was the baby. When Jack was two years old, his father died, and his mother was left alone to raise the six children.

Jack and Marge started dating in high school. After graduation, Marge got a job as a telephone operator, and Jack joined the navy. They continued to date while he was in the service, became engaged, and eventually married. During their first year of marriage, Jack was still on assignment at sea, not an ideal arrangement for newlyweds. After the navy, he decided to enroll at Ashland College on the GI Bill. Jack shared that he decided to go to college and play football because his brother was a successful football coach at Mansfield Senior, a nearby high school. Jack played offensive guard and was a defensive linebacker. He was five foot eleven and weighed 190 pounds.

Jack's older brother, Bill Peterson, was his role model. Bill became a legend among coaches of that era, as he systematically transformed college football's passing game, which at the time was almost nonexistent. His new offense added an exciting new dimension to the game. After Mansfield Senior, Bill coached at Louisiana State University, Florida State University, and Rice University, and his college coaching career included at least one NCAA national championship. He developed a reputation for winning and finished his career in the National Football League with the Houston Oilers.

In high school, Jack would single me and others out for extra work after practice. He would say, "Wile after practice." I hated to hear that phrase. He would most often run with us without saying a word. He always kept his cards close to the vest. Many times, it was just us. His thoughts were a mystery, and I could never figure him out. He was strict, disciplined, and confident. A bold but simple man of few words. The "Wile after practice" punishments bothered me so much that at the end of the season, I finally asked him why he singled me out for work after practice. He smiled and said, "I call your name because I care about you. You may not know it yet, but I believe you could have a future in college sports. Regardless, I feel like it is my duty and responsibility to challenge my best players. You should only worry when I *stop* calling your name."

I was surprised with his answer and responded. "I thought the extra practice, wind sprints, and laps after practices were punishment. All this time, I thought it was because you were disappointed in me. I guess it served your purpose because it made me work harder. I did not realize this was your way of making me a better player. I am flattered and appreciate you taking the time to care about me." Once again I had a coach taking the father figure role in my life.

We played a difficult schedule and were a good team. Our final game of the season was against top ranked Orrville High School. They were always the last game of the season, and it was a highly competitive rivalry. We were generally pretty evenly matched. This year was different. Orrville was undefeated—a big team with a powerful, high scoring offense. It was a home game for us, and although we had lost only two games and given up a total of forty four points all season, we were considered a substantial underdog.

It was a dark and stormy night, and even though it was chilly and had been raining for several days, the game was a sellout. The home stands were packed with Wooster High School General fans, and the visitor stands were full too. Despite the poor weather, the stadium was bursting with excitement.

From the opening kickoff, it was a physical game. Wooster was recognized for its tough defense and Orrville for its powerful, high scoring offense. It was a close game, and when we entered the fourth quarter, the score was Orrville 6, Wooster 0. As the game progressed in the fourth quarter, the light drizzle turned into a steady downpour. Orrville had the ball, and the game seemed to be all but over. Due to the worsening weather conditions, some of the fans were heading for the exits. The outcome looked to be as predicted, only with fewer points, which was attributed to the weather conditions and our tough defense. But with less than two minutes left in the game, things got interesting when our defense stopped the powerful Orrville offense on third down in the middle of the field. They would have to go for it on fourth down or punt. They decided to punt, which meant that we would get one final chance.

The rain picked up, and we were now playing in a torrential downpour. We called time out to evaluate our options. The weather conditions were brutal, so we decided to try to block the punt. When we lined up for the block, I went back as the lone safety. The ball was snapped. Even with the muddy field and severe weather conditions, their offensive center made a perfect snap, and we aggressively went for the block, but the Orrville punter got the protection he needed. The weather had no impact. It was perfect—a long, towering spiral punt.

I was alone waiting on the ten yard line. As the ball started its descent, I questioned whether to field the punt since there would be no blockers. *Should I just let it go and hope that it bounces into the end zone?* In that case, we would get the ball on the twenty yard line, which would give us another possession, but it would be a long way to the other end zone. Our offense had not been successful all night, and neither the weather conditions nor the clock favored our grinding offensive style. Then I thought, *What if the ball doesn't bounce and just gets stuck in the mud?* There were just too many choices, so I decided to field the punt and take control.

As I approached the ball, I could see several defenders covering the punt, but it was obvious that most had stayed back to protect the punter. The records show that the punt was fielded on the Orrville eight yard line. I initially backed up deep into our own end zone so that I could get a running start, a technique that I had practiced and successfully used all season. I timed it perfectly. I fielded the punt on a dead run in the middle of the field, easily sidestepped the early tacklers, and headed for the sidelines. Several key blocks cleared the way, which allowed smooth sailing down the sideline all the way to our twelve yard line, where I was finally run out of bounds.

We called another time out to rally the troops. This would be our final chance to score and possibly win the game. During that time out, I looked around the stadium and saw the fans returning to their seats. It was now obvious to everyone in the stadium that this game was not yet over. In the mud and pouring rain, our grinding offense took only a few plays to score. We failed to convert the extra point, and the final score was Orrville 6, Wooster 6.

Orrville would be Jack Peterson's last game as the head football coach at Wooster High School. He was a superstar just like his brother, and he was on everyone's radar screen. It was rumored that a small college in South Carolina was recruiting him. Jack had an open, honest, and caring coaching style. In his short career, he had performed well, and it was obvious that a college coaching job would be his next stop.

At home nothing had changed. I still knew everything about everything. I was stubborn, resisted authority and ignored suggestions and advice. I strongly believed that I was capable of managing my own affairs and taking care of myself. As a result, I am sad to report that a more meaningful relationship with Dad never materialized. I never gave it a chance.

The final episode came one weeknight in January. It was after midnight, and I had been out chasing girls and drinking. When I got home, Dad was waiting up for me at the kitchen table with a cup of coffee and was visibly upset. He said that we needed to talk. I knew that was code for, he was going to tell me what to do, and I was going to have to listen.

As the talk escalated, Dad lost control and suddenly leaped from his chair, stuck his finger in my face, and screamed, "You are a worthless good for nothing bum!" After realizing what he had done, he immediately sat down and looked at his coffee cup as he attempted to regain his composure.

He then calmly continued, "You are wild and out of control. You lack discipline and most of the time are your own worst enemy. You think you have all the answers, but you are too young to even know most of the right questions. You are on a collision course with disaster, and if you do not get your act together, you will never be anything except a worthless good for nothing bum or, heaven forbid, in an early grave. That's right: dead." He got my undivided attention with "dead" and I was listening with both ears.

After the lecture, completely frustrated and with nothing left to say, Dad got up from his chair, left the room, and went to bed. He left me alone to digest the essence of the message. I sat there for a long time thinking about what had just happened and wondering why. I eventually got up from the table and went to bed. I lay awake all night replaying his message and assessing my options. There was much to think about, and it was a very long night. There was no further discussion because I decided to take the easy way out.

The next morning, I packed my belongings into a duffel bag, went to school as usual, and never returned. This was a decision that I have often regretted, since Dad and I did not speak again for years.

After school, I reached out to my friend Jim Underwood. He spoke with his parents, Marvin and Hilda, and they graciously agreed to allow me to live with them while I finished my senior year of high school.

At eighteen years old, I was on my own, and it was up to me to figure things out. What concerned me the most was that Dad's assessment could be right. The events of that night certainly got my attention. Would I grow up to be a worthless good for nothing bum or end up in an early grave? I wondered what those outcomes looked like wrapped up in a gift box with a pretty bow. That created many unpleasant visuals. This painful wake-up call caused me to seriously consider the future, and it was an uncomfortable exercise as I explored those failure and death options and discovered that Dad was right. I was my own worst enemy, and I was too young and immature to understand the important issues or to even know the critical questions. Those were major revelations.

Up until then I always blamed everything bad on Dad. I could not forgive him for abandoning Diana and me as children. I carried that chip on my shoulder as a convenient excuse. I felt like we were an accident for him as a teenager and an inconvenience for him as an adult. I concluded that Dad was ashamed of us and showed up only when it was convenient for him. He rarely attended our school events and seemed to have little interest in us.

I came up with a lot of excuses for my many shortcomings, but none placed any blame on me. I never discussed my feelings with Diana. I just assumed that it did not bother her, because she seemed to take everything in stride. For her, it seemed to be no big deal. She was always in the background and never the center of attention with Dad, and I am certain that hurt, but she never complained. I wondered why none of this mayhem bothered her the way it did me.

I suddenly realized that I could no longer blame my mean, reckless, irresponsible behavior on other people, as I had done in the past. I had failed to recognize anything as my responsibility, until now. I could not change the past, but I knew that the choices and decisions I made going forward would shape the future. It was time for me to man up.

Shortly after I moved in with Jim and his family, Don Morrison, the defensive line coach, cornered me in the hall before classes for a conversation. He also coached the high school baseball team. I knew him well, but we rarely talked. "I saw you play baseball years ago in the hot stove leagues," he said. "You were a good player. I am curious why you stopped playing."

"It's a long and complicated story, but the short version is that I have to work," I answered.

"That's too bad, because I was thinking that you could really help us this season. We need players like you. You know, guys who play to win and hate to lose. I have to ask. Will you consider playing for me this season?"

Coach Morrison could tell that I was vulnerable, and he decided to fully exploit the opportunity. He wanted me, which made me feel worthy. Don was relentless, which was why he was such a good coach. After many conversations, he finally convinced me to join the team, and I was thankful for his persistence. I had forgotten how much I loved baseball.

Coach Morrison was a very good coach, and I validated his recruiting efforts. I led the team with a .421 batting average, the highest on base average, the highest slugging percentage, and the most stolen bases. I did my best to make us a better team. I was once again that nine year old making sure I was the most noticed in tryouts—only this time, I used that same tenacity to help win games for the high school team.

Mean to Meaningful

A distinguished gentleman wearing a New York Yankees baseball cap and shirt showed up at our final game of the season looking for Coach Morrison. They talked for a long time, and the conversation appeared to be serious. When I came off the field, Coach Morrison called me over and said the man wanted to talk with me. I thought that I must be in trouble. Why else would someone be looking for me at my final high school baseball game?

Then Coach Morrison told me that the man was a baseball scout for the Yankees. I thought he was joking. "You cannot be serious. *Me?* He came to see me?" I asked.

"Yes, I am serious. He had lots of questions and wanted to know all about you. I told him you were the real deal and that you were a tough kid. He is here to evaluate two players. You and the big first baseman," Coach Morrison said.

"You are kidding, right?"

"No, I am not kidding. Go talk to him," he said with a big grin.

I walked over and introduced myself. We talked awhile about the team and our incredible season, which was one of the best in school history, thanks to Coach Morrison. After a brief introduction, the scout asked, "What are your aspirations as a player?"

"I am not sure," I nervously answered. Prior to that conversation, I had never thought about baseball aspirations—certainly I had no professional baseball aspirations. All I knew was that I loved to play.

"Will you introduce me to your parents?" he asked.

"I would like for you to meet them, but they are not here," I said.

"Are you kidding me? Are they not proud of you? Where are they?" he asked.

"They are at work," I responded.

Until he asked, I never thought about whether they were proud of me or not. I guessed they were, even though they never attended games.

"Got it," he said as though he understood. "Good luck in the game; I'll be watching you." He then asked for my telephone number. We shook hands, and he returned to his front row seat in the stands.

It was a bittersweet game. I had four hits, three singles, and a double; stole two bases; and scored all of our runs. The first baseman had a good day too and hit several home runs. The longest one happened during his first at bat. Bob Fravel threw him one of his normally unhittable fast balls, and he hit a towering shot to center field. From the crack of the bat, there was never a doubt. It was so far over the center field fence that I didn't even give chase. It probably landed sometime the following morning in the next county.

It was a very memorable day, but we lost 4–3. This ended an otherwise fabulously successful baseball season.

I was excited about the New York Yankees' interest but was unsure of what to do next. I asked Coach Morrison what to expect. He said that I would have to wait and see, and if the Yankees had further interest they would contact me. I waited for the call, but it never came, and after several weeks I just assumed that I did not have the required talents for professional baseball.

That exciting experience did raise a troubling question. During the year, I had ignored several athletic scholarship opportunities because I never thought of myself as college material. Was that an irreparable mistake?

The school year was coming to an end, and graduation was just around the corner. I was bored and tired of the daily grind of school. I was already preparing for the future and had secured a job working in the shipping department at the Akron Brass Company.

When I arrived at school that hot May day in 1969, I found a pink slip on my locker. It instructed me to report to the guidance counselor's office immediately. I was accustomed to getting pink slips, but I had never received one from a guidance counselor. In fact, I had never visited the guidance counselor's office. I had no need for college materials, information or advice since I was not planning to go to college. I didn't even know where the office was located.

I had forgotten that Coach Peterson was a guidance counselor and had to ask for directions to his office. In the spirit of full disclosure, during high school, I had gotten at least one pink slip from every department, administrator, and teacher at school. Earlier that year, I had even gotten one from the school principal, which nearly ended in a fistfight. I was always in some kind of trouble, and so I naturally came to this meeting prepared for the worst.

When I arrived, Coach Peterson was smiling and asked me to take a seat in his small office. I realized that this was not a disciplinary meeting when he shared his exciting news. "This morning, I accepted the offensive coordinator job at Wofford College in Spartanburg, South Carolina, and I wanted to tell you in person." He paused for a moment as he searched for the right words, and then continued. "I know that you have your share of problems, but I want you to know that you are a good kid. You have the brains and athletic talent to go to college and play football. You should consider going to college, because I can promise you that it will change your life forever."

I thought for a moment and then responded, "Coach, college is expensive, and we both know that only the wealthy families in town can afford to send their children to college. Poor kids like me do not go to college, but I appreciate your kind words and thoughtful advice."

Then it happened: a once in a lifetime opportunity, and I never saw it coming. "I would like for you to come with me. I know that you can play for Wofford College. I checked this morning, and I am sad to report that we do not have any athletic scholarship money available for this year, but I am confident that you can walk on and earn a football scholarship. If you agree to come, I will promise you that I will do everything possible to help you find scholarship money next year."

"You want me to come with you to that college?" I asked.

"I do, and now I need your full and undivided attention."

He then stood up and leaned over his desk. I thought that he was going to grab me by the throat or punch me. I backed away because I was programmed to expect insults and violence, but instead he passionately reiterated his earlier advice. "You should go to college, Ed. I can promise you that it will change your life forever." He then paused and looked into my eyes for a long time. It was that crazy slow motion thing. He wanted to allow plenty of time for his advice and request to register. "If you decide to come with me to Wofford College, then you will have to take the SAT entrance exams and be formally accepted. I will warn you in advance that they have high scholastic standards, and it will not be easy. You may have to take the SAT test several times to earn a score good enough for admittance. If accepted, you will be expected to show up for summer football camp several weeks before school starts, and you will have to be in the best physical condition of your life. Now, I need to know. I need for you to make a decision, and I need to know right now. What do you want to do?"

After a brief discussion, I agreed to go with him to a college somewhere in South Carolina. It was a fairly complex topic but a simple decision. After I left his office, I wondered to myself, where in the heck is South Carolina.

Was this a foolish leap of faith? I told several people about the meeting and my promise to Jack. No one thought I was serious, but I proceeded as promised. If nothing else, I wanted to start being a man of my word instead of a worthless bum with a chip on my shoulder headed for the graveyard.

As I thought about my promise to Jack, I concluded that if I could be accepted into this highly respected college, then there was not that much wrong with me that, given enough time, I could not fix. Per Jack's suggestion, I took the SAT exam twice because I knew I had to score high for acceptance. Wofford College was an exceptional liberal arts college, and Jack was right about the high academic standards. I just hoped that I was smart enough to get in and that it was not too late.

That summer I worked two full time jobs and spent Saturdays and Sundays working out and running at the Wooster High School track. I would have trained during the week, but I was too busy earning money for college. I worked from 7:00 a.m. to 3:00 p.m. Monday through Friday in the shipping department at the Akron Brass Company, and when I finished that shift, I went across town to work from 4:00 p.m. to midnight in the maintenance department at Rubbermaid.

Since there were no college scholarships available, I had to earn enough money during the summer to pay tuition. It was a long, hot summer, and as it progressed, I did not hear from Coach Peterson, so I assumed, just like with the Yankees, that I was not good enough for Wofford College. I was quietly disappointed and had plenty of time to think about the future. I knew that I did not want to end up a worthless good for nothing bum or dead, so I decided to pursue a job at one of the local factories.

After considerable thought, I decided to pursue a full time job at Rubbermaid at the end of the summer. Mom had worked in their factory for years, and she seemed happy most of the time. I had all but decided, but then something amazing happened.

On July 28, 1969, the Wofford College acceptance letter arrived. I let Mom and Grandma know that I had been accepted. I still had not heard anything from Coach Peterson, but I learned that I was expected to report for summer practice on Sunday, August 19.

The acceptance letter was a watershed event—a catalyst and sign for change. It was a confirmation that I was smart enough to go to college, which would provide me a valuable pathway to opportunity. After the initial celebration, it dawned on me that I had only three short weeks to prepare for the rest of my life. Would I be ready for the journey?

At the minimum wage of $1.60 per hour, after living expenses, I had saved a total of $700 from summer jobs. The first semester's tuition was $1,250, which meant that I was still $550 short. I wondered where I would find the rest of the tuition money. Mom was an hourly worker, and I assumed that she barely earned enough to get by, but as a last resort, I asked for her help. Somehow, by the grace of God and maybe a little help from Grandma, Mom found $600 to lend me. She made it clear that it was a loan and not a gift. That would leave me with an extra $50. It would be tight, but I would have to make it work.

I went by Mom's house the morning of August 18, 1969, just before I left for South Carolina to pick up the money and say good bye. It was uneventful except for Mom's final instructions. She said, "Your grandma asked me to remind you that you have to do your best to be your best, and she sends her love. You are the first in our family to go to college, and I am proud of you. I want you to promise to work hard to get the best education possible, because an education is one of the few things in life that no one can ever take away from you." To get the cash and to make her happy, I promised that I would do my best, which turned out to be a lie because I could have done much better.

I did not have a car, so I asked Jim Underwood if he would drive me to college. Jim was slightly taller than me, with fair skin and bright red hair. He too was on the quiet side with a short fuse, and neither of us had many close friends. He agreed to take me to South Carolina, and we left Wooster, Ohio, on Saturday, August 18, 1969, just after lunch. It was a beautiful, sunny day. I was excited about college but naturally anxious about the future.

Jim was a car guy, and he had just bought a silver 442 Oldsmobile. It had black leather interior, bucket seats, and a four on the floor standard transmission. It was one of the fastest cars in town. This trip was a rare opportunity for him to take it out on the open road. We headed south through the lush farmlands and crossed the Ohio River, and then traveled up, down, and around the mountains in West Virginia, Virginia, North Carolina, and then South Carolina. We flew down the highways, but even in a four hundred horsepower muscle car, it was much farther to South Carolina than I had ever imagined.

The trip was a much different experience from what I had expected. I assumed that I would be overwhelmed with positive feelings. That was not the case. With plenty of time to think, I began to question my bold decision to leave Wooster. There were many unanswered questions. I was uncertain what to expect, which I guess was what made me so uncomfortable.

As it got dark, I began to feel like Christopher Columbus and was unsure if we would make it safely to South Carolina before we sailed off the end of the earth. We finally reached our destination. It took every bit of twelve hours. I had had no idea that it would take so long. In fact, I am embarrassed to admit that, at the time, I thought you could get almost anywhere in the world in twelve hours. I had no frame of reference, because, until this trip, I had never been anywhere outside of Ohio. I guess I still had lots to learn, including basic geography.

When we found the Wofford College campus, Jim dropped me off and headed back to Ohio. I was now on my own in a strange place. It was after midnight, and there were no people around. I gathered my duffel bag and slept on a sofa in an open building that I later learned was Shipp Hall. I was cold, nervous, and worried. There was no turning back, and the uncertainty of this new world was killing me. It was no surprise that I didn't sleep much.

Sunday morning, I was up early, walking the property to be sure that I was at Wofford College. I met a big man and introduced myself, and he confirmed that I was in the right place. His name was John Miller, and he told me that he was a junior from Dillon, South Carolina. He was six foot four and weighed 225 pounds. I had many questions, and we talked for a short while. He had a distinctive, slow southern country accent—a dialect that I had never heard before. In John's case, it was so pronounced and distinctive that I could hardly understand him.

During the course of our brief conversation, I shared my academic concerns. He said, "I was an average student in high school, and when I arrived here, I had the same concerns as you. It is different from high school because you are on your own and there are lots of fun things to do around here. It was hard for me when I first arrived, but I have done well. You will have to study, but if you got accepted, you can do the work. You will be fine, but as a new freshman football player, that should be the least of your concerns today. We are running the mile this afternoon.

You'll be there, right?"

"Yes, sir," I answered.

Our conversation went a long way toward reducing my classroom anxieties, but shortly after John left, I realized that I forgot to ask him what position he played. It would have been reassuring to know that a man of his size was not a defensive back.

Later that day, at the track, I was relieved to learn that John was a highly regarded defensive lineman.

Four

FEAR

The difference between a successful person and others is not a lack of strength, not a lack of knowledge, but rather a lack of will.

—Vince Lombardi

I showed up early at the track and immediately ran into Coach Peterson. He was surprised to see me, but he did his best not to show it. He shook my hand, hugged me, and made me feel welcome, which went a long way toward affirming the college decision.

We were scheduled to run that afternoon on the track around Snyder Field. As I looked around, I was surprised at the size of some of the players. I thought to myself, *I have to make this work. I came here to play football and am confident that I can walk on and earn a scholarship because Jack told me, back in the spring in his guidance counselor's office, that I could play college football at Wofford College.*

It was time for the first real test. Was I ready?

All players were required to complete the mile run in under six minutes before they could practice. I learned that if you did not run under six minutes, you were given another opportunity each morning until you succeeded or quit, whichever came first.

Nervous but confident, I ran a respectable time and finished second behind Mike James, another freshman, who went on to track stardom and eventually completed seven marathons including New York and Boston. We would become close friends later in life.

Mean to Meaningful

Jack was smiling and I was pleased with my performance. I had passed this first test with flying colors, but still had no idea what would be required to survive summer practice, make the team, and become a student athlete at Wofford College.

Summer practice started early the next morning. We practiced twice a day, and the temperatures were often over one hundred degrees in the afternoon sessions. At the end of the day, we crawled back to the dorm. The first challenge was exhaustion, but then came injuries and pain. There was no downtime because between practices we were eating, reviewing films or meeting in skull sessions with coaches. This was a 24-7 job.

I was assigned to the defensive back coach, Fisher DeBerry, a first year college coach. He was thirty-one years old and a former Wofford College athlete. He had played for Jim Brakefield, and graduated in 1960. Coach Brakefield recruited him back to Wofford from McClenaghan High School in Florence, South Carolina, where he was a rising star and inspirational leader.

Fisher is a high energy person who was always excited about something. He had a unique gift that allowed him to educate, inspire, and engage the people around him. I learned later in life that Fisher was an only child and had grown up in a small town in South Carolina. He grew up poor and was raised by a single mother and his grandmother.

The practice regimen was tough, and quite a few players, including many freshmen, quit. I am embarrassed to admit that on several occasions, I thought about quitting and hitchhiking home, but when I heard what was said about the quitters after they were gone, I concluded that it was not an option. At night, in the secrecy and darkness of our dorm rooms, peers discussed the possibility of being redshirted or cut. At the time, I did not know what redshirted meant, but I knew that I could not afford to be cut. I was 650 miles from home with no transportation and virtually no money.

I struggled to get through each day, one practice session at a time, and soon found myself scrimmaging with the experienced upper classmen. I survived and emerged as one of four freshmen to make the traveling team.

When classes finally started, the idea of quitting was long gone. I was now a student athlete, and I was going to get a college education with a bonus: an opportunity to play football. This realization was a turning point. I was determined to get some playing time, maybe even start a game or two, which I believed would be necessary to earn a scholarship. I was encouraged, and everything was coming together when I discovered that Coach Peterson had not told me everything about Wofford College. He omitted at least one very important fact.

It was the first week of classes when I made an alarming discovery in Doctor Tom Thurman's history class. I was totally bored, and as I casually looked around the room, I noticed something odd. I leaned over to share the observation with my friend Tom Bower, who was a teammate and standout athlete from Roswell, Georgia. As freshmen, we had survived summer practice together. I whispered, "There are no girls in this class."

He gave me a confused look and, after a few seconds, just chuckled out loud. Tom's was one of only a few fragile friendships, and he certainly understood my insecurities from our time together on the field. I cornered him immediately after class and asked, "What did you think was so funny?"

"Ed, you are going to discover that there are no girls in any of your classes," he responded.

"Are you sure? Really? No girls? Why not?"

"Because Wofford is a men's college."

I quietly thought to myself that "men's college" meant a college of men only. I did not know that there was any such thing. Coach Peterson had not mentioned this in our conversation last spring. It would have been nice to know there would be no female students at Wofford. I am not sure it would have been a deal breaker, but it would have been nice to know. I could only guess that Jack didn't think the information was material, but even without girls, I was starting to like the place, so I decided to let it go and make the best of the situation.

I got my big break during the second game of the season when Dooley Bizzell went down with a season ending knee injury. Dooley was a star wide receiver on offense, returned kickoffs and punts, and was on the kickoff cover team. He did it all. He was over six feet tall and was one of the most talented players on the team. When Dooley went down, Coach Alexander sent me in to replace him on the kickoff team. I covered two kickoffs and made both tackles.

Tom Bower played in those first two games too. He suffered from a rare disorder that caused his arm to swell, a condition the team dubbed "elephant arm." As it turned out, this was his final game, and he would eventually be medically redshirted for the season.

Even though Tom was out for the season, his parents were present. Tom Senior was a balding gentleman who ran an oil jobber business, and Shirley was a tall, attractive wife and mother. They rarely missed a game and knew most players by name. They took a special interest in me, knowing that I was from Ohio and far from home. I still remember the very first time that we met. It was the first home game of the 1969.

After home games, players went out to nice dinners with friends, parents, or girlfriends. As a loner with no friends, parents, girlfriends, or dinners I had no place to go and all night to get there. I was in no hurry to shower and get back to the dorm.

When I finally emerged from the locker room, I saw Tom standing with his parents. Their car lights were on, and they were the only people left in the parking lot. Tom waved me over and invited me to join them for a steak dinner, and I did. Tom Senior and Shirley were authentically interested in getting to know me and asked a lot of questions. I was flattered by the personal attention and their seemingly over the top interest. Being with them made me feel special. They were inclusive and treated me like family. Over the next four years, I spent a lot of time with the Bower family and was blessed to learn much from, and about, them. They were kind people, and I saw them as perfect parents.

During halftime of the next game against Presbyterian College, Coach Peterson told me that I would return punts in the second half. It was a wonderful opportunity to prove myself. I returned the first punt 48 yards and the next game I had a 61 yarder for a touchdown. Returning punts was my first real progress toward earning a scholarship and would lead to other valuable playing opportunities.

During the first quarter of our sixth game, the tight went down with a season ending injury. Coach Brakefield was visibly upset. He took his hat off; threw it on the ground; stomped on it in disgust, scratched his balding head; and then finally called for Coach Peterson. "Can your little man play tight end?" he asked.

"Yes, he can play anywhere you need him," Jack said.

I overheard the conversation and felt good about Jack's response; however, I couldn't believe that Coach Brakefield had referred to me as the "little man." At five foot eleven, I was four inches taller than him and outweighed him by at least twenty pounds. I think the truth was that he simply couldn't remember my name in the moment. The nickname stuck, and I was always the "Little Man" to Coach Brakefield.

We finished the season 9–2, but did not qualify for the national championship playoffs even though we had won our last nine games in a row, most by landslides. Our offensive yardage and points scored were among the best in the nation. Jack's powerful wishbone offense—with Harold Chandler, our star quarterback, at the helm—was turbocharged and running on all eight cylinders. In researching the facts for this book, I discovered that many of those 1969–70 team records still stand today. We had become a world class band of brothers, and almost everyone was returning the next season.

As promised, Coach Peterson aggressively searched for financial solutions. He helped me get a student loan for the second semester tuition, and got me a small work study job in the library. It was helpful, but it would not be nearly enough. I would require a scholarship to return.

Time was running out when Coach Peterson asked me to come by his office. I assumed that he was going to tell me we had reached the end of the road and there would be no scholarship then or ever…no hope, no help, and no future. That was what I had come to expect in my world. However, that would not be the case today. When I arrived, he did not offer up the expected bad news but instead gave me a much needed ray of sunshine. "I think I may have found you a scholarship," he said with a smile. "I have arranged for you to meet an important lady. She goes to my church, and she may be able to provide a scholarship, but she wants to meet you. She insists on knowing all of her student athletes. I will pick you up in front of your dorm tomorrow morning at eleven thirty sharp. We are going to her house for lunch."

I showered and put on my best clothes: a T-shirt and a pair of clean blue jeans. When Coach Peterson arrived, he took one look at me and shook his head in disgust. "Ed, this is an important meeting, and you should wear a coat and a tie."

"Well, Coach, we have two problems," I said.

"What are they?" he impatiently asked.

"I do not own a coat nor a tie."

He thought for a moment. "That is not a problem. Just go back in the dorm and borrow what you need from the guys on your hall, and do it fast. I worked hard to get this meeting, and we cannot be late."

I rushed back into the dorm and did exactly as I was told. We got into his truck, raced down Main Street past the shops, and arrived a few minutes early. We were meeting with a lady by the name of Vera Parsons. She met us at the door with a smile, invited us into her home, and led us through the spacious living room into her lovely dining room. We talked during lunch, but I noticed that Jack hardly touched his food. He was quiet, analyzing everything while Mrs. Parsons queried me about my personal history and some about my dreams, which were few at the time.

Mrs. Parsons was a small, attractive widow in her seventies. In many ways, she reminded me a lot of Grandma, which made me unusually comfortable. I would later learn that Vera was an heir of the Winn Dixie fortune. She was the youngest of five children and the only girl. She was a generous lady with a long history of philanthropy and was known to provide a hand up to financially stressed student athletes. She was pleasant and asked a lot of questions. The visit turned out to be fun, and Jack was pleased. I would learn later in life that Mrs. Parsons loved men. She married four times, and those marriages resulted in her helping each husband find his way, just as she was trying to do for me as a struggling student athlete.

The coat and tie must have worked, because the next day, Coach Peterson informed me that I would be a Vera Parsons scholar the next year. I did not know what all that scholar stuff meant, but what I did know was that Mrs. Parsons was going to pay for me to go to school and that I was probably going to be able to return. I later learned that she would provide me with a full scholarship—including books—for the balance of my time at Wofford. This was an unbelievable gift that I clearly underappreciated.

I had no further contact with Mrs. Parsons during my time at Wofford College. I got what I wanted, and frankly I never felt the need to see her again. I was just happy that she was paying my college tuition. I did not fully appreciate the value of her generous support. In hindsight, I am surprised at my lack of awareness, maturity, and gratitude.

There were many generous people making significant sacrifices for me. They were handing me the world on a silver platter, and I did not even know it. I was blind to the significance of what was happening to and for me. Once again an outsider was helping me find my way along the path of life. This time it was not a coach but a kind generous lady who made the difference.

A more pressing issue surfaced as the second semester progressed. It was still uncertain if I was going to survive academically. If I failed, I would not need a scholarship. Fortunately, I discovered a new advisor who would become an important ally and friend.

When I went to breakfast that spring morning, I stopped by the post office to pick up my mail, as I did every day. There was usually a letter from Grandma and occasionally one from Mom. Although I had moved on, I still looked forward to those letters from home. On this day, I found an invitation to report to the dean's office at my earliest convenience, which I learned from my roommate meant immediately. I thought, *uh oh, this is not good.*

During that first year, I played football and then baseball. Fisher DeBerry also coached the baseball team. During his time at Wofford, he had been a two sport letterman. We had a wonderful relationship, but he played no favorites. His coaching style was aggressive and competitive. Practices, just like in football, were focused and highly disciplined. As in high school, I played in the outfield, but my baseball star did not shine as brightly in college because all my teammates had been high school superstars. We had a game almost every day. When there wasn't a game, we practiced. I considered sports my full time job and rarely attended classes. I had yet to discover what was expected of a student athlete, but the message was on its way.

At the time Joe Lesesne was the dean of students, and it took me a long time to work up enough courage to walk over to his office. I concluded that just as the Vera Parsons scholarship door had opened, Dean Lesesne was going to close it. There was no mistake, and it was clear from the very start that this was a serious meeting and I was in big trouble. I had never had much guidance at home; once again, I was receiving critical survival guidance from an outsider.

His office was nothing like I had imagined. It was small and modest with old pictures and worn out furniture. When I arrived, he jumped up from his desk, welcomed me, and asked me to take a seat and get comfortable. Dr. Lesesne was a tall, thin, nice looking southern gentleman. After a few introductory pleasantries, he said, "You are probably wondering why I asked you to stop by this morning. Well, I am sad to inform you that we have a serious problem; however, before we get to that, I want you to know that the coaches here really like you, and I believe that Wofford College is fortunate to have you on the campus as a student athlete. We are proud of our athletic programs and pleased with their achievements. That being said, it is important to the success of the college for our student athletes to attend classes, make good grades, and earn a degree. It is most important that all of our student athletes graduate. If they do not graduate and go on to successful careers and happy lives, we have failed our mission. You have to understand that there is more to college than just sports."

He paused for a moment, rubbed his chin, and then continued. "Now to the problem. I would suggest that you go to your classes and spend time getting to know your professors a lot better, because at this college it does not really matter how much the coaches like you. As a student athlete, you are expected to be a student first. I can promise that if you do not attend classes and get to know your professors, and do the required work, then you will not be invited back as a sophomore. In fact, you will not be invited back at all. And one more thing. If you survive, I would suggest that you focus your energies on football. Do you understand what I am saying, and am I clear?" "Yes, sir," I responded.

"Do you have any questions, or does any of the message need further clarification?" he asked.

"No, sir," I answered. With the message kindly delivered, he stood up, looked me in the eye, shook my hand, wished me the best of luck, and dismissed me.

The message was loud and clear. I attended classes and did what was required to get invited back. I decided to focus on football. That was an easy decision since I could not return the next year without the Vera Parsons scholarship.

Dr. Joab Mauldin Lesesne Jr. would go on to be the ninth president of Wofford College and successfully guide the institution for almost three decades. We developed a wonderful relationship of understanding, and I visited Dr. Joe's office regularly, mostly at his invitation. I am blessed that he took a personal interest in my survival.

On April 24, 1970, Mom called to tell me that grandma had passed away. She had a heart attack and died suddenly following a church sponsored sightseeing bus trip to Florida. She was sixty-eight years old. I had never been on an airplane, but I made a reservation on Eastern Air Lines and flew home. I attended the services, but I kept to myself. I was totally devastated and knew that I had lost a wise lady who really cared about my personal well-being and my future. I was an emotional wreck and decided to return to Wofford immediately following the funeral to focus on academics and survival.

I was able, with Dr. Joe's advice, to survive my freshman year. Even though I had a scholarship and could have stayed and worked in Spartanburg, I elected to return to Wooster for the summer. I took the Greyhound bus home, and the trip took almost forty hours. When I arrived home, I learned that Jim Underwood had taken it upon himself to get me a job at Snyder Brothers, where he worked. I moved right back into my old bedroom with him. The job was heavy duty road construction. It was a physically demanding job and was like working out ten to twelve hours every day. The workday began at six in the morning, and the pay was outrageous, with an almost unlimited opportunity for overtime.

The men I worked with gave a full day's work for a great day's pay, and they each made it perfectly clear from the beginning that they expected the same of me. I quickly learned that I would not survive if I did not bust my ass every day. I liked the work and discovered that the more I worked, the more I made—and I learned to appreciate the money. That summer, I learned many valuable life lessons, including the importance and value of hard work.

I worked long hours, saved some money, and purchased a 1965 Ford Mustang. It was racing green with mag wheels and bucket seats. It was an active summer that included plenty of fun. We met old friends and partied every night. I made the same mistakes I'd made in high school all over again, doing a lot of dumb things, which were not limited to all night parties—smoking, chasing wild and crazy girls, and fighting with anyone who looked at me funny.

By the grace of God, I avoided most lethal situations, but toward the end of the summer, my luck ran out. It was two in the morning on a Sunday. Jim and I had been drinking and were cruising for fun. We passed a car, and the two male passengers motioned for us to pull over with the familiar one finger signal, which lit us up. When we reached the next stoplight, they jumped out and charged our car. We naturally got out to engage, but it turned out to be a brief encounter. They were no match for us. There was a lot of blood, and we left them unconscious face down in the street. When it was over, we got back into the car and went home.

I would later learn that one of the men and I had met a year earlier. I was headed to the off campus lunch hangout, the Shack, for a hamburger and a cigarette. He was hanging around just looking for a fight. It all started with casual name calling and a shoving. One thing led to another, but I never saw it coming: a perfectly executed sucker punch. When the blow landed, I immediately lost consciousness and fell hard to the ground, with my head bouncing off the concrete. When I regained consciousness, I had a badly swollen face and two black eyes. It was clear that I lost. That one punch victory had never been avenged—until now.

The police came to the Underwood house later that morning before sunrise and took Jim and me to jail in handcuffs. I assumed the guys were dead and that we would eventually be charged with murder and that the local jailhouse was just a brief stop on our way to the big house. We were released later that day. I asked the policeman why we were being released, and he told me that there was an eyewitness at the other stoplight who reported that Jim and I appeared to be only defending ourselves. The men recovered, and we were never formally charged.

I worked and played hard that summer, but when it was time, I was ready to go back south. I was excited to resume the challenges of school and football. I was sad to leave Jim, the wild parties, and girls, but I was eager to return to college.

The 1970 season included Wofford College playing for a national championship. We were undefeated and dominated our opponents with Jack's powerful wishbone offense. Many articles were written about our team's success in the *Daily Record*, Wooster's community newspaper, and the local residents finally learned how to properly pronounce *Wofford*.

At season's end, the polls ranked Wofford College as the number one small college team in America, which earned us a place in the national championship playoffs. As the top ranked team, we received a bye in the first round. In the next round, we played our most uninspiring game of the season and squeaked by West Liberty College 12–6, which qualified us for the national championship game.

Game day was a beautiful Saturday afternoon. It was December 12, 1970. We got on the bus early that morning and traveled an hour south to Sirrine Stadium in Greenville, South Carolina. It was Furman University's home field, an undistinguished football stadium with a simple dressing shed and no showers. We had played there several times that season, once against Furman and most recently in the semifinal game the previous week against West Liberty College. Our opponent today would be Texas A&I, a school ten times our size. Most of the team's players were shaving, and many already had young children.

Mean to Meaningful

They were a talented team, and it was 14–0 before we knew it. Our powerful wishbone offense moved the ball but could not score. With three minutes and twelve seconds left in the second quarter, Karl Douglas dropped back and threw a forty two yard touchdown pass to his speedy wide receiver, Dwight Harrison, which made the score 21–0. That pass capped a ninety five yard, seven play drive and was a perfect spiral that traveled almost seventy yards in the air. Dwight caught the ball in full stride in the back of the end zone. I will never forget that play, and neither will my teammate and friend Jimmy Johnson.

When we returned to the sideline bench, Fisher DeBerry was sprinting wildly up the sidelines toward us as though his hair were on fire, and was screaming, "Great garden seed, great garden seed," over and over and over again. *Great garden seed* was his colorful substitute for profanity because he did not swear. When he got to us, he asked, "Guys, what happened?" Dean Lemler, Chuck Whitt, and I looked at each other, and after a short period of processing, we all shifted our attention to Jimmy Johnson. He sat with his head in his hands, looking at the ground in shame. The wide receiver, Dwight Harrison, was his man. Jimmy was a gifted athlete and the biggest of the defensive backs. Coach DeBerry waited impatiently for a response. He looked at Jimmy and asked, "Great garden seed, Johnson, what happened?"

After what seemed like an eternity, Jimmy lifted his head, looked Coach DeBerry in the eye, and in an unusually calm voice, he said, and I quote, "Coach, nobody can throw the ball that far. It is just not possible." Jimmy's slow and distinctly southern response allowed Coach DeBerry time to gather his thoughts and regain his professional composure. After digesting Jimmy's response, he patted each of us on the back and returned to his coaching duties.

In Jimmy's defense, Karl Douglas, the quarterback who threw that pass, was drafted in the third round by the Baltimore Colts. The wide receiver, Dwight Harrison, the flanker who caught the pass, was equally talented and was drafted in the second round by the Denver Broncos. Their team was loaded with talent, which included eight players who were drafted by teams in the National Football League. In total, eighteen of the twenty two starters went on to play some level of professional football. They won the game 48–7.

That would be Fisher's last game at Wofford. He was destined for greatness and would ultimately have a long and successful Hall of Fame coaching career. After the season, Jim Brakefield accepted the head football coaching job at Appalachian State University, a larger school, in Boone, North Carolina. Fisher followed him the next day. Jack Peterson was promoted to head coach at Wofford College, and he quickly assembled a new coaching staff.

Many of the leaders on the 1970 team graduated and moved on with their lives in professional careers or graduate school. Fortunately, we had many outstanding players emerge on the 1971 team. The most noticeable was my good friend Tom Bower.

We were rebuilding a team that had lost many of its great players. With a new coaching staff and many rookie starters, it turned out to be a challenging season. We lost four of our first five games, but it ended well, as we won our last five games to finish the season 6–4.

In 1972, we lost our first two games, and we were preparing to play nationally ranked and undefeated Presbyterian College. Tom and I were studying the previous year's game film, and I watched as he blocked a field goal, picked it up, and returned it seventy yards for a touchdown. I asked, "How are you able to block so many kicks?"

He answered, "You have to study the films for player tendencies and weaknesses, but at the end of the day every opportunity requires a lot of luck." From his success, I assumed that he had a pocket full of four leaf clovers.

I would not have to wait long for an up close and personal demonstration. During the Presbyterian College game with just under a minute left in the half, Tom burst past the big lineman like a jaguar, blocked the punt, picked it up, and ran the final twenty five yards for the touchdown. We went into halftime with a 14–10 lead. The game included much second half drama, including a Wile interception with 1:26 left in the game, which sealed the deal and ended any hopes of a comeback. The final score was Wofford 28, Presbyterian 23.

Mean to Meaningful

Even with that win, we lost three of our first four games. We seemed to be improving and had won our last two games to improve to 3–3. This weekend, we were playing Elon College in Burlington, North Carolina. It was a night game, and we started the long bus ride in the pouring rain on Saturday morning. We arrived midafternoon. As we approached game time, the temperature dropped, and the field conditions were wet and muddy. As we went through our pregame warm ups, it was clear that the weather was more fitting for duck hunting than football. On the first Wofford possession, Ricky Satterfield broke free for a fifty two yard touchdown run. It was second and eight. Ricky broke a tackle at the line of scrimmage and headed down the left sideline, getting a final block from the tight end, David Creasy, which assured him clear sailing into the end zone.

The rest of the night was just dirty work in the trenches. Neither team was able to mount much offense due to the sloppy field conditions. We had viewed a lot of game film that week and were well prepared. It helped that veterans Terry Laney, Tom Bower, Dale Vezey, and I had all played in the 1971 game and remembered the devastating 7–6 loss that had ended our twenty game regular season winning streak. We were eager to avenge that loss and defensively were always one step ahead of them. The halftime score was 7–0, but it was still anyone's game.

Early in the second half, we forced their offense into their less favored shotgun formation. They made the change to combat the fierce rush and allow the quarterback more time to pass. Tom made sure that we were prepared for their favorite plays run out of that formation. They were driving, and it was first down and ten at the Wofford forty six. The Elon quarterback, Joe West, took the snap from center and rolled to his right but immediately ran into a bunch of my friends, so he decided to throw to his wide receiver in the left flat. Although I was best known as a standout tackler, primarily because I liked to hit people and hurt them, I was there and ready. With 6:34 left in the third quarter, those long hours in the film room were about to pay off.

I recognized the play, so when Joe looked in the flat and made the pass, I proactively broke on the ball and knew that I was about to get lucky. I timed it perfectly, stepping in front of the receiver for an easy interception. I coasted down the field untouched for a sixty one yard touchdown. The final score was 17–0. It was a significant win because Elon was a great team; in fact, the next year they would play for the national championship.

I was humbled the following Monday when I was named the South Carolina Defensive Player of the Week. This bittersweet celebration was short lived because we lost the next game to an inferior team. We won our final two games to finish the 1972 season 6–4, equaling our 1971 record. Only after the final buzzer sounded and the lights went out did it dawn on me that I was done with college football. I would never wear the pads again.

At the end of the 1972 season, my friend, mentor, and coach Jack Peterson was named the National Association of Intercollegiate Athletics District Six Coach of the Year. He is a good man, and I was proud of him. Tom would return in 1973 for his final year of eligibility and continue his superman feats, receiving every athletic and academic honor possible, including Phi Beta Kappa. He would then go to law school at the University of Georgia, pass the bar, and go to work with his father. One precious gift did not change. We would remain lifelong friends.

The finish line was in sight as I headed to the last exam. It was a sociology class taught by Dan Maultsby. He was a young professor who seemed barely older than me. I enjoyed his lectures on the days that I made it to class. The final exam was three hours, starting at nine o'clock. I got there early so I could get a desk in the back of the classroom. When the tests were distributed, I discovered that it was a one question exam. I was excited because I knew a good bit about the topic and feverishly began to record my unorganized thoughts with a number two pencil in the provided blue books. I was fully engaged, and my brain was running full speed because I wanted to include everything that I knew about the subject. I knew that I needed to pass this exam to graduate. I first looked up from my desk at ten o'clock to discover that everyone in the class was done and gone.

A few minutes before noon, I filled up the final blue book and carried the collection to the professor's desk. After handing in the stack,

I stood there for a few seconds thinking about whether there was anything else I could do or say to advance my cause. Dan noticed that I was awkwardly lingering and asked if there was something else. I had no immediate ideas, so I just started talking. "I really enjoyed your class; however, I am not sure that I fully understood the test question. I included a lot about the subject, and I hope that you can find what you need because I have to pass this class to graduate." Dan listened, and when I finished throwing myself under the bus, he smiled and assured me that I would be fine and wished me the best of luck.

Five

EXCITED

*Find a place inside where there is joy
and the joy will burn out the pain.*

—Joseph Campbell

Average is the worst of the best or the best of the worst. Looking back, I am ashamed of my academic performance at Wofford College. The work was difficult, but I was an empty seat in the classroom and struggled as a result. It was my own fault and I should have done better. I believe that it was harder for me because, as John Miller said, "There were so many other fun things to do."

One of those fun things was a pretty girl. Her name was Vickey Key from Atlanta, Georgia. She was a cultured southern belle, like no one else I had ever met. I was smitten, and she became a huge distraction.

Vickey stood out in a crowd. She was almost six feet tall and strikingly attractive, with dark skin; silky hair; a great figure; and long shapely legs. She had a kind demeanor and a bubbly personality, which reminded me of Mary Poppins. At a party she was like a magnet—people were simply attracted to her.

When we met, I made a poor first impression. Without thinking I made insulting comments about a former boyfriend. My mouth was racing ahead of my brain, and before I knew it the toothpaste was out of the tube. It was not my best moment, but there was an attraction, and we became friends. We spent time together at the El Cid, a popular bar, and we occasionally helped each other get dates. We were like today's

Match.com, and I dated many of the cute girls on her hall. When I got her dates, I handpicked the guys because I wanted her to be treated well.

She begged me to get her a date with David Murphy. She told me that he was her dream date. David was a tall, good looking Pi Kappa Phi fraternity brother and a star basketball player from Greensboro, North Carolina. He was six feet seven inches tall and drove a Citron, both of which fascinated Vickey. They went to a drive in movie, and the experience was not as she had fantasized. Fortunately, they became friends and only dated once.

Vickey was a nice girl with an impeccable reputation. We started officially dating in January 1973 after she broke up with an on and off boyfriend, who attended the University of Florida. Despite our cultural differences we enjoyed being together and our relationship dangerously progressed into the serious red zone.

After graduation, I worked two jobs in Spartanburg, and Vickey decided to attend summer school so we could be together. I worked as a management trainee with the Harley Bag Company during the day and tended bar at the El Cid at night. As the summer progressed, Vickey suggested that we schedule a weekend trip to Atlanta to meet her parents. I had met her mother briefly that spring, but I had not met her father. We settled on a date that worked for everyone. We got a late start from Spartanburg, and the traffic coming into Atlanta was heavy and slow. We were over an hour late. Her father was gracious about our tardiness. He was an Atlanta native and understood heavy traffic.

Their home was a large, two story brick Georgian that sat on over two acres and was surrounded by other mansions. It was one of the nicest homes I had ever seen. There were no homes or neighborhoods like it in Wooster. As we pulled down the long driveway, I got a knot in my stomach. This was quite different from what I expected. Vickey's mother and father were waiting to greet us at the end of the driveway. Her father, Ernest D. Key Jr., was a tall, trim, gray haired southern gentleman who was smartly dressed in a blue blazer. Her mother, Barbara Jeanne Key, was a beautiful, tall, thin, dark haired lady dressed in a Lilly Pulitzer shift. They were a handsome couple and appeared much too young to have a daughter in college.

Although I was an unsophisticated redneck, Mr. Key and I hit it off. He suggested that we have a drink before dinner. We followed him to the house bar, and he prepared drinks. We then walked down a long hall and through the living room to the sunroom. When we arrived, I noticed that there were several silver trays with cute little sandwiches. Fannie, their longtime maid, passed the trays. After visiting awhile, Vickey's mother suggested that we move into the dining room.

I followed Vickey and her parents through the living room and into the hallway that led to the banquet sized dining room. The room had beautiful floral wallpaper and a crystal chandelier, and there was a gorgeous arrangement of flowers on the sideboard. The long mahogany table was set with Waterford crystal, Wedgewood china, and a full arsenal of Gorham silverware.

When we sat down, I was puzzled by all the cups, plates, spoons, forks, and knives. The setting was overwhelming, and I had no idea where to start. It was obvious that Vickey's mother was testing my level of sophistication.

She would quickly learn that I had none. That is right: I had no southern sophistication and no education or experience to guide me. I did not know where to start, so I followed Vickey's lead every step of the way and successfully navigated the dinner experience without embarrassing her. I noticed that Mrs. Key kept a close eye on me. I was not sure what to think, but it was obvious that she had me under the microscope. She kept her cards close to the vest, and I would not get her assessment until much later.

After dinner, I went to a friend's house to spend the night. The good news was that I had survived dinner. The bad news was that I still had another day and a half to screw up. I returned after lunch on Saturday. We sat and talked with her mother and father all afternoon. They were curious about me and naturally asked a lot of questions. We excused ourselves around six o'clock and went to dinner with friends at a popular bar. I made sure that I got Vickey home well before her midnight curfew.

The Keys took us to the Capital City Club for lunch on Sunday before we returned to Spartanburg. It was a beautiful property two blocks from their home. This was my first time at a private country club. We sat around the pool after lunch. Mr. Key and I talked while Vickey visited with her mother. The first visit went well and was fun. I thought her parents liked me. As we were leaving, Vickey's dad asked, "Would you like to come to Atlanta and interview for an executive sales position with our company?" I was caught off guard by his offer.

"Maybe. Can you tell me about the job?" I asked with a well concealed hint of excitement.

"It is an attractive commissioned sales position in an established territory. You should know that our sales professionals are very well paid. In fact, they are some of the highest paid people in the company."

"It sounds like a great opportunity, and I am quite honestly flattered. Can I take some time to think about it?" I asked, intentionally slow playing the answer, not wanting to appear too eager.

"Sure, take all the time you need. I understand this is an important decision, but you should know we currently have a rare opening in the Florida sales territory, so don't take too long," he said.

It was an interesting proposal and one that intrigued me. On the drive home, Vickey and I discussed the events of the weekend. When we got to the interview offer, she seemed surprised. When I got home, I thought long and hard about the best course of action. I was not that happy in Spartanburg, so the next day I called Mr. Key and accepted his offer. I set up an appointment, went to Atlanta the next week, and interviewed with the management team at the Atlanta Belting Company. During the interview process, I was informed that the Florida job had been filled that morning and that I would be interviewing for a new sales trainee position that involved working in the plant.

The final meeting of the day was with the president, an older gentleman by the name of Ed Patton. He was a short, round, balding man who had been with the company most of his career. He was no politician but was a well-respected, honest, matter of fact type guy. I liked him. The interview was intensive, and at the end he asked, "Why would a college educated boy like you take a job like this? It is a trainee job that pays minimum wage." This question was revealing, because he knew I was dating the owner's daughter and would be leaving an attractive salaried job in South Carolina. I hesitated for just a moment to gather my thoughts before I answered.

"I am a poor kid just trying to get ahead. I am still trying to find my way, and I see this as a wonderful opportunity to prove myself. I am not afraid of hard work and am more than willing to do whatever it takes to get the job done. I believe that if I can consistently perform at the highest levels, one day I might earn the right to sit in your chair," I humbly responded. I saw this as a rare chance to enter an opportunity rich life in a new world.

He smiled and then asked, "When can you start?" It was an easy decision, and I accepted his offer on the spot. We shook hands and agreed that I would start in three weeks.

Vickey was enrolled in a semester abroad with her college. She would leave in September to study and live in London for three months. I returned to Spartanburg and put in my resignations. Several weeks later, I rented a small U-Haul trailer and moved to Atlanta.

I started work in August 1973 at the bottom of the organizational hierarchy. I earned minimum wage, and my first jobs were sweeping the floors and cleaning the bathrooms. I was really good at these jobs. The floors were always clean, and the urinals and toilets never had it so good. A college boy sweeping the floors and cleaning the bathrooms— that expensive liberal arts education was really paying off!

I settled into an exciting new life. A friend, Kirk Morton, and I roomed together in a nice apartment complex and played in a flag football league with some old Wofford College buddies. I liked Atlanta and it was an interesting time, but I really missed Vickey. She returned from London just before Christmas. I was glad to see her. We celebrated New Year's together and then she returned to college. That was a bad day. I had her back and then just like that she was gone again. I was in love and wanted Vickey to be a part of my life. We never discussed getting married, but I knew that before I asked I would have to get her parents' permission. I learned that was the way it was done in the South.

I invited her father to dinner to ask for permission. Even though I knew he liked me, I was anxious about the whole process. I could not sleep the nights leading up to the dinner, and I practiced what I planned to say over and over again. I wanted to be sure to get it right. I worried about his possible responses. What if he said no, or, even worse, what if he said I was not good enough?

We met and had several drinks before dinner. I was not sure that Mr. Key was fully aware of my agenda, but as we finished the meal, I finally got up the courage to ask the million dollar question. "I would like to marry your daughter. She is a wonderful lady and I want to share a life with her. She makes me happy and accepts me for who and what I am. Will you give your permission?"

He smiled at me and asked, "Do you love her?"

"Yes, absolutely! I cannot imagine life without her," I responded.

"Will you take good care of her?" he asked.

"I can promise that I will do my best," I said. I was now sweating, and he had to see and feel my growing anxieties.

He thought for a moment and then gave his final answer. "Yes, you have my blessing, and as a formality let me talk with Barbara Jeanne. I am certain that she will approve. We are both very fond of you, although you are quite different from most of the boys Vickey has brought home."

We talked a lot more about his expectations as a father, but in the end, I got what I came for. I was so excited that when I got back to my apartment, not realizing the time, I called Vickey and proposed, and she graciously accepted. It was two in the morning on Thursday, January 17, 1974, Vickey's twentieth birthday.

We were engaged and going to get married. For me, this would be a significant life changing *God wink,* a term originally coined by SQuire Rushnell in his book "When God Winks" in 2003. It refers to those moments when we feel touched by God in a unique and unexpected way. It is an event or personal experience, often identified as coincidence, so astonishing that it is seen as a divine intervention, especially when perceived as the answer to a prayer. Additionally, it is often used to recognize other significant life changing discoveries or gifts.

Whenever I hear Van Morrison's 1967 hit song "Brown Eyed Girl," it sends chills up my spine and often brings tears to my eyes. I know that without Vickey, I would surely be in a different place. She allowed me see the world through her beautiful brown eyes and encouraged me to be a better person. With love, she skillfully pushed hard when necessary, and over time she would gently reset my failed compass.

Shortly after we were engaged, Mr. Key purchased a company in Memphis, Tennessee, and within a few weeks, Mr. Patton offered me a sales territory just as he had promised. It was in northern Mississippi, which I would soon discover was the poorest state in the country. I had no idea what to expect, but I accepted the offer anyhow.

I moved to Memphis in the spring of 1974 after six months of working in the Atlanta plant. During the time in Atlanta, I had swept floors, cleaned bathrooms, and worked throughout the plant to learn the products and their industrial applications. These experiences uniquely prepared me for the new sales role. I loaded everything I owned, including that duffel bag, into the car and headed to Memphis. I found a small modest apartment near the airport and went to work.

I did not know what I did not know about the job, but that did not deter me. I went to the chamber of commerce in every little town in my territory, got a complete list of the businesses, and systematically located and called on them one by one. They included cotton gins, sawmills, cotton mills, grain storage facilities, cottonseed and soybean processors, and a few manufacturing plants. I called on the maintenance people or plant superintendents, who were generally not the business owners. I had to learn to connect and bond with people from all walks of life. I worked long days and developed a lot of new business, which surprised the management in Memphis, since they had been covering this same territory for years. Work became my life, and I used the strong work ethic that I had learned at Snyder Brothers to thrive. I traveled during the week, spent Saturdays in the plant, and used most Sundays to plan the coming week's work.

Several months before our wedding, Vickey and her mother came to Memphis. It was their first visit, and from the very beginning they made it clear that they were disappointed with my apartment and its collection of Goodwill furniture. They liked the neighborhood even less. After a brief inspection, they informed me that I would have to move.

"Vickey will not be safe in this place, and she cannot live here. We must find another apartment," Mrs. Key said. After a brief, educational discussion, she convinced me that I could do better and then offered her help. I agreed to move and appreciated her guidance because I had no idea where to start. I discovered that Mother evaluated apartments by the types of cars in the parking lot. The complex we ultimately selected was brand new and in a nice part of town.

In hindsight, the original apartment worked for me but was a cheap dump in a bad neighborhood, and there were more than a few cars up on cement blocks in the parking lot. Vickey and Mrs. Key returned the next month to help me move and prepare the new apartment. While I moved, they went shopping. They spent the entire weekend furnishing and decorating. The resulting living accommodations were classy and looked like the work of Martha Stewart on steroids.

Vickey graduated from Converse College on August 9, 1974. She took course overloads every semester, attended summer school, and graduated a year early because her mother would not allow her to marry without a college degree. She made it clear that the wedding was off if Vickey did not graduate. "You may marry, but you will get your college diploma first. I married early and did not graduate from college. I am a few courses short of a degree, and it is something that I have always regretted. I am not going to allow any of my girls to make that same mistake."

We were preparing to marry on Saturday, September 7, 1974. I returned to Atlanta the week of the wedding to a full slate of parties. As always, I was excited to see Vickey, but I knew the week of parties would be overwhelming and challenge my fledgling social skills. The eleven groomsmen arrived on Thursday for a casual party that night for those involved with the wedding. The party was graciously hosted by Roger and Jill Smith, who lived across the street from the Keys and were kind enough to allow me to stay with them in their lovely home that week. They were an attractive young couple fifteen years or so older than us. Roger was a handsome and successful stockbroker, and Jill was a beautiful blonde. The elder of their sons, Bear, who was five, was the ring bearer in our wedding.

I had selected the groomsmen earlier in the year, but I had no idea whom to ask to be my best man. Dad was not an option. He wasn't even on the guest list. Months earlier, I had discussed this quandary with Mr. Key, and he suggested several options. I ultimately decided to ask Jerry Richardson. As a Wofford College alum, I had come to know him well, and he was friends with the Keys. Both Jerry and Mr. Key were members of the Young Presidents' Organization.

Jerry and his lovely wife, Rosalind, graciously assisted with wedding parties and helped keep the plans and people, especially me, on track. As we prepared to go into the sanctuary for the wedding ceremony that evening, Jerry pulled me aside, put his hand on my shoulder, looked into my eyes, and said, "I am proud of you. You have come a long way in a short time. You will discover that today is one of the most important days of your life. Vickey is a nice girl, and you are a lucky man. I have gotten you this far, so please do your best to not screw it up." "Yes, sir. Got it." I knew exactly what he meant. With nothing left to say, we headed into the Northside Methodist Church sanctuary to join the others and get married.

The wedding was followed by a lovely reception at the Key home. We survived a week of alcohol rich parties with only a few minor incidents and married in southern fashion.

Six

LOVE

You are amazing just the way you are.

—Bruno Mars

On Sunday morning, we boarded a plane for our honeymoon destination. It was a bumpy two hour flight with a rough landing, which made Vickey nervous because she hated to fly. I was eager to get our bags so we could make our way to our honeymoon hotel at the beach. We were exhausted from the nonstop wedding celebrations and ready for a break. When we picked up the rental car, I discovered that we had a two hour drive to the Hilton Hotel in Ocho Rios. I should have known, but I was still geographically challenged. The trip would take us on a narrow two lane road, and along the way, the road often narrowed into one lane on treacherous cliffs several hundred feet above the blue ocean water. It was an uncomfortable drive.

When we finally arrived and started unpacking the car, Vickey looked to me and asked, "Where is my jewelry bag?" I had no idea what she was talking about.

I honestly did not yet entirely understand the husband role. I thought it was simply living and sleeping together and sharing expenses. That was all I ever saw and all I ever knew. It was a difficult stretch for me, and the learning curve would be steep. Over the next few years, I would have many opportunities to learn, grow, and do better.

During the honeymoon, we would discover that we were not a perfect pair, which I think was a bit of a surprise to both of us. It started when Vickey left her jewelry bag in the Montego Bay Airport. We did not discover that it was missing until we reached our hotel, and we immediately got back into the car and made the two hour trip back to the airport to retrieve the bag. When we got there, I noticed we were low on gas and discovered that we had to rent another car in order to get a full tank. It was during the oil embargo, and gasoline stations were closed on Sundays. When we finally got back to our hotel that evening, the dining room was closed. That was a disappointment, since dinner was included with our hotel package. I was frustrated and angry and lost my temper.

The many glaring differences between me and Vickey began to come into focus that week. She was good, and I was bad. She was kind, and I was mean. She was generous and thoughtful, and I was cheap and selfish. I was a hard ass, and she was a mama's girl. I was poor, and she was rich. We agreed on little, and our backgrounds clashed. She had strong political views, and I had none. She was a religion major, and I was a heathen. We were both naïve, and it was shaping up to be an interesting journey.

On a positive note, the hotel was luxurious, and the staff was attentive to every detail and need. We had a wonderful Jamaican bellman and waiter who took a special interest in Vickey. He took a shine to her southern belle personality and made it his job to give us a delightful experience. We took advantage of the beach amenities, the daily excursions, the sunset cruises, and the many other hotel activities. Even with the distractions and our subtle disagreements, the honeymoon was fabulous. A relaxing trip that ended too soon.

When we returned to Atlanta, we went directly to the Key home. On Sunday morning, we got up early, packed our U-Haul trailer, said our good byes, and began our trek to Memphis. We arrived home later that day just before dusk.

I got up the next morning at six o'clock. It was Monday and time to go back to work. I had been off for almost two weeks. I showered and packed a suitcase like I did every Monday morning, went into the bedroom, and leaned over the bed to kiss Vickey good bye. "What are you doing?" she asked.

"I am going to work."

"Why do you have a suitcase?"

"I am going out of town. I will be traveling all week calling on customers, but I will return Friday night in time to take you out for a nice dinner."

"Please don't leave me. I am all alone in a strange place. Don't go. Please stay with me," she pleaded.

"I have to go. You will be fine," I said. She then looked up at me and began to cry. I felt bad but ignored the emotions and went to work.

This uncomfortable scenario occurred every Monday morning. I was not a good communicator, nor was I equipped to deal with a needy wife. I knew that she was lonely and missed me during the week. I never told her, but I missed her too. Each Monday, I endured that same pain, but I still had to go to work.

I felt bad for Vickey, and I know it was a difficult time for her. I think my time away from home was part of the reason she did not enjoy her time in Memphis. She was lonely and unhappy. Things got a little better when she found a job teaching high school English. It got even better when they asked her to coach the girls' basketball team. At almost six feet tall, she had been a star player in high school.

We were blooming where we were planted. Vickey was enjoying her new teaching and coaching roles and I loved my sales job. We were both thriving beyond our wildest dreams.

While at a sales meeting at Walker's Cay, between the deep sea fishing trips and business meetings, I learned from some of the senior sales guys that we were in a recession. I am not sure I knew exactly what a recession was or what caused it. That was a new term to me, so I thoroughly researched it. My territory was northern Mississippi, the poorest state in nation. Businesses there were always in recession, or at least they seemed to be. The guys continued to ask me questions and were curious what I was doing to increase sales. I didn't feel like I had anything revolutionary to share, so I kept quiet.

They were all good salesmen. In fact, many of them were the same guys who had trained me. Our training program simply included traveling with our top salespeople for a week at a time. During my training period, I had traveled with several of them. I learned so much, which, of course, included all their best practices. I am not the smartest guy in the world, but I was bright enough to recognize good ideas and know what was necessary to succeed.

After much coercing, I finally agreed to share my secrets. As a twenty- four year old rookie, I shared these thoughts at the final dinner. "You asked how I was doing so well during these difficult times." I hesitated uncomfortably for just a moment. "Well, it is really pretty simple. I do exactly what you guys taught me to do when I traveled with you. First, I mail my appointment cards one week in advance of my planned visit. Second, I make my sales calls religiously. I even call on some of the most difficult prospects in the territory over and over and over again, even though they never buy anything. Third, I work twelve hour days on the road, and I ask for and expect an order and sale on every appointment." I then humbly added, "That's it, except for a healthy dose of discipline and an ever present fear of failure. The fact is that I cannot afford to fail because I have too much to lose."

When I returned to Memphis, I realized that I had become a workaholic—not a bad disease, but tough on relationships. It was good for me, but bad on Vickey. I could sense the significant tolls levied on her. I knew that the work habits and family last attitude created undue stress in our marriage, but I did not care and did it anyway.

With both of us working, we decided to purchase a home in Germantown, a conveniently located suburb of Memphis. Mrs. Key came to town to be sure that there were no cars up on blocks in the neighborhood. She liked the house, blessed the purchase and then stayed on to help Vickey move, decorate and furnish our new single story, traditional home.

In 1976, I was offered a promotion to run the business in Memphis. It was a difficult decision, but after talking with Mr. Key, I concluded that this opportunity was the most direct path to the presidency, so I accepted the challenge. I believed that the General Manager duties would teach me what I needed to understand and know to lead the company. The new job came with substantially more responsibility and considerably less pay, but it allowed me to sleep at home with my wife every night, a good trade. I was confident that I could do the job and, with Vickey's support, we could make it work financially. The next few years were quite challenging for both of us.

We all have skeletons in our closets. I am cursed with more than my share. There are many deeds that I now regret and lots of personal incidents that are not on the résumés of men of good character. Some of them might even warrant jail time. Anger and rage were my daily enemies, and I still lived a fight or flight life. With Vickey's care and influence, the episodes were far less frequent, but when they showed up, they were explosive and uncontrollable.

We had been in our Germantown home for just a few months when an alcohol related disagreement over nothing escalated into a shouting match. Vickey eventually stormed out of the kitchen, went into our bedroom, and locked the door. She left me sitting all alone at the kitchen table, just like dad had done years earlier. It was like pouring gasoline on a blazing fire.

I was locked out of my own bedroom which really pissed me off. Before I knew it, I knocked down the bedroom door and found myself towering over Vickey in a blind rage with cocked fists. I have this horrible memory of my half naked wife curled up on our bathroom floor, covering her head with her hands, helpless and crying.

At the very last moment I heard a familiar voice whisper in my ear. "Please stop! This is wrong. You are out of control and have no idea what you are doing. When you drink you are just like your grandfather. I know that you are better than this. You will discover that the girl on the floor is your greatest advocate. She is a good person and will love you unconditionally despite your many weaknesses. Get off of her right now! This is not your destiny." Was it Grandma?

I left Vickey crying on the bathroom floor, got into my car, and drove around for hours. As I emerged from the apparent out of body experience and slowly regained my sanity, I asked myself, *why would I ever want to hurt her?* It was a good question, but I had no answers, not even bad ones.

I was concerned about Vickey's current state of mind and our future. Would she or could she forgive me? At the time, I believed the chances of that happening were unlikely. I then questioned whether this might be the beginning of the end.

When I returned to the house in the early hours of the morning, I decided to sleep in one of the guest rooms, which would become my new bedroom. I did not sleep but instead continuously replayed the events of the evening.

The next day, I asked Vickey if we could talk. She said, "No, absolutely not. I am scared of you and uncertain of my feelings. I need some time to process the situation and evaluate my options." For me, this was a painful period of serious soul searching. I realized that without Vickey's forgiveness and significant behavioral changes, I was going to lose everything.

After several weeks, Vickey agreed to discuss the incident. She shared how she felt that night. Her feelings of fear and the resulting images were quite disturbing. Until then, I never thought much about or cared how others felt in my fits of rage. Vickey was quick to point out the many possible scenarios that would change our lives overnight.

During the conversation, there was no finger pointing and no hostility or anger. It was a constructive dialogue, but she did most of the talking. "I love you, but you know only hate and hurt. I believe it is important that you learn to love. You must learn to love me and others like I love you. That is where you have to start. You must acknowledge that love and kindness are good and that hurt and hate are bad. You must know that, in a good man's heart, love and kindness will always trump hurt and hate. It is your choice. You will be challenged to *pay forward* kindness instead of *paying back* hurt. In the past, hurt was all you ever knew. It was all you ever saw, and it was all you ever felt. Your circumstances are now different. You have all the love in the world. Anger and the resulting rage no longer serve a purpose. I know that my love for you is real, and in our wedding vows, I agreed to love you until death do us part, and I will." As we concluded, I realized how blessed I was to have such a wise, strong, and forgiving wife.

I wish that I could say the anger problem was cured and that we lived happily ever after; however, that is not the case. I struggled badly for years, but over time, Vickey's unconditional love and patient care ultimately prevailed. She was right. Love trumped hate as she gradually reset my failed compass, and then together we tamed the anger demons.

On August 15, 1978, we had our first child, a baby girl. She was perfect, and we named her Laura, after her great grandmother. Shortly after she was born, our national sales manager had a tragic automobile accident, and Ed Patton asked me to come to Atlanta and take the national sales manager job. It included a substantial pay raise and a vice president title. I accepted his offer. I was excited about this new opportunity, and Vickey was overjoyed to be returning to Atlanta.

Shortly after we arrived, Ed Patton was diagnosed with terminal cancer. He died a short time later and Mr. Key allowed James Beard and me to run the company. James was responsible for operations, and I was responsible for sales. I was sad about Ed Patton's death, but the new position was a dream come true, and I took full advantage of the opportunity.

We aggressively expanded sales. I split the Georgia territory and trained a new salesman. We then added a warehouse in Orlando, Florida and hired two young salesmen Don Stanford who played baseball at Georgia State University, and Karl Cone, an accounting major from Wofford College. They worked in the plant and then trained for a month with our best salespeople. When they finally got to Florida, they were good to go.

We lived with the Keys while we searched for a home in Atlanta. We finally settled on a conveniently located cute bungalow on Allison Drive. It was the last house on a dead end street in an excellent neighborhood with many small children and good schools.

When we returned to Atlanta, Vickey was invited to join the Converse College Alumni Board. The first meeting date was approaching, and she was looking forward to a quiet weekend getaway with no baby. I agreed to stay in Atlanta with Laura, but at the last minute we decided to go with her to Spartanburg. Vickey reluctantly accepted the change of plans with mixed emotions as she imagined the loss of a quiet weekend alone with her fluffy pillows and magazines. At the time, she was eight and a half months pregnant.

We drove to Spartanburg on Friday evening. On Saturday morning Vickey gave me my instructions for the day. I was to take care of our baby daughter. I knew I could do it, even though I never had. After breakfast, Laura and I drove Vickey to her meeting at Converse College. As she got out of the car, she said, "Please take Laura to the mall and get her a nice winter coat with a hood and heavy lining. It is cold, and she is going to need a coat."

"Consider it done," I said. This was a pretty simple assignment—or so I thought. Laura and I were off for our first ever daddy daughter day. We went to the shopping mall and looked around, and I permitted my fourteen month old daughter to pick out her winter coat, as if she knew what she was doing. It was Carolina blue with a thick, soft rabbit lining and a nice little hood. I thought it was perfect, and it fit, so we bought it. I later learned from Vickey that it was a boy's coat.

Alfred North Whitehead said, "No one who achieves success does so without acknowledging the help of others. The wise and confident acknowledge this help with gratitude." Fortunately for me, there is another chapter in the Vera Parsons story. To be brutally honest, I hadn't thought about her since our lunch meeting in 1969. I had never had a reason to see her again after I got the scholarship money.

After our shopping excursion and a light lunch, we were headed back for a nap when I had an epiphany. I decided to see if I could find Vera Parsons's home. I told Laura we were going to see someone special, but she was sound asleep in her car seat.

I am not sure why, but I suddenly realized the significance of Mrs. Parsons's gift and had an overwhelming need to see and thank her. The emotions were powerful and free flowing. I can only assume it was Grandma again. She was active in my life right up until the day she died. After her death, I believed that she often mysteriously appeared and whispered into my ear, but today she was on a mission to awaken my sometimes absent sense of appreciation. She seemed to know when I needed a nudge, and she was not going to allow me to miss this rare opportunity to personally thank someone who had unselfishly provided a hand up.

Regardless of the origin, the gratitude that had been absent in the past suddenly was overpowering, like nothing I had ever experienced. With tears running down my cheeks, I drove straight to the house where Jack and I had met Mrs. Parsons for lunch ten years earlier. It was just as I remembered—a nice home on a large private lot with a distinctive entrance. It was in the best part of town, down the street from the high school. I was surprised that I could find the house, because I had only been there once. I drove right up, parked, walked to the front door, and knocked. There was no answer.

I knocked again harder, and a frail voice on the other side of the heavy door responded. "Who is it?"

"My name is Ed Wile, and I am a Vera Parsons scholar from Wofford College. I had a nice lunch at this house a decade ago, and I wanted to come by today to personally thank Mrs. Parsons for her generous help. Is she at home and available?" I asked, assuming that I was speaking with the maid.

She cracked the large heavy door and said, "I am Vera Parsons, and you are welcome."

As she was preparing to dismiss me, Laura awoke in the car and began to cry. Hearing her, Mrs. Parsons swung the front door wide open. "Is that a baby I hear crying?"

"Yes, ma'am, it is my daughter, Laura."

"There is a chill in the air, and she is probably cold. Please bring her into the house," she said. Her demeanor changed instantly when she opened her home. She was now warm and friendly. With Laura in the equation, it was suddenly like we were family. We spent an hour visiting. She still asked a lot of questions but had a much different agenda from our meeting ten years earlier. She was interested in why I decided to come to see her that day and was curious about me and my family. I shared that we were expecting our second child in a few weeks. She wanted to know all about my wife, who was also a Vera. She was very inquisitive, and I was humbled by her genuine interest.

"I am sorry that it has taken me so long to realize the value of your generous gift, and I am ashamed that I did not come to see you sooner. My mom and grandmother raised me better than that," I said apologetically and then continued. "I was fortunate that Jack Peterson brought me to Wofford College and then was kind enough to introduce me to you."

"Oh, Jack is such a fine man. I know him and his wonderful family well," she said.

Struggling through emotions, I continued, "I want you to know that I would not have come to Wofford College without Jack, and I could not have stayed here without you. Your scholarship was critical to my collegiate survival, and for that I am eternally grateful. Thank you!"

She thought for a few seconds, and then in her frail voice, she said, "You are welcome, and I want you to know that no one has ever come to my home to personally thank me before. You are the first. I am proud of you, and so are your mom and grandmother." She paused, smiled, and then continued, "This has been a wonderful visit. I am so happy that you and Laura decided to come to see me today, and I cannot tell you how much I have enjoyed this time together."

Before we left, she helped me connect with Coach Peterson, whom I had not seen since 1973. He still lived in Spartanburg, and he and Marge attended Vera's church and they were friends. As our time together concluded, she picked up the phone and called Jack. She told him all about our visit and let him know that Laura and I were on our way to his house. She gave me detailed directions. When we departed, Vera kissed Laura on the cheek and gave me a big hug.

Jack and Marge were pleased to see us, and we spent the rest of the afternoon with them catching up. They were both excited to see Laura but still curious to meet Vickey, the miracle worker. It was a wonderful visit, but during our conversation I was surprised to learn that Jack was oblivious to his impact on me and others.

I used this opportunity to enlighten him. "You changed my life when you invited me to come with you to Wofford College."

"I am flattered, but I just encouraged you. It was your choice. You took all the risk, and when you showed up, you came ready to play," he said. "You earned your place on the team. As the coach, I was just doing my job."

I responded, "You know that I would be in a different place today if it were not for you. You are responsible for giving me the chance to attend college and play football. You believed in me, a rare and precious commodity for me in those years. College changed my life forever, just like you said it would that spring day in your guidance counselor's office. I know for a fact that you changed other lives too. My high school friends and teammates Jon Viar and Larry Durstine are perfect examples. They told me how you helped them. Where would they be today without your influence, guidance, and encouragement? Would or could they have gone to college without your help?" He sheepishly smiled but said nothing.

Jack is a humble man, and I believe those flattering accolades embarrassed him, which abruptly ended that part of the discussion. In hindsight, I was shocked at his assessment, but his message was clear—he saw himself as a modest man just doing his job to help young men advance their lives.

When we picked Vickey up, I shared our day's activities. I told her about the powerful emotions that led me to Mrs. Parsons and eventually to the Petersons. Vickey had never met Jack or Marge, and it would be many years before they would become formally acquainted, but she was thankful for his presence and influence. Unfortunately, she would never get the opportunity to meet or thank Mrs. Parsons.

In December 1979, we were blessed with another child. The doctor prepared us for a daughter. We had considered several pretty names for our precious unborn girl. We never settled on one, nor did it matter, because we got a healthy boy. He was born early in the morning on December 4, 1979. We named him Edward Bryan Wile II and decided to call him Chip. With two beautiful, healthy babies, Vickey had her hands full, and since she only had two hands, we decided that our family was complete.

That same year I became reengaged with Wofford College. It was the beginning of my work of paying it forward. After all, this small college had changed my life. Years later, I would be asked to serve as the president of the National Alumni Association. I accepted the assignment and transformed the committee and association to one of education, inspiration, and engagement. I served a productive and rewarding two year term, and learned much about the college. By the end of the second year, I was a lifetime ambassador. In the future, I would get the opportunity to serve the institution in a variety of meaningful ways.

When I was on campus, I often had the good fortune to bump into Dan Maultsby. He always appeared glad to see me and acted like I was someone important. Dan continued to grow with the college and was regularly recognized and promoted. Over the years, Dan and I became friends, and today he is one of my favorite people on campus. Every time I see him, I am reminded of how important it is to do your best. I know now that if I were given the chance—a do over—I would do much better, but unfortunately, life rarely gives us second chances.

I would not get a do over with Dan, but when I attended graduate school, I would not make the same mistakes. I was no longer an immature boy just trying to find my way. I was now a man with two precious children, a lovely wife, and a dog, doing his best to make a better life.

Mr. Key was a supportive father in law and encouraged me to attend graduate school. In many ways, he became the father I never had. I took great joy in pleasing him and worked hard at whatever role I was assigned.

At a family dinner, Vickey learned of her father's vision for graduate school. On the way home, she was curious to know what I was thinking and was surprised that I was even considering graduate school. I told her that it was her dad's idea and that I was only lukewarm to the idea. I figured that graduate school would be difficult academically, and I had not been that good of a student the first time around. I was surprised that she liked the idea and insisted that I apply. As the head of sales, I traveled extensively and was rarely at home during the week. Our marriage was good, but I knew that the time commitment of graduate school would be challenging for us. As the wife of a demanding husband and mother of two children under three years old, she was already overwhelmed on a good day. Piling on more responsibilities would not be fair to her. I was naturally suspicious and unsure of why she was so supportive. It never occurred to me that she wanted me to take advantage of every opportunity to better myself because she loved me.

After much discussion, I applied for admission into the Georgia State University Executive MBA program. It was a long shot, and I was confident that my undergraduate records would keep me out, but I took the GMAT anyway. To my surprise, I was accepted and started graduate school in the fall of 1981 while continuing to work full time.

Georgia State University is a large college in downtown Atlanta with a sprawling urban campus and thirty thousand students. The Executive MBA program was in its second year. The exclusive class included forty two executives from Atlanta and the surrounding area from prominent businesses like Coca Cola, IBM, General Electric, Southwire Company, and Georgia Power Company, to name just a few. My classmates were senior executives looking to advance their careers. I was the youngest in the class and initially was intimidated. I was unsure if I could do the work and keep up with them, knowing that I had never been a great student. The program's structure and schedules were designed to accommodate a full time working schedule. I had classes from eight to five every Friday or Saturday, and with the other regularly scheduled classes, study groups, and my job, I had no time for anything else.

During graduate school, we were very busy and always stressed. Vickey took care of the house and the children. We found it difficult to balance our school, family, and work time because there was always something that needed special attention. Our marriage grew stronger, and I made some lifetime friends. Unlike my time at Wofford, during graduate school I was all in. I went to every class, read every book, completed every assignment, prepared for every class, and studied for every test, and it showed. In the do over, I proved that I could do better, and I was able to prove to myself that I *was* a good student.

Graduation was just around the corner, and I would be attending the last lecture before final exams. The lecture was given by Dr. Mike Mescon, and the topic was the secrets to business success. Mike was short, muscular, middle aged, energetic, and balding, a dynamo in the classroom, and well respected and successful in the business consulting community. It was an 8:00 a.m. class, and I got there early to get a front row seat. I was eager to learn what Dr. Mescon was about to share. Every chair was filled, and the room was bursting with excitement. He shared some personal thoughts and then jumped right into the lecture.

The message focused on three simple but fundamental principles. Mike said, "Success is simple, but these three things are essential to get to the top of the class. First and foremost is that you must show up. If you show up, you will be better than half of your peers. The second point is that you must be on time. Showing up and being on time will make you better than 75 percent of your peers. The third point is that you must come dressed and ready to play, which will put you at the top of the class." That was it: a simple lecture that lasted no more than twenty minutes.

At the time, I was unimpressed and thought his suggestions were too simple. Now, after watching people struggle to navigate their careers, I share these secrets with people I care about. They are easy to understand, control, and execute, and I know from experience that they can change outcomes.

At work, we discovered that our plant manager was stealing. After he was fired, Mr. Key became engaged in the business for the first time since I had been in Atlanta. He wanted to make some drastic personnel changes that made no sense. We discussed the situation, and I encouraged him to consider other options, but his mind was made up. I strongly disagreed and quickly learned the golden rule: he who has the gold makes the rules.

My relationship with Mr. Key deteriorated rapidly, and almost overnight we were adversaries. Work was miserable, and I hated to go to the office. I would lie awake at night wondering what had gone wrong. He sought me out when I was in the office and said ugly things about me in front of the employees. After much soul searching, I decided to quit. I tried several times but could not pull the trigger. It was a never ending battle with myself. I continued to evaluate how quitting would impact the company, our employees, and Vickey and children. After yet another incident, I decided it was time.

I took my personal items from my small office at the end of the hall, quietly loaded them into my car, and headed home. About halfway home, I pulled over to the side of the highway and brought the car to a stop. I was an emotional wreck, but I concluded that I was neither a quitter nor a coward. I turned the car around and returned to work. I decided that if Mr. Key wanted me out, then he would have to fire me.

And that he did. He fired and rehired me twice over the next three months. He fired me for a third time on the night of my graduation party at the Piedmont Driving Club. An incident after the party at the Key home resulted in a heated discussion, and many unkind things were said. The events of that night ended my ten year career with the Atlanta Belting Company for good.

After all the dust settled I wondered how these events would look on my new résumé as I pursued other career opportunities. Would they make it impossible to find another job?

Seven

ANGRY

That which does not kill us makes us stronger.

—Friedrich Nietzsche

I spent the first ten years of my working career at the Atlanta Belting Company, a family business that was owned by Mr. Ernest D. Key Jr., my father in law. As a son in law, I moved through the ranks quickly, gaining priceless knowledge and experience.

Getting fired left me uncertain about almost everything, including Vickey. I was an outsider, and the Keys were a close knit family. I subconsciously wondered if Vickey might choose her family over me once the dust had settled. I was pretty sure she would choose me, but the jury was still out.

On the day I was to receive my master's degree in business administration, I woke up to a future that looked bleak from every perspective. I had lost not only my job but also the man who was the closest thing to a real father that I had ever had. Ernest D. Key Jr. had set my future in motion when he recruited me to his company. We became close as he nurtured my career. He affirmed me, and I thrived under his direction. It wasn't just the challenge or success that I relished; the trust and approval had been equally important, if not more so.

It's funny, but as close as I felt to him, I never called him by his first name, nor did he invite me to: my in laws were "Mother" and "Mr. Key" from the start and remain so to this day. Despite the odd formality, Mr. Key and I were alike in so many ways—stubborn, hot tempered, and driven—that I honestly felt like his son, minus the DNA. I viewed him as a mentor, much like the coaches who had pushed me to be a better player. I don't know if I would describe it as love, exactly, but I definitely felt validated by the way Mr. Key would listen to me, provide advice, and set standards he expected me to meet. Deviate from his prescribed path, however, and there was always hell to pay. As both a son in law and employee, I could generally count on a double helping of his venom. To avoid these situations, I learned to hold myself to a higher standard. At work, I would try to do more than he expected. It did not matter, sometimes there was nothing that could satisfy him, and I still received my share of irrational criticism and punishment.

I'm no Dr. Phil, but I suspected from the get go that his volatility stemmed from insecurity, with his ADD adding fuel to the fire. I had wrestled with that same dangerous duo myself since childhood. Until Vickey came along, rage had been my default emotion. Love turned out to be the only thing that could match its intensity.

Over the years, I had weathered plenty of Mr. Key's infamous storms, but this one, I knew, was different. This wasn't just a few thunderheads passing over. A tornado had touched down at my graduation party the previous night, and our family landscape was forever altered. My father in law's drunken rampage nearly turned into a fistfight. I woke up that Saturday morning thankful that I had kept my own temper in check, but anxiety quickly replaced the relief. The MBA I was being awarded that afternoon was a degree my father in law insisted I earn to prepare to take the reins at his business. Now I was crossing that finish line, but the trophy had been snatched away. In a heartbeat, I had gone from the chosen one to a thirty-two year old nobody with a wife and two babies to support, a mortgage, no medical insurance, no severance pay…and no prospects.

Although they all lived within minutes of us, none of the Keys showed up to celebrate or offer congratulations on one of the proudest days of my life. Vickey came alone to my graduation and reception. It looked like that was how things were going to be from now on. Even Vickey's closest sister, Miff, was absent.

Miff and her husband, Karl, had just bought a house a mile from us, and we were excited to have them nearby. Karl Cone was a fellow alum from Wofford College, where he majored in accounting and began courting Miff. In 1980, I hired him at Atlanta Belting Company, and he quickly became a star. He soon became my brother in law as well. Vickey and Miff had a strong sibling bond, and Karl and I forged a close friendship over the years too. The four of us got along well and enjoyed spending our free time together. Karl helped me paint the outside of our house on Allison Drive and I agreed to return the favor by helping him paint the interior of their new place. I showed up when they closed the loan on the house, which was not long after the big fight with Mr. Key.

Karl and I went to work without saying much. It wasn't a hostile silence, just awkward, and I figured it was best to just let it work itself out. Karl and Miff had been staying with her parents until their house was ready, but I knew they went to a Holiday Inn the night of the blowup, hoping things would cool down the way they usually did after one of my father in law's tantrums. Karl physically held back Mr. Key when he tried to charge me like a deranged bull. In retaliation, Mr. Key tossed all of Karl's and Miff's clothes out onto the front lawn in the rain. Karl quit the next day. They headed to Karl's parents' home in Hampton, South Carolina, to try to figure things out and decompress. After deep reflection, Miff decided to go to work with her father, thinking she could right the ship. Karl had no choice and reluctantly followed her. What else could he do?

That Sunday, while we painted, Karl seemed morose and uncomfortable.

"Karl, what's going on?" I kept asking. "What's wrong?" But he wouldn't—or couldn't—answer.

"Nothing. Nothing's wrong," he insisted, his eyes fixed on the wall he was painting. Finally, I gave up and went back to my own wall. When we were done painting that day, I could tell Karl wanted to say something but was nervous. There were tears in his eyes when he finally blurted it out: "You know, it's probably best for us not to have much interaction for a while." I nodded, knowing that he had been given an ultimatum. Mr. Key was still his boss, after all, and Karl's livelihood depended on him, just as mine had for the past ten years.

The news that we were being shunned didn't even register with me, let alone deliver the crippling blow it was meant to. I had considered it a given that Mr. Key would be vindictive. It was his style. This was war, in the old man's eyes, and if asserting control over his family meant deeply wounding

Vickey, her mother, and her sisters, he didn't care; I had to be punished no matter whose blood was shed.

"I'm sorry. This is all my fault," Vickey tearfully said after we got home from the disastrous party. I knew she would be devastated by her father's excommunication decree, and I was filled with a sickly hate for someone who could do that to his own daughter, but dealing with this melodrama would have to wait. I had to find work and find it quick. We had no source of income or insurance, and if I didn't land a new job pretty soon, I might not have any walls left to worry about painting. Weirdly enough, the prospect of imminent homelessness didn't send me into a tailspin. I knew this drill from childhood, when my single mother seemed to teeter on the brink of destitution while moving us from one ramshackle rental to the next.

Divorce had pulled the rug right out from under Mom, and the bitter experience of watching her start all over from scratch caused me to be a disciplined saver. Fortunately, Vickey was too, and we had faithfully saved 25 percent of every paycheck, even when we were only making minimum wage. We lived below our means, and had managed to build up a modest savings account, which now became our emergency fund. We sat down together and reviewed our budget and determined that we had enough savings to last about a year.

I tried not to let Vickey see how terrified I was. I didn't want her to know that being fired was doing a real number on my ever shaky sense of self-worth. I couldn't sleep, and when I did manage to drift off, I often jolted awake again in a cold sweat. I thought, *how did I take such a good thing and let it go bad? Was it because I didn't deserve it? Or wasn't thankful enough? What's wrong with me? Am I just a bad person, a fraud who can be successful only if he marries into a family business? Mean Wile. Remember when they used to call you that? Maybe that's all you ever were and ever will be.*

Vickey was torturing herself as well, putting on a good show for my sake just as I was for her. Her mother had returned from a horse show in Kentucky that fateful weekend to find Ernest seething and the family in ruins, but Barbara Jeanne's usual attempts at diplomatic mediation had failed. At her urging, Vickey had gone to her father's office that following week to extend an olive branch. She was not sorry that she had defended me; Vickey tried to explain, but the way she had said it was disrespectful, and she *was* sorry for that.

"I don't accept your apology!" her father bellowed. "Get out of this office, and get the hell out of my life!"

Most of Vickey's old school friends had moved on with their lives by the time we had returned to Atlanta five years earlier. Once she became a mother and stopped teaching, her world revolved almost entirely around family. When I got fired, Chip and Laura were just three and four years old, and Vickey's youngest sister, Elizabeth, would come after school to help out while Vickey made supper. Barbara Jeanne would also often drop by with bags of groceries or just to visit over a glass of iced tea or to play with the kids. Chip and Laura noticed her sudden disappearance. "Where's Mimi?" they kept asking. "Why can't we see Mimi? Why can't Mimi come over?" I knew my mother in law ached for life to go back to normal too, but Vickey's two youngest sisters still lived at home, and Mother knew Ernest would turn their world into a daily hell if they all didn't bow to his will. She might be able to sneak in little visits now and then, maybe meeting up at the zoo with the kids or grabbing a quick cup of coffee with Vickey, but she didn't dare openly defy her tyrannical husband's no contact edict.

"I've got to look at the bigger picture," she said by way of apology.

"I understand," Vickey said, but that didn't make the reality any less hurtful.

Getting a job had to be my top priority, and I couldn't begin to fill the void her family had left in Vickey's day to day life. Vickey and Miff were accustomed to seeing or speaking to each other every day; it wasn't so much separate, distinct conversations that they had as it was one long, continuous chat threading through their intertwined lives. Now Vickey was the pariah, and as I would only learn years later, she would wait for the kids to go down for their naps and then spend hours curled up in bed crying her eyes out. The sheer loneliness was killing her, but I was too consumed by the frantic search for work to notice how bad it was. It is a testament to both her kindness and her strength that she somehow managed through her own pain to give me just what I needed just when I needed it. I relied more and more on her insight and intelligence, and she became my most important confidante and advisor as I cast about for a new career. I grew up with emotional trauma, but Vickey, by her own admission, was so sheltered that her biggest dilemma up until now had been deciding whether to wear pink or blue shoes to church. This was trial by fire, and Vickey quickly proved herself a natural survivor. We had been husband and wife for ten years, but for the first time, we truly became partners. She was my personal Mary Poppins with her sunny disposition and can do attitude. Knowing that I wasn't in this alone went a long way toward stitching up the self-worth my father in law had left in tatters.

Within days of my firing, I was at home researching companies and people I might contact when the phone rang.

"Is this Ed Wile?" a stranger's voice asked.

"Yes, it is. May I ask who is calling?"

The caller identified himself as a headhunter for a company he wasn't at liberty to name. "Our client has an interest in talking with you. You are on their short list, and they asked us to call you to see if you would be interested in an attractive senior executive position." "If this is a joke, it's not a funny one," I snapped.

"It's not a joke," the headhunter assured me.

Once I was convinced that this wasn't a hoax by some rival at the Atlanta Belting Company who wanted to rub salt in my wounds, I agreed to talk. I eventually learned that the company was Rhoads Belting Company, which at the time was the oldest incorporated business in America. They were looking for a new president. Rhoads was a financially strong, highly regarded business. I knew them well as my father in law's biggest customer.

This wasn't merely a job opportunity, I quickly surmised. This was redemption, with a side order of revenge on a silver platter. I licked my lips at the thought of serving that dish, stone cold, to Mr. Key.

Of course I was interested, I told the headhunter.

Not long thereafter, I traveled to Wilmington, Delaware, so eager to find out more that I took the early bird. The Rhoads chairman picked me up, and I spent the entire day interviewing with the family, testing, talking with employees, reviewing the company's financial records, and touring the facilities. It was a good operation, and I was impressed. I could easily picture myself at the helm. The company owner, Dick Rhoads, was a legend in the industry, a grandfatherly gentleman in his seventies who proved easy to talk to and good at listening. He wanted to know all about me and was keen to hear the circumstances surrounding my exit from the Atlanta Belting Company. As a customer, he knew my father in law well—they had done business together for several decades. As the wise patriarch of a family business, he knew how complicated things could get when personal differences boiled over into the workplace. After our conversation, I felt as if he understood my departure on a deeper level than even I did. My wounds were raw, and my emotions were clouding reason. There was a genuine sense of connection with the Rhoads family, and I started to get excited that this might be the perfect opportunity for me as well as for Vickey and the kids. We could start over in a nice place that could become ours, without the constant reminders of the painful feud with the Keys. I would be well compensated, and Wilmington promised a lifestyle we hadn't dreamed of in Atlanta.

On the flight home, though, a familiar seed of insecurity sprouted, and I began to second guess everything. Were they really serious about hiring a thirty-two year old as their next president? *Don't get your hopes up,* I cautioned myself. When Rhoads called me the next day, I had already steeled myself for the big letdown, mentally rehearsing how to conceal my disappointment with polite gratitude at having been considered for the position in the first place. Instead, I was invited back for a second interview. This time, they suggested that I bring Vickey along.

Vickey proved far less enthusiastic about meeting the Rhoadses than they were about meeting her. The belting industry was too small for her father not to catch wind of my recruitment, she knew, and while her dad didn't have the power to make things worse for us anymore, she was certain that he could—and would—aim his renewed wrath at her mother and sisters. In the end, she agreed to go with me for the second interview and to keep an open mind.

We flew to Wilmington the following week. The Rhoads folks met us at the airport and gave us a grand tour of their city. We were shown the schools, which were good, and pastoral neighborhoods with big beautiful houses on large parcels of land. We even visited several attractive homes that were available for purchase. Somehow they knew traditional homes were Vickey's favorite. Atlanta couldn't hold a candle to what we might have in Wilmington! We wrapped up with a dinner at Dick Rhoads's home. The family was there, along with senior management and their spouses. It was a delightful dinner, and everyone was convivial. There was none of the stiff formality or five fork pretension that marked Key family dinners; on the contrary, the feast the Rhoadses treated us to included corn Vickey had helped pick fresh from the field that day. It was as if we had somehow been painted into a Norman Rockwell canvas, and the glances Vickey and I exchanged said it all: *Why can't our family just be like this?*

I had a conversation on the porch with Dick Rhoads before dinner. "Ernest called me today," he said. Vickey must have told her mother about the trip, I realized, and news that I was being courted by his biggest customer probably sent my father in law into the kind of head spinning, bile spewing fury that had made Linda Blair famous in *The Exorcist*.

I smiled at my host.

"Oh, really?" I said. "What did he say?"

"He was emotional and said unkind things that I prefer not to repeat."

"I guess that is no surprise. I know this has been particularly hard on Vickey. Well, after talking with him, what do you think?"

"I understand why he is upset and I hope that if we make you an offer, you will take it."

Once we were alone, Vickey had to admit that as much as she wanted to hate Wilmington, she was impressed. It was a good place to raise a family. She sounded tentative, but at least the window was open now. I could barely contain my excitement. The moon and the stars seemed to be slowly lining up. I pictured us in a big house with a huge grassy yard where I could toss a football with Chip or kick around a soccer ball with Laura. There would even be a brand new company car in our garage. A runaway imagination saw a new black Mercedes Benz two seater coupe with tan interior. We could become significant again, and I wanted this job now more than ever. As we were boarding our plane back to Atlanta, Vickey turned to me. "This is a great opportunity," she said, "but please don't take it."

It was a quiet trip back to Atlanta. Vickey and I barely spoke on the plane, both of us processing our thoughts of the day. Enticing as Wilmington was, Vickey knew that it would mean crossing paths with her father again, and even if I held all the cards, it wouldn't make it any less painful for her. The fact that Mr. Key had called Dick Rhoads to discredit me had only confirmed her worst fears: this was going to set Daddy off more than ever. wouldn't have admitted it out loud then, but she was right to also suspec that I savored the prospect of revenge as much as the promise of success. Working for Rhoads would finalize our personal estrangement with Mr. Key while keeping us professionally entangled. Late that night, Vickey quietly gave me her verdict: "I don't really want to do this, to go there, but I will let you make the decision."

I was surprised by her feelings, but the job hadn't even been offered, and we agreed to keep talking. And if I did land the position, I knew Vickey would be true to her word and accept my decision with every ounce of optimism she could summon. I hoped to win her over in the meantime; I wanted her to want the fresh start as much as I did. I even tried to convince myself that leaving Atlanta was a selfless, noble thing to do for my mother in law and Vickey's sisters. With us far away, I reasoned, there would be no catalyst for the hostility and dysfunction that prevailed under the dictatorship of Mr. Key. You cannot carry on a state of war when the enemy has decamped, it stood to reason. I went back to my fantasy of a perfect life in Wilmington. Vickey and the children would be happy, and we would be successful.

Shortly after we got home, I heard from Rhoads. They advised me that they were interviewing other candidates. They wanted to know my level of interest; I shared my thoughts without committing. At the end of the conversation, I was told they expected to make a decision within two weeks and that I would hear back from them. I hung up, not sure what to expect. This could go either way. As much as I wanted to go to Wilmington, I dove right back into mining for prospects in Atlanta. My strategy was to visit the senior trust officers at every local bank in the city, looking for a family business for sale that needed a new leader. I felt confident that I could buy— and run—a company of my own.

Not many real businesses were available, but after rummaging through a lot of garbage, I discovered a gem. It was a family owned granite company in Elberton, Georgia, a profitable business on its own. I could envision several markets and products that could be developed with minimal capital investment. There was just one problem: it was valued at $6 million. Our entire net worth and available resources were insufficient, and I knew it would take additional equity capital to make the deal work.

I remembered an old friend, Phil Lundquist, the former managing partner of the E. F. Hutton office in Atlanta. Phil had been one of my sponsors for the Capital City Club in 1980, and I knew his connections included private equity sources. I decided to seek his advice. We met at his offices in the Piedmont Center the next day. I gave him the granite company's financial statements and shared my ideas. He promised to look over the information, and we agreed to meet again the following week.

"Ed, will you do me a favor?" Phil asked as I was leaving.

"Sure, anything. You name it."

"I want you to visit with Bob Varn," Phil said. "Bob is a good friend of mine, and he's the managing director at Kidder, Peabody & Company, a boutique investment firm here in Atlanta. I've known you for a long time, and I sense that you would be a good investment guy." I wasn't keen on the idea at first—the field was so far removed from my knowledge and comfort zone that Phil may as well have suggested I become a marine biologist—but once he told me how much a good investment broker could earn, I decided I owed it to my family to at least research it. As a favor to Phil, I agreed to go see this Bob fellow and ask a few questions.

That proved easier said than done. When I called Bob the following morning to set something up, we had barely exchanged greetings before he started pushing me to attend an informational seminar later that month. "Thanks," I said, "but I just want to make an appointment to talk with someone about how the business works and what it takes to be successful." Bob ignored me and urged me once again to attend the seminar. I politely refused—again—and pressed for an appointment. "I'm willing to come down there and sit in the office lobby until someone can see me," I said, thinking I could probably chat up passing brokers for the inside story.

"Come to the seminar," Bob insisted. After I rebuffed his seminar pitch for the third time, he hung up on me. Five minutes later, the phone rang. It was Bob's right hand man, Lewis Holland.

"Are you the guy who wants to come sit in my lobby?"

"Yes, I'm that guy," I said. Lewis invited me to drop by for a visit that afternoon at the Kidder, Peabody & Company offices in the First Atlanta Tower downtown at Five Points, which was the heart of the financial district. With his premature gray hair and courtly manner, Lewis was the epitome of the southern gentleman. He spent several hours telling me what the investment business was like and what it took to be a good broker.

"It's a very risky career," he said. "The failure rate for new people is high, and fewer than 10 percent do enough business to prosper." If those odds were meant to scare me off, it didn't work; now I was really intrigued.

Lewis was kind enough to introduce me to the other branch managers in town, and within a week, I had interviewed and tested with them all. All but one made me an offer. It was going to be a hard fall, though, from the executive ranks I considered my natural habitat. I would not be a president, CEO, or even vice president. I would be a stockbroker trainee. The training, I surmised, would be thin and the salary guarantees minimal. Despite the high risk and low pay, I liked the job flexibility and was excited by the opportunity to change lives. I was undaunted by the high failure rate because it made success that much sweeter: within those elite ranks, there was unlimited income potential.

Maybe this was fate. Back when I graduated from Wofford, I had interviewed with Smith Barney in Spartanburg. It was a last minute interview, and I went only because I needed a job. I didn't get an offer, but I did get some useful advice from its long tenured manager, a fellow Wofford alum named Marion McMillan. "Go out into the world and get some successful sales experience and come back to see me in five years," he said. "You're too young and inexperienced to survive in this business at this time."

But now, I was starting to feel the time might be right. I felt ready. I would have to make sure Vickey was on board, given the necessary family sacrifices and potential risks this career change entailed. You were more likely to crash and burn on the launching pad than rocket to the moon, but what a thrill if you made it. Vickey was gung ho. "That sounds great!" she said. I knew her enthusiasm was probably less about the job than it was about staying in Atlanta, but it felt good to have her endorsement after our impasse over Wilmington. I ditched the granite company idea and started mulling over the trainee offers from investment firms. The deals were pretty much the same, so it came down to which company I liked best. My favorite was Kidder, Peabody & Company, the boutique firm. I trusted Lewis Holland, and the company's philosophy, people, and culture seemed to be a better fit for me. So it was settled.

Or not.

The telephone rang. It was Dick Rhoads calling to update me on the job. "We have completed our search, and the committee met this morning and unanimously agreed that we want you to lead our company. We need your energy, enthusiasm, and experience at Rhoads. We want you. As I said at our dinner last month, 'If we make you an offer, I hope that you will take it.' I am making the offer. Would you like to come to Rhoads as our president?"

I was speechless and struggled to control the overflowing emotions of joy, but I remained poised and calm long enough to hear him out. We discussed the responsibilities of the job and the detailed terms of the agreement. It was an exciting opportunity. There was still one hitch: I could not make a final commitment until I had talked to Vickey. I promised to let Dick know by the end of the week, which gave me three days to convince her.

Sometimes there are things in life that happen that we cannot understand or explain at the time of their occurrences. People sometimes refer to them as *God winks*. Vickey had made it clear that she didn't want to move to Wilmington, but she told me once again that it was my decision, and she would support me no matter what. I had decided and was about to call Dick Rhoads a day early to accept the offer when Vickey's mother showed up at the house.

Two months had passed since the firing, and while Mother had managed a few stolen outings with Vickey and the kids, this was the first time she had crossed our forbidden threshold since Mr. Key had banished us. We were surprised and happy to see her. Her kindness, warmth, and wisdom had been constants in our lives, and we missed her terribly. But her welcome reappearance wasn't to signal any cracks in the Berlin Wall that Mr. Key had built around us. She was on a different mission today and asked to speak to me alone. We retreated to the living room while Vickey entertained the children.

Mother settled onto the sofa, and before we even had a chance to get comfortable, she began to cry. I sat there awkwardly, uncertain of what to do. Mother was the rock in the Key family, the one who picked up the pieces and figuratively put everything—and everyone—back together after her husband's rampages. I knew that she blamed herself for not being home to keep Mr. Key in check that night, and the feelings of guilt and the outcome of separation were weighing heavily on her heart.

"You are a good husband, father, and son in law and one of the hardest working men I know," she said. "I have no doubt that you will be successful at whatever you decide to do." She paused and then got to the important part of her message. "Laura and Chip are my only grandchildren, and they are special to me. I love all my girls, but I am especially close to Vickey. Heck, I even love you, as hard as it is sometimes. I know that you have a job offer in Wilmington. Delaware is a long way from here. I need for you to know that I would like for Laura and Chip to grow up in Atlanta, if at all possible." She paused for a long moment as she regained her composure. "You are a smart man, and I know that you will make the right decision. I love you." When she finished, she immediately got up, hugged me, and left.

This left me confused and angry. I understood the emotional family attachments but resented the bigger selfish message. I felt like it placed an undue burden on me to stay in Atlanta. I thought what she was asking of me was unreasonable and completely out of character. I was destined to spend the rest of the day and a sleepless night in gut wrenching torture.

I could stay in Atlanta, where we could be family outcasts living on ramen noodles with my stockbroker trainee paycheck. Or I could move us to Wilmington and live the good life as president of a company owned by good, normal people.

I could reinvent myself at Kidder, Peabody & Company or redeem myself at Rhoads. I picked up the phone, dialed a familiar number, and asked, "When can I start?"

Eight

CONFIDENT

Success is the best revenge.

—Abraham Lincoln

I started as a stockbroker trainee at Kidder, Peabody & Company on Monday, August 22, 1983. I had gone from a vice president to a trainee in less than ninety days, which had to be some type of record. At thirty-two years old, I was going backward in my career. To make things even worse, I noticed after several months that my name was not on the local organizational chart, nor was I listed in the company telephone directory.

During the first month on the job, a senior financial advisor in the office ordered me to hand deliver invitations to business executives in downtown Atlanta for an investment seminar that he was sponsoring. I knew no better, so I did what I was told without question, but I resented the request. Another trainee who started a few weeks after me refused a similar request from the same senior advisor. I witnessed the interaction and was shocked when, without a moment of hesitation, I heard him tell the senior advisor that he could put his invitations where the sun doesn't shine.

Allen Wright, a fellow second career trainee, and I discovered that we had a lot in common. I quickly learned that Allen was not afraid to say what he believed—even when it was unpopular. He was a southern gentleman and a man of character who was also tall, handsome, and smart. He had a lovely wife and baby daughter who were counting on him too. He was the one who informed me that we were not on the organizational chart or listed in the telephone directory. At this point, I felt insignificant, and the new employment circumstances were far more humbling than I had ever imagined.

There was one bright spot during those times. In the fall of 1983, I was named to the Wofford College All Time Football Team, which recognized Wofford College's forty best football players of all time. The list of players included Jerry Richardson, Tom Bower, Charlie Bradshaw, and Harold Chandler, who were all now outstanding business leaders. Vickey and I attended the event. It was rare air, and I was humbled by the recognition. It culminated with an awards celebration that included recognition plaques and a wonderful luncheon. It was a sorely needed pat on the back for a broken spirit in a dark and uncertain transitional period of life. We attended with our peers and accepted the prestigious award, but when it was over, I immediately returned to work.

You have to be licensed to sell securities, and I had been employed with the firm for 120 days, the minimum required waiting period for the licensing exam. During those four months, I went to work every day and studied the voluminous preparation materials from dawn to dusk. In December, I took the all-day written test in a monitored college classroom setting with forty other people. It was a grueling examination exercise, and it took a week or so to get the final test results.

The wait was intense, and I heard in the office break room that the firm fired anyone who failed the exam, which only added to my already elevated anxieties. Was I was going to get fired again? I patiently sat at the desk in my small cubicle, which had been my office for the past four months, just waiting. When the test results finally arrived, Lewis Holland called me to his office. When I arrived, he seemed to be frowning, which I felt was a bad sign. He slow played the results, which kept me on the edge of my seat, and just when I thought he was about to drop the hammer, he suddenly got up from his desk, smiled, and extended his hand in congratulations.

In three months, I would be on my way to New York City for a month of comprehensive sales training, the next phase of the program. Until then, I would spend time cold calling strangers with investment ideas. I used this time to practice various sales techniques and was able to open some small accounts.

Our marriage was fragile, and now I was leaving for a month—not the best of circumstances. My flight arrived early Sunday morning. I took a cab to the firm's brownstone and met my three roommates, all smart men.

On Monday morning, Edwin Lee Solot, the director of advisor training at Kidder, Peabody & Company, opened the session and outlined our agenda for the month. After staff introductions, he said, "Kidder, Peabody hires only the best and the brightest. We are committed to providing the most comprehensive training in the business. Our success rates are the best of any firm on the street, but even so, it is a fact that 25 percent of you will fail in the first year. Half of those remaining will fail by the end of year two, and only a handful of you will ultimately succeed." I was unaware of those specific facts and figures. I knew success would be difficult, but I had no idea that it was virtually impossible.

That first morning scared the heck out of me, but I had earned the right to compete, so I just put my head down and did my best. After a difficult month, I was more than ready to get back to Atlanta. That first night home, I sat down with Vickey after the children went to bed and reflected on the training events and then shared the failure rates. She could hear the anxiety in my voice and see the fear in my eyes.

When I returned to the office Monday morning, I visited with Lewis, and we discussed the training experience. I focused on the low probabilities of success. I admitted to him that, after the month of training with the best and brightest, I was scared. As we concluded our conversation, I said, "Vickey and the children are counting on me. Right now, I am all that they have. I grew up with an irresponsible father, and I clearly understand the perils of a father's failure. I want to do well so that my family will be proud of me. I cannot afford to fail again." Then I asked him one final question: "What do I have to do to succeed?"

I could tell that he was pleased that I asked that final question. He smiled and said, "Success is very simple, but most still fail." He paused for a moment and then continued. "You will have to make a minimum of five hundred phone calls per month. You will have to open a minimum of ten new accounts each month, and you will have to generate $100,000 of sales commissions during the first twelve months." "What else?" I asked.

He thought for a moment and then said, "That's it. If you can do that, then you will be successful, very successful."

I had run a small company, and after training in New York, I somehow believed that it would be more complex and difficult than just a handful of tasks and a series of activities that I controlled. I understood what I had to do, so I wrote a short business plan and went to work to establish myself as a successful stockbroker.

I was still confused about my relationship with Mr. Key, past, present, and future. At the time, I hated him for what he had done to our family. To keep these emotions ever present, I purchased a wooden plaque and placed it on my desk. It read in big bold letters: **SUCCESS IS THE BEST REVENGE**. During difficult times, I would look at it and slowly read the words out loud. It was therapeutic, and helped me navigate the mental anguish that continued to haunt me.

The guaranteed salary part of compensation package would be exhausted in less than a year, so I knew that I had to get started right away to survive. I had no personal or family money and no wealthy friends, so I purchased a local business directory and began cold calling strangers.

My peers in the bull pen were rookie brokers dressed in thousand dollar suits with Hermès ties, each of whom believed they were the next investment superstar. They were the cream of the crop, most straight out of graduate school but inexperienced in life and still wet behind the ears. I knew that I was better suited for the job as a thirty-two year old, seasoned business guy with average intelligence who was organized and motivated, and I had one other significant difference. I had two small children at home who were depending on their dad, which motivated me to aggressively pick up the telephone and sell, 24-7.

I cold called business executives in the Southeast all day long, which I discovered is a brutal way to make a living. People are rude, they hang up on you, and they sometimes even call you ugly names. I lived on the telephone. I hated it, but I knew I had to do it to succeed. They say that practice makes perfect. I got plenty of practice, and although I was far from perfect, I became pretty good at the job.

I worked long hours, which included Saturdays and Sundays. Most weekends, I was the only person in the office. I depended on Vickey to handle the children and pressing family duties. She was becoming my best friend and confidante and happily did her part. We were a good team, and she was happy to lead the way. At work, I had a disciplined daily schedule. I arrived at my desk early every morning and went right to work. I got on the telephone and enthusiastically called people. I wasted little time in the break room at the coffee machine or in idle conversation, and it worked. I earned an assistant vice president title, which came with a small private office.

I proved that I could follow simple instructions. I had done everything according to Lewis's plan. There was only one problem: I was not having fun. I did not want a long term career as a cold calling salesman. I made an appointment with Lewis to review my progress and share some thoughts. I always looked forward to our meetings. Like Coach Baus, he encouraged and never criticized. When I arrived at his office that morning, we went to the break room, got some coffee, and visited for a few minutes. When we got back to the privacy of his office, he said, "I want to congratulate you on a great year. Your results are nothing short of amazing. I wish that I had more people like you."

I was flattered and responded, "I cannot thank you enough for your support. You are a good leader, and I consider you a friend. You helped me get here, and I am honored to work with you. I've appreciated your thoughtful guidance and advice this past year, but I must tell you that I am not having any fun." I paused for a moment to get his reaction, which I interpreted as mostly confusion. "I have decided that I am not going to sell stuff that I don't understand to people I don't know anymore. My current duties are not fun, and this will never be my dream job. It is not something that I plan to do for the rest of my life. I want to make a difference, and I need for work to be fun."

I was right about the confusion. It was obvious that Lewis was caught off guard by my bold summation. Once he regained his composure, he asked, "What are your plans?"

I responded without hesitation, "I have been studying a new business model where we work for clients as investment consultants. In fact, it will allow us to partner with them. It will not permit us to serve as stockbrokers or promote the firm's products or agenda under any circumstances."

He then asked, "What are you going to do?"

"I plan to take a week off to see if I can write a simple business plan," I said.

"What if you are unsuccessful in your efforts?"

"That is a tough question and one that I have given much thought. The short answer is that if I fail, I will not return to work here. I will probably seek out more suitable career options."

After further discussion, he stood up from his desk, shook my hand, and said, "I wish you the best of luck, and I have no doubt that you will succeed. Please keep me informed and let me know how I can help."

I took the week off and wrote a simple plan that worked for me. The business model uniquely packaged the firm's investment resources, capabilities, and research into a fee for services offering. We would no longer earn commissions on every sale. We would be working with larger, more sophisticated clients, and our compensation would be tied to their successes. We did not win if they did not win first.

The value proposition focused on four simple concepts: (1) processes that were both disciplined and systematic; (2) proactive investment strategies, communications, and reporting; (3) performance oriented functionality, with required quarterly performance updates and personal reviews; and (4) partnership behavior with client centric functionality.

These four Ps were the foundational pillars of the offering. It was a very simple win-win business strategy. When I showed Lewis the final plan, he approved and we launched. The first year, we struggled and were marginally successful but strongly encouraged. We were retained by a handful of publicly traded corporations and several large private companies, clients the firm would have never attracted without us.

We were no longer viewed as stockbrokers buying and selling stocks. We were professional partners, protecting precious assets and promoting the interests of our clients. We focused our initial marketing efforts on trusteed assets with fiduciary responsibilities, which included foundations, endowments, and retirement plans. I was eager but struggled and did not open an account for several months.

Each night I would share my frustrations with Vickey. As with every new business, there was always a problem to solve or details to resolve. We were a highly regulated business, so the frustration was multiplied by one hundred. It was a never ending battle, and it was killing me. I could not always help our regulators and compliance folks understand what we were trying to accomplish, and as a result we were always swimming upstream.

Vickey was patient and listened. I found her to be a fabulous sounding board and problem solver. She usually let me vent endlessly, but one night was different. I came home upset and began to share the problems of the day. She was tired and uninterested and stopped me midsentence to say, "That is not my problem." When I pushed, she stopped me again and said in an unkind voice, "You need to get a real job." She then proceeded to tell me about her day, which was far more challenging than mine. As we crawled into bed, I once again tried to engage her, and she repeated, "That is not my problem and you need to get a real job." She then smiled, leaned over, kissed me on the cheek, fluffed her pillows, turned out the light, pulled up the covers, rolled over, and went to sleep. Fortunately, over the next year, I established a handful of substantial new account relationships. To this day, we still joke about that night.

As the source of my identity, success and significance were extremely important. I still had much to prove, and I worked long hours, which included dusk to dawn days and most weekends. I would see Vickey when I got into bed each night, but I rarely saw the children except during an occasional late night dinner or a rare afternoon rendezvous. I knew the lack of regular interaction would yield bad outcomes. I longed to talk with Vickey about these feelings, but I did not want her to think I was insecure or weak. Even so, I knew that I sorely needed her guidance.

I finally marshalled the nerve to speak up. "I have to talk with you about some things that are keeping me up at night. It has become obvious that I still have a lot to learn about being a husband and father. You understand these things better than I do, and I need your help."

She smiled and asked, "How can I help?"

"I know that I am not living up to your expectations. I work extremely hard to make you proud of me, but then I am an absentee husband and father. I want to do better, but I am confused and must admit to you that I do not know where to turn or what to do. I need your guidance."

Vickey waited for me to complete my thoughts and then patiently responded. "I thought you would never ask. Yes, I agree that you do have a lot to learn. Most important, you are not showing up for your work at home, and I am disappointed in you. We need you in our lives, and you will eventually discover that you need us in yours. Hopefully sooner rather than later."

"I am embarrassed to admit that I am unaware of the children's needs. Heck, I am not sure that I even know what you want, need, or expect of me. How can I become a better father and husband? Please tell me what I need to do."

"You need to figure out the parent piece first. Laura and Chip need your influence. They need an engaged father. I can help some, but I have yet to discover a step by step manual on raising children. You have to do what you feel is right, and you must be present. In terms you understand, you have to *show up*. The more, the better. You lead by example at work, but you are missing in action at home. You must start leading by example here, too." After a short pause, she continued. "I believe that parenting is more art than science. You will not get a second chance to do it right, and we will not get any regular report cards along the way. We will not know how we did until later, much later. In fact, we will not get our final grades until they are adults and have their own careers, lives, and families. You must recognize that parenting is an important job. It is far more significant than your work at Kidder, Peabody."

After our conversation, I realized that I was selfishly absorbed. I focused exclusively on success, money, and personal recognition. It was all about me. I felt guilty and then stupid. I aspired to be an engaged parent and husband and was failing. I knew that I could not fulfill my family responsibilities unless I reorganized priorities. I had to make our family the top priority. They could no longer get what was left over, because that was virtually nothing.

I was now certain that Vickey had chosen me over her family. The ugly and uncertain times had passed. Our relationship was thriving, and our marriage seemed to grow stronger every day. She was my sweetheart, but as a man of few words with guarded emotions, I always struggled to show the proper gratitude and affection. Then I stumbled on a sensational idea.

We were about to celebrate our tenth anniversary, and I decided to plan a surprise trip. In the past few years, Vickey had endured two years of graduate school, two babies fifteen months apart, a devastating family separation, and a stressful job change—all with a smile. She never once complained, and I wanted to do something nice for her. We needed some special time for us. I found the perfect trip and kept it a secret since I knew how much Vickey enjoyed surprises.

On Wednesday, September 5, 1984, I got up early and went to work just like every other day. I left the office to return home around ten in the morning. On the way home, I picked up Mae Upchurch, a nice older lady who babysat for us regularly. She was a grandmother and was experienced at looking after young children. Vickey and the children loved her. Mae and I drove to the house, and she slipped in the front door undetected. Vickey was in the backyard with the children working in her garden. She was covered in dirt but was more beautiful than ever.

When she saw me, she asked, "What are you doing home?"

"It is a surprise," I said.

"Did you get fired again?" she joked.

"Not this week. And for the record, I do not think that is something for us to joke about, nor do I find it funny considering what we have

Edward B. Wile

been through. I am here for you! Go take a quick shower and get cleaned up, because we are going on a surprise anniversary trip."

"I have to pack and get a babysitter," she said with excitement.

"No, you don't. I packed for you last night, and I included those sexy panties and sheer, skimpy negligees, and Mae Upchurch is here to take care of the children."

She quickly showered, and we were on our way. She seemed happy but had many questions. We got into my sporty green BMW and left the neighborhood. She immediately asked, "Where are we going?" I told her it was a surprise. When we got on I-85, she asked, "How far are we going?" I told her it was a surprise. In a few minutes, as we were going through town, she asked, "Are we going to the airport?" I told her it was a surprise. When we passed the airport and got on I-75 south, she stopped asking questions, put her seat back, and relaxed.

I was pleased with her response. I had planned everything down to the last detail, and we were on our way to spend a long romantic weekend together. As we passed by the airport on our way out of town, I looked over at her and winked, and she smiled back. The next time I looked over, she was napping in the warm sunshine. We arrived in Savannah, Georgia, later that day after a delightful stress free drive. We talked more that day than we had in a long time. At home, we always seemed to be too busy with life, work, and the children to really share or talk much.

I had booked a room at the Savannah Inn and Country Club, the nicest hotel in town. When I made the room reservation, I must have told them that we would be celebrating our tenth anniversary. On arrival, I could see that Vickey was thrilled with the hotel selection. As the bags were being unloaded, I checked us in and made a dinner reservation with the concierge for that evening. Vickey casually walked around admiring the beautiful hotel lobby. The bellman gathered our bags, and we proceeded to the elevator. I noticed that he pushed the button for the top floor and appeared to wink at me. I thought nothing of it at the time, assuming it was just an eye twitch. When we got off the elevator, we proceeded down a long hall with our bags in tow to the last room on the floor. I remember thinking, *a long walk back and forth to the elevator.*

Mean to Meaningful

When we entered our room, we were pleasantly surprised. It was a suite, and my first thought was that this was not our room, but I said nothing, fearing that I would ruin the moment. The bellman took the time to show us around; I was excited to see that the accommodations came with a king size bed and a luxurious, oversized bathroom. The living room table had a colorful assortment of roses, carnations, and hydrangeas. Vickey stopped and admired the arrangement. She loved flowers and lingered a moment to let the fragrances catch up before turning to me and smiling. It was clear that the flowers made quite an impression. As we walked around the spacious bedroom, I noticed a bottle of champagne on the nightstand. I knew that I had not ordered any champagne and was now absolutely sure that the hotel had made a mistake. This was obviously someone else's room. What was I going to do?

When I picked up the bottle of champagne, I noticed a small envelope on the silver tray beneath the bottle, addressed to me. When I opened it, I discovered a handwritten note of congratulations from the general manager of the hotel. He offered his best wishes on our tenth anniversary and advised that since the honeymoon suite was available, he wanted us to enjoy the upgrade as the hotel's gift to us. We were both excited with the suite, and I noted how much Vickey enjoyed the other special touches and committed those observations to memory for future use.

The general manager's kindness and that first nights romantic dinner got the trip started off on the right foot. But when I got up early the next morning, Vickey asked, "What are you doing?"

"I am going into Savannah to make some sales calls. You can sleep in, have breakfast in bed, relax, have lunch, get a massage, and lounge by the pool. It is going to be a beautiful day."

"When do you think you will be back?"

"I will be back in plenty of time to shower and dress for our seven o'clock dinner reservation."

"Safe travels and good luck." She said nothing else, but I could feel her disappointment. I had no idea that working on this trip would diminish her joy. It was too late to change my plans for today, but I would never make that same mistake again.

Except for my bad business decision on Thursday, we had a fabulous trip and did things that we would never do for ourselves at home. We slept in and enjoyed breakfast in bed. We visited historic sites and had leisurely lunches. We sat by the pool, sunned, and drank margaritas. We brainstormed about the parenting duties and responsibilities. We shared our most intimate feelings and concerns over quiet dinners. It was a much needed romantic getaway.

On the drive home, we talked about the significance of the weekend and decided to make the anniversary trip an annual tradition. We agreed that we would take turns planning the trips. I would plan trips on the even years and she on the odd years—and we would plan each trip as a surprise with the other in mind. We would establish a date to get it on the calendar, but no other details would be disclosed.

This tradition evolved into more than we ever imagined. We have traveled to many wonderful places around the world, sometimes with family or friends. It is an intentional act of love and something that we look forward to each year with great anticipation. A time when we discuss important issues and share private thoughts. It is a selfish luxury that allows us to further discover the joys of our precious relationship. Those times and trips have made us better people, better partners, and better parents.

As we pulled the car into our garage at the end of that first trip, Vickey mentioned that Chip was starting Northside Youth Organization baseball in the spring and suggested that I consider coaching his team. I initially thought it was a bad idea. I was too busy at work and believed that I would not have the time.

The idea percolated until I recalled how a few coaches turned me around. They were role models and mentors, and I learned many valuable lessons on the field about character, success, and life from them.

Would this be a perfect opportunity for me to share those same precious teachings with Chip?

Top: John and Laura Little, 1926
Bottom: Aunt Mary and Mom, 1933

Mom and Dad's Wedding Day, 1950

Ed and Diana, 1953

Laura Little with Grandsons, 1955

Ed, 1956

Edward B. Wile

Jack Peterson and Ed Wile, 1969

WOFFORD COLLEGE 1969 FOOTBALL SQUAD

First Row: David Currie, Dooley Bizzell, Larry Forgacs, George Tyson, Clifford Boyd, Bobby Jordan, Mike Lunsford, Jim Johnson; Second Row: Bill Fenters, David Williams, Herb Peebles, Randy Bringman, Harold Chandler, Bill Heath, John Miller, Ronnie Wilson, Rick Burns; Third Row: Boogie Ayers, Dean Lemlier, David Miller, John Wall, Glenn Reese, Sterling Allen, Henry Medlock, Chuck Whitt, Keith Dyer, Sidney Allred; Fourth Row: Gordon Koleznar, John Harris, Jim McCabe, Bruce Johnson, Mike Roebuck, Monty Allen, Larry Robbins, Steve Williams, John Borror, Tom Bower; Fifth Row: Bill Calhoun, Gregory Turner, Ed Wile, Richard Mollett, Stan Scarborough, Skip Corn, Scooter White, Mike James, James Oatway, Donald Robinson, Dale Vesey; Sixth Row: John Spakes, Jimmy Taylor, Eddy Woody, Jeff Butts, Tommy Durham, Coach Jim Brakefield, Coach Jack Peterson, Coach Fisher DeBerry, Coach Gene Alexander, Doc Stober, Peg Boothe, Equipment Manager, Charles Ramsey, Tim Hulings, Sports Publicity.

Edward B. Wile

WOFFORD COLLEGE 1970 FOOTBALL ROSTER

No.	Name	Hgt.	Wgt.	Class	Letters	Hometown
	QUARTERBACKS					
11	George Tyson	5-10	175	3	1	Florence, S. C.
12	Eddie Woody	5-9	175	2	0	Marietta, Georgia
16	Jimmy Johnson	6-0	176	4	2	Waynesboro, Ga.
18	Harold Chandler	6-1	167	4	2	Belton, S. C.
	BACKS					
20	David Currie	5-9	188	3	2	Norfolk, Va.
21	Ed Wile	5-11	170	2	1	Wooster, Ohio
22	Bobby Jordan	5-11	180	4	2	Florence, S. C.
24	*Scooter White	5-7	165	2	1	Sumter, S. C.
25	*Randy Bringman	5-9	190	3	1	Anderson, S. C.
27	Dean Lemler	5-10	195	3	1	Avon Park, Fla.
33	Stanley Scarborough	5-11	195	2	0	Baxter, Ga.
40	Ray Monroe	5-8	150	1	0	Spartanburg, S. C.
42	Chuck Whitt	6-1	185	3	1	Atlanta, Ga.
45	Clifford Boyd	5-10	197	2	2	Fort Mill, S. C.
46	David Miller	5-11	178	3	1	Canton, N. C.
	LINEMEN					
51	Sterling Allen	6-3	230	4	3	Florence, S. C.
52	Boogie Ayers	5-10	185	3	1	Marietta, Ga.
53	Bill Reese	6-0	205	4	1	Thompson, Ga.
60	Scott Morris	6-3	230	3	0	Spartanburg, S. C.
63	Ronnie Wilson	6-0	200	3	1	Gainesville, Ga.
64	Keith Dyer	5-11	215	4	2	Norfolk, Va.
65	Dale Yezey	5-11	187	2	0	Gainesville, Ga.
66	Tom Bower	6-0	180	2	0	Rosewell, Ga.
70	Bill Fenters	5-11	220	4	3	Manning, S. C.
71	Pete Nixon	5-11	210	2	0	Virginia Beach, Va.
73	Mike Roebuck	6-1	230	4	2	Shelby, N. C.
75	Monty Allen	6-3	200	3	1	Augusta, Ga.
76	John Harris	6-1	204	4	2	Springfield, Va.
77	John Miller	6-3	250	3	1	Dillon, S. C.
	ENDS					
80	David Creasy	6-2	175	1	0	Highland Springs, Va.
81	Terry Laney	5-11	192	2	0	Virginia Beach, Va.
82	Dooley Bizzell	6-2	180	3	2	Norfolk, Va.
83	Henry Medlock	6-5	200	4	2	Clemson, S. C.
87	Skip Corn	5-11	170	2	1	Spartanburg, S. C.
88	Glenn Reese	6-1	192	3	2	Thompson, Ga.

*Kicking Specialists

Glenn Patterson, Spartanburg, S. C., Manager

WOFFORD COLLEGE FOOTBALL STAFF

This Staff, considered to be one of the most able and versatile staffs in small college circles, is composed of sports men who combine exceptional balance of athletic talent and experience.

Duane Stober, Mankato State "53", Athletic Trainer and Track Coach; Fisher DeBerry, Wofford "60", Defensive Backfield and Baseball Coach; Eugene Alexander, USC "40", Defensive Football and Basketball Coach; James A. Brakefield, Center "41", Head Football Coach; Jack Peterson, Ashland College "59", Offensive Back and Tennis Coach.

Doctor Joe Lesesne and Family

Barbara Jeanne Key

Jerry Richardson, Ernest Key, Jon Richardson, and Ed Wile
The Famous Marathon Tennis Match, 1975

Laura, Ed, and the Famous Coat, 1979

Vickey, Mother, and Laura, 1982

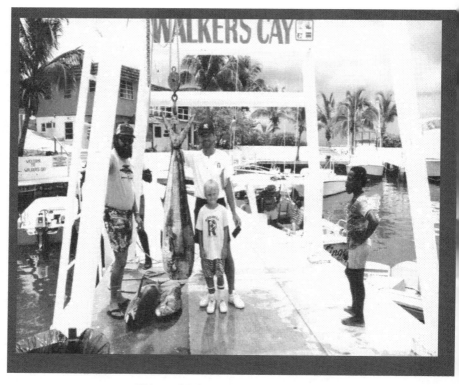

Chip and Ed, Walkers Cay, 1986

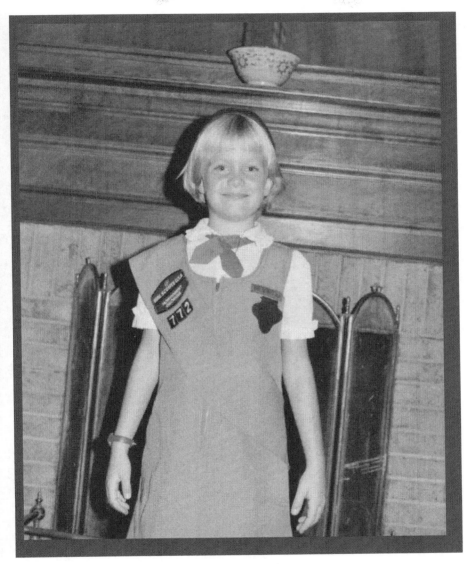

Laura Wile, 1986

Diana Montgomery Promotion Ceremony, 1986

Chip Wile, 1987

Chip Wile, 1989

Laura Wile, 1992

Laura Wile, My Precious Junk Yard Dog, 1994

Top: Laura's High School Graduation Day, 1997
Bottom: Kiawah Cup Group at the Broadmoor, 1999

Albert Harris and Bill Ervin, Kiawah Cup Champions, 1999

A Yard of Beer at the Golden Bee, Kiawah Cup, 1999

Laura and Robert Wellon Rehearsal Dinner, 2001

Top: Chip and Catherine's Rehearsal Dinner, 2003
Bottom: Chip, Catherine, Robert and Laura on our
30th Anniversary Trip, 2004

Phil and Mom's 50th Anniversary, 2004

Ed and Vickey with Allen and Cecilia Wright
UBS Chairman's Club Meeting, 2006

Vickey Wile, 2010

Parks and Tyler Wellon
Flower Girls at Whitney Horton's Sea Island Wedding, 2013

Edward B. Wile

Ed Wile, Jack Peterson and Harold Chandler
Wofford College Donor Dinner, 2014

Mount Kilimanjaro, Uhuru Peak, Elevation 19,341
July 21, 2014

Vickey Wile with her Student Athletes and Prema Samhat
Wofford College Donor Dinner, 2014

UBS Wile Consulting Group, 2016

Robert and Laura Wellon and Family, 2016

Chip and Catherine Wile and Family, 2016

Nine

STUNNED

You can teach and win with kids with no ability,
as long as they do not know it.

—Coach "Bear" Bryant

I joined the Northside Youth Organization (NYO) board a short time later. I immediately rolled up my sleeves and helped raise funds to build a *Field of Dreams* baseball complex. In the spring, I volunteered to coach Chip's team.

There were tryouts and a draft, and I discovered that the assistant coach's son was automatically on the team. After the tryouts, I called Carlton Fry and introduced myself and asked him to be the assistant coach because I wanted his son, Walker, on the team. I knew that Carlton had been an outstanding baseball player in high school and was a good dad. His son, Walker, was a quiet, smaller kid, and I was attracted to his gritty determination. He was a good player and smart. He had an all in personality, and I saw him as an undiscovered talent. He was a loner who was determined and stubborn, and he had an explosive temper. In many ways, he reminded me of me. Chip came to me as a respectable third round pick.

Immediately after the draft, I wrote each boy a personal letter on my Kidder, Peabody & Company stationery. The letter would become a tradition. I thought it would be a classy touch and would differentiate our team from the others. In the letter, I told the boys that they were drafted by our team because they were talented and that our team picked only the best players. The letter explained that they would be expected to attend every practice and game, and there would be no excuses. They were instructed t bring their parents to the first practice, where we reiterated the expectation and addressed any and all questions. I must admit that my coaching styl was more dictatorial than collaborative, and I made it clear to everyone that was not interested in every player in the league getting a trophy. I wa interested only in winning championships. The rules were clear, and rarel did we have anything less than perfect attendance.

Our kids came to believe that they were good players. Our first seaso was a learning experience, and it was quite different from what I ha expected. We practiced hard, had fun, educated several parents about th value of showing up, and won the first of many league championships. A the end of the season, I wrote a second letter, which took much longer. Ther were many drafts—it had to be perfect to be effective. Years later, I woul learn by coincidence just how significant those letters were to the players.

I coached for years and became known as a disciplined, creative, an demanding coach who thrived on competition. I naturally drew on the man lessons I learned from my childhood coaches. It was all that I knew, and believed that many of their teachings were timeless. Coaching turned out t be a blessing, and those rich experiences allowed me to grow as a man father, and husband.

Peter Cwalina, a college basketball star from Carnegie Mellon, joine our firm, and when he learned what we were doing with the boys, he aske to join our coaching staff. Pete was smart, athletic, and handsome, and h knew computers. He joined the coaching staff and agreed to help us build computer program to statistically evaluate each player.

Pete's program became informally known as GLM, which was a acronym for good looking moms. It was an effective tool, and here is how i worked: During the tryouts, our coaches evaluated and scored each player o the technical skills of hitting, running, and catching. One of our coache made it a point to personally talk with each player to evaluate his general attitude. We wanted only players with good attitudes. They received possible ten points for each skill. After a player completed his tryout, I would follow him to his car to meet his parent, which was almost always his mother.

This confused Pete. "I get the tryout part, but why do you insist on meeting their mothers?" Pete asked. "What purpose does that serve?"

"We want the good looking ones on our team. We want them in our stands, cheering for our team at our games," I joked. "Seriously, think about it. When it is our turn to draft and the available players are all equal in talent. How do we decide whom to select?" I responded and continued with a big smile. "The mom is the tiebreaker."

Pete smiled and said, "Oh! Got it and agree."

Behind the scenes, the magic began with getting the right players and then spending a lot of quality time with them. We practiced any time we could get a field, day or night. We focused on helping our players believe in themselves first, and then we taught them to play, how to wear the stripes, and finally how to win. What no one tells you is that these teachings all took place during the long, hot sessions on the practice field. As an insider, I knew that for them to succeed, care and practice were the essential secret ingredients.

Chip spent Friday night with his friend Reed Walden against my advice. We had practice the next morning at seven, so I picked him up at six thirty. We got to the field a few minutes early, and as we unloaded the equipment, I noticed he was limping. We usually began our practices by loosening up and running the bases. I noticed that Chip was dogging it around the bases, and I assumed he was tired from the night before. This upset me, so I told him to pick it up. He was my son, and he knew that I expected him to lead by example. After a second warning, I decided to send him to the dugout for the rest of the practice session.

After practice, Chip helped me gather up the equipment, and we were talking. I was over the silly pouting spell, and things were back to normal. He apologized for dogging it in practice. He told me that he was having trouble running because he had cut his knee on the ping pong table at Reed's house. I asked him to show me. When he pulled up his baseball pants, what I saw was a huge gash across his entire kneecap. It was a clean razor cut and went all the way to the bone and was slightly bloody. It was bad. I explained to him the difference between a cut and a gash, and we went directly to the emergency room. It took a lot of stitches to close the gash, but to his credit, he never missed a game.

Chip was a good player and helped us win many championships. He was a star, even though I never told him, something I have always regretted. was naturally much harder on him than others because he was my son— held him to a higher standard. Right or wrong, that is the way I am wired. I a do over, I would change only one thing: I would spend more time wit Chip.

After a few seasons, Chip saw that many of his NYO baseball teammate also played basketball. He knew that his mother had played basketball i high school, so he asked her if she thought that he was good enough to play and she encouraged him to try. He was eight years old. They needed a coach and Vickey volunteered me. I cautioned NYO that I had never coache basketball. It did not matter, because they were one coach short. Vicke helped me with the draft. We had some great kids, but it was an averag team at best. Chip was one of the biggest and best players, but he fell dow the stairs at our New Year's Eve party and broke his right arm just before th season started. The league allowed him to play with a cast, and he did th best he could. He scored nineteen points in his first game with a cast from his hand to his elbow. It was an amazing effort, and I was proud of him, bu we lost.

Our record was not very good, and we were in the lower bracket for th end of season playoffs and had little chance of advancing. We were playin the number one seed, and it was no surprise that we were losing by twelve points with less than two minutes left in the third quarter. Rip Sartain, one o the assistant coaches, called a time out. He smiled at me and said, "I have ar idea." As the boys gathered, I heard him say, "We have them right where we want them." Rip was sometimes a little out there, and I concluded that he must have been drinking in the parking lot during halftime. He laid out a strategy that worked perfectly. We stole the inbound passes, and Chip scored three times in those final two minutes. He went on to score nineteen points in the fourth quarter, and we won. It seemed to be a different team.

We went on to win all of our playoff games and the NYO basketball championship. Our team had come together and matured nicely at just the right time, in spite of me.

As a reward for winning the tournament, I was asked to coach the NYO all-star team in the all city championship tournament. Chip was selected for the team. I had to be in New York on business that week and had to decline the honor. I hated to miss this opportunity, but it would turn out for the best.

The team practiced together, won every game, and advanced all the way to the finals. When I heard the news, I changed my flight so I could be back in time for the Friday night championship game. I rushed from the airport and arrived as they were announcing the players. The game was at the Martin Luther King Center downtown. It was a cold and rainy night. This was a big game, and even though the weather was horrible, the stands were packed.

The whole experience did not start well for me when I saw that the coaches were starting Chip at center. He played guard for me and was an amazing offensive weapon. The seat wasn't even warm when I jumped up and screamed, "What are you doing? Chip is a guard." Vickey asked me to be quiet and calmly motioned for me to sit down. She knew basketball and as a good mother had attended all the playoff games.

I sat down but continued to think: "Chip is a guard, not a center. He never played center, and he is definitely not one of the taller players on the floor." After much pain, I decided to take Vickey's advice. It was an exciting game, and the score was tied at halftime. I was on the edge of my seat the entire game and had a difficult time containing myself, and I must admit that Chip was a surprisingly good center. He blocked out well, got his share of rebounds, and scored a lot of points.

It looked like the game was all but over. The other team was leading by three points, and they had the ball with thirty one seconds left in the game. They brought the ball down the court and made a pass inside. Chip stepped in front of the opposing player and stole the ball. He was immediately fouled, and the clock stopped.

Chip calmly went to the foul line and made both ends of the one and one. They were now down by one point with only twelve seconds left in the game. As they inbounded the ball, Chip instinctively turned around and stole the pass, because that was what Rip Sartain had coached him to do in that amazing comeback. The frustrated opposing player fouled him in retaliation.

With the game on the line Chip went to the foul line and made both shots. They won by one point, and Chip received the tournament's Most Valuable Player trophy.

While we were enjoying our baseball and basketball activities, difficu times were brewing with the Keys. They separated and eventually wei through a horrible divorce. A short time later, Mother was diagnosed wit lung cancer. We made ourselves believe that she could win the battle although most did not.

Mother now visited with us daily. She was anxious to catch up and eage to share time with Vickey and the children. Time was precious. She was beautiful grandmother, was always dressed to the nines, and had not a single gray hair. Laura and Chip enjoyed her renewed daily presence in their lives as did Vickey. She and Mother were very close and were the best of friends.

We shared many dinners together those final years, and during a cheerfu night, I decided to ask her several questions that only she could answer. knew it was probably now or never, so I asked, "Why did you set the tabl with every piece of silver, china, and glassware you owned that first night came to dinner with you and Mr. Key? You had to know it would be ai intimidating setting for me."

"No, I did not. That was never the purpose. You were different from Vickey's other boyfriends. I was not trying to make you uncomfortable, but wanted to know where I would have to start in order to make you into a southern gentleman. From our frequent telephone conversations, I knew that Vickey loved you and that there was a good chance you would become my son in law."

I smiled and said, "I wish I had known. I thought that you were trying to run me off. You do realize that I nearly crashed and burned on the dining room floor that night." A colorful discussion followed, and when the humor subsided, I continued. "I have another question that has troubled me for years. Why did you encourage me to remain in Atlanta and pass on the opportunity of a lifetime in Wilmington? It seemed so out of character."

"That one is a little more complicated. You are correct—it was not my best moment. I was blinded by love, and I will admit that, at the time, it was a selfish request. I could not bear the thought of Vickey, Laura, and Chip living in Delaware. It broke my heart knowing that they might be so far away. Yes, I wanted them close to me. On the other hand, I felt like you had to find your own way. I knew the Rhoads opportunity, although very attractive, was not your answer. You would remain in Ernest's shadow and still have to deal with him. It would not have been a good situation. You needed your own journey to prove yourself. Thank goodness it worked out, but I always knew it would," she said with a mischievous smile.

Had we moved to Wilmington, we would have missed the precious luxury of time and intimacy with Mother during those final years. Her wise guidance turned out to be a priceless gift. It was another precious *God wink*. Mother was a wonderful parent, a loving grandmother, and a one of a kind mother in law. She was a remarkable lady, and I loved her.

As time passed, she lost weight, and her condition worsened. In 1990, Vickey's sisters gathered in Atlanta for Thanksgiving, which would be their last visit. Early Thanksgiving morning, Mother lost her battle with cancer.

Prior to her death, she rarely missed one of the grandchildren's events. They were a source of joy in her life. She was a big baseball fan and attended most games with Vickey. This was our final season. Chip was twelve, and Mother was gone. I suspected that she had met Grandma and that they watched all of the games together from their skybox in the heavens.

Throughout Chip's Little League career, he aspired to be a pitcher. He had a great arm, but he lacked control. He played center field, and to keep him relevant, Carlton made him the captain of the outfield. He had a strong arm and could throw the ball to home plate from the deepest parts of the outfield. We built a pitcher's mound in our backyard when Chip was seven, and he would practice pitching whenever he had the chance. In a moment of weakness, I promised that I would let him pitch when he was ready. He was now twelve years old and in his final season.

Teams often struggled during spring break because many players would go to Sea Island or to the beautiful white sand Florida beaches with their families. It always confused me why families placed vacations ahead of baseball. We had never had an attendance problem until then. I guess that at twelve years old, boys find the beach more attractive because of the girls. That week, we had only nine players available, so everyone would get to play the entire game.

This was my last year of coaching, and this was not our best team, but we worked well together. We were playing a good team, and it was a must win game. Our season had gotten off to a slow start, but we had won six of

our last seven games and were on a roll. Unfortunately, all of our startin
pitchers were gone on spring break. Today's game would be a challenge.

Pitchers are critical to winning, and I planned to use Jeremy Casey, on
of our backup pitchers, for the entire six inning game. I usually only allowe
pitchers to pitch for three innings per game. Jeremy was a strong, reliabl
player and our only regular pitcher. He had pitched in previous seasons bu
had pitched in only two games that year. I could only hope that he woul
step up, because he was all we had.

Jeremy pitched well but got little support in the field. We gave up on
run in the first inning and two runs in the second inning. As he came off th
field in the second inning, he let me know that his arm was hurting.

In the third inning, he started looking at me after every pitch. When th
inning was over and the other team had scored two more runs, he made it a
point to tell me his arm was worse—a lot worse. I assumed it was jus
nerves. We scored four runs in the first, three runs in the second, went dow
in order in the third, and were leading 7–5.

As Jeremy left the dugout to start the fourth inning, he once agai
reminded me that his arm was getting worse. At this point, I realized it wa
more than just nerves. He was almost out of gas. He had a difficult time wit
the first batter but eventually got him to ground out. He grimaced and looke
over at me before and after every pitch, so when we got the groundout,
called for a time out. I could see that he was struggling. When I got to th
mound, I noticed that he looked sad. I asked what was wrong, and he said
"My arm is hurting, and it is getting worse with every pitch."

I thought for a moment. "Jeremy, you are all we got. I need for you to tr
to finish this game. Do you think that you can continue?"

He looked up at me and said, "I'll try."

During the next batter, he continued to look over to me in pain afte
every pitch. I thought we were out of the woods once the batter went 0–2
Then he lined the next pitch over the left field home run fence—but it wa
foul. The batter fouled off several more pitches but finally hit a slow roller
down the third baseline and beat it out for a single. When Jeremy looked at
me, I knew that he was done. I called for another time out and walked slowly
to the mound. I asked Jeremy if he could continue. With tears in his eyes, he

shook his head and said, "No, sir, I cannot." I put my arm around him to ease his pain even though that was not exactly what I wanted to hear.

I carefully looked over the field and studied our options. I looked toward center field and thought to myself, "Is it Chip's time?" It was a tough question, but the answer was pretty easy since the bull pen was empty.

I motioned for Chip to join me on the mound and sent Jeremy to center field. I still had some concerns and wondered whether this was a good decision. I was not concerned that Chip lacked the strength to pitch or that he was not fast enough. I knew from our long hours of practicing on our backyard pitcher's mound that Chip had a strong arm. In fact, he had one of the strongest on the team, and his fastball had plenty of pop. I was not concerned that he was not prepared. After all, we had been preparing for this day for over five years. If anything, he was over prepared. I was not concerned that Chip lacked the required self-confidence or that he was not mentally prepared. None of those things really bothered me. What concerned me the most was that I knew from our many years of practice in the backyard that Chip had mastered every pitch in baseball except the strike.

Chip trotted calmly in from center, and when I handed him the baseball, all my concerns disappeared. I could tell from the look in his eyes that he was good to go. He was ready to make his pitching debut. He looked like a pitcher, and as he warmed up, I thought about ideas that might relax him, be fun, and help establish his confidence. As we all know, a twelve year old can be a real head case. I knew Chip was nervous even though he showed no signs. He looked as cool as a cucumber. I looked into the stands and saw Vickey covering her eyes.

When he finished his warm up pitches, I said, "Chip, this is your big chance. You look really good. Are you ready?" "Yes, sir," he said.

"Sounds good. Now I need for you to listen closely. You will have to dictate the tempo of the game and focus on your pitch control. You must throw strikes, and under no circumstances can we walk batters. If you walk one single batter, it is all over. It is one and done. Do you understand?"

Chip nodded. "Got it, Dad. No walks, no problem. I got it, I got it." He was ready to get on with the game.

As I prepared to leave the mound, I said, "Now, Chip, let's have som
fun. On the first pitch, I want you to take a big windup and throw the ball a
hard as you can at the backstop. Make an intentional wild pitch. Do not eve
try to throw a strike."

He gave me a confused look. "Why would I do that?"

"Because you want them to think that you are wild. Just do it. Th
runner can advance only one base, so it's no big deal. You are going to hav
to trust me on this one. I know you can do it." At first, he seemed confuse
and frowned, but on my way back to the dugout, I heard him chuckle.

He executed the wild pitch perfectly, and it seemed to relax him. Afte
that, he came back with his favorite pitch, a blazing fastball right down th
middle, which was followed by another good pitch that was just outside. Th
count was now two balls and one strike. The next pitch was a heater righ
down the middle. It was so fast that the batter never even tried to swing. Th
count was now 2–2. His next pitch was center cut but just high. The coun
was now 3–2, and everyone was on the edge of their seats as we anxiousl
waited for the payoff pitch. It was another fastball, but it was way inside an
hit the batter in the middle of the back. I jumped up from the bench an
headed for the dugout steps. Chip saw me coming, but before I could get ou
of the dugout, he threw his glove on the ground and raised his hands in th
air and yelled, "Whoa, whoa, whoa, whoa! Stop! You said a walk was on
and done. For the record, I hit him, and that does not count."

The home plate umpire, Bo Wilkins, a Georgia Tech student and son o
Jane Wilkins, the executive director of NYO, slowly walked to the edge o
the dugout to observe my reaction. I stopped when I realized that he wa
right. After a few moments, once he knew that I was back in control, Bo
smiled and said, "Coach, for what it's worth, I believe that Chip is correct."

"What do you mean?" I asked.

"He didn't walk him; he hit him, and that shouldn't count."

I remained in the dugout and watched Chip strike out the next two
batters. We threatened but did not score in the fourth. In the fifth, Chip gave
up a single to the leadoff hitter and then handily struck out the next three
batters. We went down in order, and the score was still 7–5. As we entered
that final inning, Chip confidently walked out to the mound, put on his game
face, and retired the side with twelve good pitches.

I enjoyed coaching, and I learned more during those years than I ever thought possible: much about coaching, but more about life. I had experienced the power of coaching character and meaning into the lives of our players and witnessed its amazing impact. I would use those prized discoveries in business to help develop people and advance careers.

Coaching made me a better man, but the best part of the whole deal was bonding with Chip. It was great fun, and I have often wondered why neither of my dad's ever wanted to coach.

Ten

RESTLESS

*There is a major difference between intelligence and stupidity;
intelligence has its limits.*

—Albert Einstein

Let's get back to October 19, 1987, which became known as Black Monday: the stock market crashed as the Dow Jones Industrial Average plunged 508 points, the largest single day percentage loss in history. It was far worse than 1929, and I questioned whether we were standing at the gates of another depression. I then wondered: was the world coming to an end, or was this just an incredible once in a lifetime fire sale?

The powerful bull market began in the summer of 1982. During those times, much of the growth was fueled by hostile takeovers and leveraged buyouts. Every day, the market went higher, and in April 1986, General Electric (GE) joined the party and announced that it would purchase 80 percent of Kidder, Peabody & Company, a move that made GE one of the nation's leading securities firms. Kidder would retain its name, management, and compensation structure and operated separately from GE's other financial services units. From the beginning, there were significant cultural challenges. Even though the deal looked good on paper, the organizational synergies and scaling opportunities never materialized.

Shortly after the deal closed, we began receiving subpoenas in the government's widening investigations of insider trading on Wall Street. We were implicated in one of the most publicized scandals. A former star banker, Martin Siegel, admitted to selling inside information to Ivan Boesky. The firm paid a large fine to settle the charges. On a call with employees the next day, Jack Welch said, "We would have never touched Kidder, Peabody with a ten foot pole had we known a skunk was in the place. Unfortunately, we did, and now we have to live with it. But we're as committed to winning as we were on day one. We'd love you to win— more than any mother in the world."

Black Monday was my first major market challenge. The Dow lost $500 billion in market value in a single day. I sat at my desk staring in disbelief as I watched the quote machine screen all day, monitoring the unprecedented free fall.

According to the October 20, 1987, *New York Times*, "business leaders were shaken by the collapse which wiped out huge amounts of market value of their companies. And they seemed to have been caught by surprise, but many leaders were confident that the panic would pass."

There are several theories on why the stock market crashed. Some believe the market had gone too high and the steep decline was a correction. Another popular theory was that the crash was exacerbated by computer programs designed to sell stocks as they dropped in price. These computer driven selling programs were affectionately known as portfolio insurance. They were popular with large institutions and pension funds. In theory, they were designed to get money out of the market before major declines, but in practice, once they were triggered, they just fed on themselves. Without the influence of structured buying programs, there was no other possible outcome. There were no buyers, so the market had no bottom. I believe that the massive portfolio insurance programs were the primary drivers of the crash. Thank goodness the market closed at 4:00 p.m.

Despite fears of recession, the stock market quickly rebounded. The Dow made record gains on Tuesday and again on Thursday. By the end of the year, the Dow was slightly higher than it had been at the start of the year and returned to its pre–Black Monday levels less than two years after the crash.

Investor behavior is a powerful weapon. After studying the impact, we concluded that most investors, left to their own devices, bought at the top when they felt good and sold at the bottom when they felt bad. Buy high and sell low was a bad strategy. If we permitted clients to do that enough times, then they would eventually run out of money and no longer need us. It was a fatal flaw that impaired investment performance and would eventually destroy capital. We made enhancements that allowed us to exploit market opportunities by taking emotions out of the equation, which turned out to be another terrific improvement.

Volatile capital markets were good for business. Most advisors did not proactively call clients when things were not going well. They hovered around the coffee machines in the break room and made small talk. They seemed paralyzed. I guess it was easier to be missing in action than to make outgoing calls and talk with confused and angry clients. To me, the advisory business was just another brutal contact sport. I lived on the telephone and used the bad times to aggressively communicate with clients and prospects. I established many meaningful relationships, and made exciting but modest progress. I had learned to *reach higher* and discovered that my goals, aspirations, and dreams were bigger than most, and I am embarrassed to admit that my results fell far short of significant success for almost a decade.

It was now the spring of 1993, and we were focused on getting our children into the right schools. We had submitted an application to Pace Academy for our daughter. Laura and Chip had been at Woodward Academy, an excellent private school in South Atlanta, for the past four years, but we decided as a family that the one hour daily commute each way was too much. They would board the school bus at the Cherokee Plaza Shopping Center at sunrise and return at sunset. It was a long day for them, and it was difficult for us to attend school events. As the children got older, it became more important for us to be involved in their schools and activities. We lived in Brookhaven, and Woodward Academy was geographically unfriendly.

For many reasons, including superior academic credentials, we thought that Pace Academy was a good choice for Laura. Chip had already been accepted at Saint Francis Academy, an exceptional school for children with ADD type learning challenges.

Mean to Meaningful

Vickey was a Pace alum, and her father was a former chairman of the board and had hired the current headmaster, George Kirkpatrick. As an alum, Vickey was involved at the school and knew many of the faculty members and staff—we believed we were pretty well connected. Even though ninth grade was a transition year and admission was competitive, we felt as though we knew the right people and that Laura would have little difficulty being admitted. We were in for a big surprise.

We finished the application process far in advance of the deadline. Laura was smart and made good grades, but she often struggled on standardized tests. We knew this was a challenge but hoped that as a prominent legacy with strong recommendations, her acceptance would be no more than a formality.

Several weeks had passed when we received a letter from Pace Academy. At that time, I thought nothing of it because we got alumni mail from them all the time. Vickey, on the other hand, knew something was wrong when a thin envelope appeared instead of the thick enrollment package. She quickly opened it and found not a rejection letter but an invitation to meet with George Mengert, the director of admissions.

It was a beautiful day in the neighborhood, and I was headed out the door to work when Vickey casually mentioned that she was going to a meeting at Pace Academy to discuss Laura's application. I had a busy day, but I volunteered to rearrange my schedule to join her, something I did not do often. We agreed to meet at 2:15 p.m. I assumed that the purpose of the meeting was to welcome us as new parents and for them to learn about Laura—I figured we were good to go.

We met in the lobby and immediately ran into our old friend George Kirkpatrick, the headmaster. I had not seen him since our wedding almost twenty years earlier, when we had played golf at the Capital City Club. He asked about Mr. Key, and after a brief conversation, he escorted us to the boardroom. It was a large room with a huge mahogany conference table and twenty four intimidating high backed leather chairs. The setting was uncomfortable, and something did not feel right, but Vickey said nothing. She was nervous, and I suddenly realized that this was not a simple glad handed acceptance conference. We would soon discover that we were not as well connected as we thought and were in for a fight.

George Mengert joined us promptly at 2:30 p.m. He was a tall, gangly professorial type. In addition to his admissions duties, he was a talented drama teacher. We seated ourselves across from George at the long table. We passed pleasantries for a few minutes and then, got around to Laura. George started off by informing us that Pace Academy had never accepted a student with standardized test scores as low as Laura's. I believed this was his shot across the bow to let us know that he considered Laura a substandard candidate for admission. George continued, "We have worked very hard to become one of Atlanta's most exclusive private schools, and our admissions standards are strict. We do not make exceptions for anyone under any circumstances."

Vickey immediately responded with the beaming pride of a mother. "You must know that Laura is an excellent student. This is accurately reflected in her transcripts, but she has always struggled on standardized tests."

George seemed uninterested and continued with his critical assessment. His comments were harsh and rubbed me the wrong way, but I said nothing. His condescending attitude naturally placed Vickey on the defensive, but as a determined competitor, she passionately put her head down and just pushed harder. As the conversation progressed, little seemed to change. It was obvious that George had already made up his mind. He was not listening, nor was he really interested in what Vickey was saying. He acted as though we were wasting his time as he just kept repeating in many different ways that he did not think Laura would be successful or happy in the rigorous academic environment at Pace Academy. I had finally heard enough. I threw my hands into the air in disgust and halted the dialogue. I had listened attentively, and believed that it was now my turn to talk. I told George that we knew that Laura was a bright student and could do the work.

After a short moment to gather my thoughts, I said, "I feel bad for Pace Academy. You have spent most of our valuable time today telling us all the reasons why you should not accept Laura for enrollment. I think what bothers me most is that you have yet to ask a single question about Laura or her qualifications. She has always thrived academically and is an excellent student. You can see that in the academic records. I can assure you that she will always be a good student because that is just who she is. We are here today only because we want Laura to get a quality education, and we know that she will be happy here. We chose you first for a reason, but if you do not want her, I am pretty sure the other private schools would be willing to jump through hoops to have her on their campus."

It was still my turn, and I was feeling good, so I decided to play the sports card. I asked, "Did you know that Pace Academy hosted a citywide girls' basketball tournament last weekend?

He frowned and seemed confused. "No. I would have no reason to know. I have no personal interest in athletics."

"That's interesting. Then you do not know that Laura plays basketball for Woodward Academy? Then I can assume that you do not know that her team played in the tournament this weekend and lost a heartbreaker in the finals. Do you have any idea who was the tournament's most valuable player?" He admitted that he had no idea. "Laura Wile, the same person whom we have been academically dissecting for the last hour."

He smiled and leaned forward. The MVP award must have piqued his interest, because his body language changed and indicated that he wanted more. He had overcome his snobby academic biases and was now ready to listen with both ears.

After an hour of intense dialogue, which included begging, reasoning, and even a few gentle threats, George finally agreed to a conditional acceptance and proposed that Laura attend a mini summer school session. Laura completed the session, did well, and was admitted in the fall.

School was in session, and the Pace Academy soccer season was upon us. Laura did not start the first game and was bummed, but she was only a freshman. She worked hard and was disappointed to be, as she put it, "riding the bench." Midway through the first half, the coach put her in. She made the most of this opportunity and played the rest of the game. They won 4–3, and Laura scored three goals.

I was pleasantly surprised to see George Mengert at the game. We spoke briefly and shook hands. Over the next four years, the team enjoyed much success. I often saw George—the man who had told us that he had no interest in athletics—in the stands cheering. His attendance made a lasting impression and spoke volumes about the character of the educators at Pace Academy.

They had an exciting team, and over the next four years, they won two state championships and tied for another. During Laura's senior year, *USA Today* ranked Pace Academy as the third best women's high school soccer team in the nation, and Laura was the second leading scorer. She was an amazing player. When that ball was anywhere near the goal, our blond, blue eyed little girl morphed into a ferocious junkyard dog and found ways to score. That national ranking was an amazing feat given that Pace Academy's total enrollment was fewer than three hundred.

Laura's basketball teams were good too. She was the starting guard for four years. Those teams were highly regarded but never made it to the dance.

In 1994, I decided to pursue additional investment education. I researched the many options and settled on the Certified Investment Manager Analyst curriculum, more commonly known today as CIMA. It is an exclusive advanced designation offered only at the Wharton Business School. Only a handful of competitors spent the time and money to complete the comprehensive curriculum, which had a pass rate of less than fifty percent.

For acceptance, I was required to provide college transcripts. I ordered them, and they coincidentally both arrived the same day. Vickey opened them with the other mail and left them on the dining room table. When I arrived home that night, Laura was sitting at the table carefully reviewing the transcripts. She looked up and smiled but never said a word. I am thankful, because I am not sure how I would have responded. Though I didn't dare risk asking, I did wonder what she was thinking. I would find out soon enough.

Mean to Meaningful

Vickey and I both emphatically embraced education. We wanted our children to have the best possible and were willing to sacrifice because we strongly believed that it would dictate their place in life, ultimate happiness, and degree of success. We preached to our children the importance of doing their best. As parents, we all do it. *Do your best in school. Do your best in sports. Do your best at work. Do your best to be a good friend.* I could go on and on. I often wondered how I would explain my Wofford College academic record and grades to the children, because the results were inconsistent with our messaging and expectations. I was clearly an underperformer. I did not lead by example, nor did the records reflect that I had done my best.

Several weeks later during dinner, Laura asked if we could talk about school. I assumed that she meant her school, and I was excited. She was a teenager, and I found it thrilling that she would seek my advice. I had broad school of hard knocks experience that I could share, and I believed that I could offer invaluable guidance on almost any topic, even boys. After the dishes were cleared, we made our way into the living room. We got comfortable, but that didn't last very long. I was not prepared for the ensuing cross examination—I didn't even see it coming.

She looked at me with those striking blue eyes and said, "I saw your college grades. You and Mom tell us to do our best, but you did not. There has to be more to the story. Can you explain what happened and tell me why?" I was speechless; I'd had no clue until that very moment that our talk that night was going to be about *me*. Frankly, I was a little shocked by her bold and direct approach.

When I regained my composure, I responded, "I can understand your curiosity, and I appreciate your need for an explanation. I am not sure that I have all the answers, but here is what I know for sure. I was a troubled young man. I had many problems as a new college student, the least being that I was angry, naïve, and immature. On my best days, I was an average student just trying to fit in and survive. I maximized the sports opportunities, but I did not thrive in the classroom. I was more of an empty seat, bored and uninterested, which is reflected in my grades. If I had it to do over, I can promise you that I would do better. The bottom line is that I failed to do my best work at Wofford College." I paused to organize my next thoughts on what I believed was the more important part of the answer and then continued. "I did much better when I went to graduate school because I was eight years older and more mature. I had you, Chip, and Mom and wanted all of you to be proud of me. I could not afford to fail because I had too much to lose. I was driven to do my best while working full time. Those results accurately reflect my abilities as your father."

She listened intently, processed the message, and smiled. "I appreciate the explanation and understand." A wonderful father daughter conversation ensued that included many more difficult yet important questions.

I completed the CIMA advanced degree designation in 1995. The course work was grueling, and the examination process was brutal. The CIMA experience and the feedback of peers further confirmed that it would take a team of highly trained professionals to deliver the world class results and personal services that clients needed.

I read that collaboration divides tasks and multiplies success, and that made perfect sense to me. At the time, I did it all. I was the salesman, relationship manager, research analyst, operations person, and investment manager. On a good day, I was going a hundred miles an hour, and it was obvious that this one person business model was unsustainable and that I was headed for certain burnout. I concluded that I could not do everything well. I could never make a difference for clients or achieve any real personal significance alone, so I slowed down, stepped back, crafted a long tailed strategy, and began to seriously build a team.

A short time later, I hired Stacy Womble as an investment associate. She joined me from the bank across the street. We met and talked many times, and during our final meeting, I told her what I expected and then proceeded to ask one final question: "If you work for me, you will be required to save 15 percent of your gross salary. Can you do that?" She was leaving a bank position for a job with me, which included a substantial pay raise. She agreed to save as requested, if hired. I then asked her if she wanted the job, and she said yes. I slept on it and hired her the next day.

Over the years, I had broadly researched and settled on a handful of best practice ideas. The "savings plan" was the first to be implemented. I believed that saving was one of the most fundamental components of personal success. This simple forced wealth accumulation discipline would change her future and influence her quality of life. It worked, and she remained in her seat for a long career with the firm.

I now want to share a true story that proves no good deed goes unpunished. Stacy had worked with me for two years. One day after lunch, she stormed into my office and yelled, "You lied to me!" I had no idea what she was talking about and calmly asked her to be more specific. She said, "I just went to lunch with the office administrator, and she said that the firm did not require me to save." Her face turned red, and she once again blurted out, "You lied to me."

I asked her to sit down and relax. When she was comfortably seated, I said, "You are correct about the firm's savings requirements, but first, before I address that, I want you to know that I did not lie to you. As it relates to firm savings, you are right. The firm does not require you to save. Retirement plan and stock purchase savings are completely optional.

Now, I want you to listen very closely as I repeat exactly what I said to you during your final job interview. I said, 'If you work for me, you will be required to save 15 percent.'" I then compassionately added, "I require you to save because I care about you. You must save if you are going to work with me. You may not agree, but I do not care. I feel it is my responsibility to require you to do what is best for you. You can hate me today, and you can thank me later." I paused for a moment and then asked if she had any other questions. She sheepishly looked at me and shook her head no. With that she excused herself and went back to work. Knowing Stacy, I am sure that she dissected our entire conversation word by word because she is a perfectionist, and that is what I loved about her.

I replayed that conversation many times over and discovered that I had made a mistake. The right number should be much higher than 15 percent to really make a life difference. I asked myself, "How much does someone have to save over twenty-five years, with a reasonable rate of return, to retire comfortably?" I did the math and decided that we would ask all new people to save 25 percent. I decided several years later to match a portion of every dollar saved as a year-end bonus with no vesting schedule. The goal was to help make them wealthy.

Kidder was on the ropes and continued to be weakened by lawsuits, Securities and Exchange Commission investigations, and fines. The company managed to survive until 1994, when GE sold the assets to PaineWebber.

By acquiring Kidder's 1,150 brokers in fifty US offices, PaineWebber would have a total of 6,700 brokers and become the nation's fourth largest investment brokerage firm. There would be massive layoffs and restructurings, and the Kidder, Peabody name vanished after 130 years. GE's common stock rose slightly on the news of the sale.

PaineWebber had a much different feel. It was not a boutique firm like Kidder, serving wealthy individuals and large institutions. It served a broader client base and its slogan "Thank You, PaineWebber" was widely recognized. It had a good reputation, excellent research capabilities, good client service tools, and information systems that were much improved. It would turn out to be an excellent merger.

In 1996, after Kidder had died, I got a call from Marie Wile. She said Dad was sick and I needed to come to Wooster right away. I'd had minimal contact with Dad over the years. We would talk occasionally, but that was about it. Neither of us had much invested in the relationship, and we were now very different people with very different lives in very different places.

I had not talked with Dad in quite some time, but I had heard that he was involved in a real estate investment that went bad. It was rumored that he had lost everything.

We left for Wooster the following day. It was a 650 mile drive, so I had plenty of time to think about the past. I was now much older and wiser and wondered how I might have been a better son. We arrived late and checked into the Best Western Hotel in downtown Wooster. We got up the early the next morning and had a big breakfast in the hotel restaurant. The children wanted to see their grandmother, so we went out to Mom's house first and, after a pleasant stop, headed for Dad's new place in Shreve.

I was nervous and had no idea what to expect. On the short drive, I realized that Dad had never met Laura or Chip. In a way, I was excited that they would get to meet their grandfather that day. When we arrived, we discovered that Dad and Marie were living in a rental house. Marie met us at the door with a smile and invited us into a small room that served as the main living area. It was nothing like I had expected. It felt more like some of the bad places on North Street.

Dad was nowhere in sight, so we visited with Marie until Dad could join us. I was surprised when he finally rolled out of his bedroom in a wheelchair with his oxygen tank in tow. We shook hands, and Vickey introduced him to his grandchildren. She had met Wilbur and Marie only once, twenty-three years earlier, at my college graduation. After a brief exchange of pleasantries, Dad talked almost nonstop for the rest of our time together. Laura and Chip never said a word beyond hello. They were curious teenagers who had a lot of questions, but they sat patiently and listened. It would be the only time they would ever see their grandfather Wile.

In a perfect world, I had hoped that we might reconcile that day, but even after all these years, with the end of life in sight, nothing had changed. On the drive home, I relived the details of the visit many times over, just trying to understand. As I pulled into our driveway in Atlanta, mentally and physically exhausted, I realized that during our visit, Dad had never asked a single question about Vickey or his two grandchildren. At first, it made me mad, but after further reflection, it made me sad—very sad.

Dad died on July 26, 1996, before we made it back for another visit. He was sixty-six years old. When Diana and I attended the funeral's visitation services, we discovered that few people in town, including dad's closest friends, knew that Diana and I were his children. Some did not even know that we existed. That was no surprise since Diana and I both left Wooster after graduating from high school. Diana joined the

Air Force, married a wonderful man, traveled the world, retired after serving the United States for twenty years, settled in Oklahoma City with her husband and two children, and I left for college.

Diana was a thoughtful sister. She and her husband Dan called me from Maine on their wedding day to let me know they had gotten married. Our sibling relationship is best described as close, but distant. Coincidently, we would share the same wedding day, September 7. I always knew Diana would find happiness wherever she landed. She is an extraordinary person, and I often felt guilty that I was not a better big brother.

The next day after the burial service Diana and I went by mom's house for a brief visit before heading home. When we got to the airport we said our good byes and then went our separate ways. I would not see Diana again for years. On the flight home, I gently closed the dad chapter. It was over and there was nothing in the world that I could do or say to change the outcome. Albert Einstein said, "Life is like riding a bicycle. To keep your balance, you must keep moving." With that in mind, I offered a final prayer, and then quietly moved on to the many important duties ahead of me at home and at work.

I made it known throughout the firm that I was building a team and was looking for a few good people. I had a reputation, and as a result, I had two or three interviews each week. Most turned out to be a waste of time, and I discovered that it was hard to find good people when you knew what you wanted.

Jan Pendleton was moving to Atlanta from Valdosta, Georgia, and was looking for a job. She had investment office experience and was referred to me. When I interviewed her, I discovered an experienced, smart, tall, attractive blonde who wore crazy colored platform shoes. The soles were three inches thick, and I had never seen anything like them. I assumed they were a fad. Jan's professional experience and warm can do personality were perfect. Once she agreed to save, I offered her a client service associate position. She joined the team in 1997.

Our branch manager, Lewis Holland, suffered some serious health issues and retired after a successful career. I enjoyed his friendship and respected his straightforward approach to life. I found him to be a great mentor and leader who had laid a solid foundation to support the many great things to come.

George Longino was recruited by the firm to replace Lewis. He was a well-known and respected branch manager at another firm. He grew up in Atlanta but managed an office in Texas. He accepted the job and immediately made some valuable changes, which included allowing some people to move on. His greatest contribution was establishing a board, a brilliant idea that gave a voice to the ten largest advisors in the office. I loved his motto: "Do more business, make more money, and have more fun."

Larry Radford followed George, and he would manage the office for many years and mold Atlanta into one of the top offices in the world. He was a workaholic. I would see him on Saturdays, and he would come to the office early on Sundays with his wife, Vickie. She read the newspaper while Larry prepared his work plan for the coming week. They were usually gone by 3:00 p.m. Larry was a professional manager, highly structured and organized. I enjoyed working with him, and we made enormous strides under his leadership.

I worked hard and continued to aggressively grow within the firm. It is true that success is the best revenge. The desk plaque served me well as our once irrelevant small group of advisors grew into one of the firm's top producing offices. I was fortunate to be a significant part of that growth as one of the senior leaders.

In the fall of 1997, the children began to leave the nest. Laura graduated from high school and decided to go to Wofford College and play soccer. She was a walk on just like her dad and was thrilled to have the opportunity to play NCAA Division I soccer. The next year Chip would leave for the College of Charleston.

The soccer experience was frustrating for Laura because she did not get the opportunity to play much; however, she did get plenty of opportunity to practice and "ride the bench," which built character. We attended many games, and toward the end of the season, we decided to go to the Furman University game. We loaded the Tahoe with a group from the neighborhood, including mom who was visiting from Ohio, and drove to Greenville, South Carolina.

Even though the Wofford coach knew that we had driven up from Atlanta with a crowd, Laura did not start. She sat on the end of the bench for most of the game, but with two minutes left, Laura entered the game. The Atlanta crowd cheered when her name was announced. It was a bittersweet moment because I knew Laura was considering a transfer to the University of Georgia, where she would not play soccer.

With just over a minute to go Wofford stole the ball and passed it to Laura. She dribbled down the sidelines. The scoreboard showed a score of 1–1 with fifty eight seconds left. It was go time, and when the defender slipped, Laura dribbled around her. I knew what was on her mind as she headed down the field toward the goal. Then it happened. From twenty yards out, the junkyard dog took the shot on goal. The ball left her foot like a rocket and soared past the goalie into the back of the net. Wofford won the game 2–1, and Laura's college soccer career was complete.

The children were flourishing and business was heating up, but I was burning out. I had two full time team employees: Jan Pearlman, a sales assistant, and Stacy Womble, an investment associate. It was a good start, but at a minimum, I still needed an analyst, an account officer, and a solid business development person. I continued to interview, and much to my disappointment, I found that most of the candidates were unwilling to start at the bottom and work their way up. This simple task had become far more difficult than I had anticipated.

In the fall of 1999, I invited John Nix, a friend from Gainesville, Georgia, to join me for a Pro-Am golf event at Arnold Palmer's Bay Hill Golf Club in Orlando, Florida. John was two years older than me and was a former high school quarterback. He was a man of principle, and we had developed a friendship over a twenty year period, since we had "the jock thing" in common. He managed an accounting firm in Gainesville, and he occasionally referred clients who were seeking more sophisticated or personalized investment relationships. During our flight to Orlando, I shared my frustrations about finding good people. John was a thoughtful, smart man, and he listened intently. At the end of our conversation, he confirmed the job requirements as he heard them, and then, after many questions, he mentioned a local young man who he thought might be a candidate. I respected John's opinion, so I asked him to send the young man's work history and résumé to me. I asked John to send it only if, after further thought, he was willing to personally recommend him. I made it perfectly clear that I was tired of interviewing losers.

John sent the résumé, and I immediately called the young man for a short telephone interview. I liked him, and at the end of our call, I invited him to the office for a personal interview. Stacy Womble conducted most of the interview, and she liked him too. That day, I met with the young man for only a few minutes at the very end of the interview. Even though he was frumpy, we invited him back for another interview. I spent a long time with him during this visit. After considerable thought, I offered him an entry level position as a sales assistant. It is an important role but generally not a high skill or prestigious job.

Before he even had time to respond to my offer, I outlined my long term vision, the opportunities, and a potential career path. I was testing what I thought was the ideal team model. I wanted to get his reaction. He would be leaving a management position where he had done well. I felt that if he took this job it would confirm some of my observations. He took the offer, and we agreed that he would start on March 20, 2000. His name was Harris Gignilliat, a University of Georgia graduate. On his first day of work, I was pleased to see that he came dressed to play and showed up an hour early.

On November 3, 2000, PaineWebber merged with UBS, and the stock skyrocketed. The merger made the new firm an 800 pound gorilla. Initially, the firm was known as UBS PaineWebber, but the 123 year old PaineWebber name disappeared in 2003 when it was rebranded as UBS Wealth Management USA.

Our director of operations, Patrick Brisse, and I had an ongoing dialogue about his joining the team in a newly created position as a senior analyst. He came to me when the merger was announced and shared that several firms had approached him with attractive offers. He just wanted me to know that he was weighing his options.

Patrick had started with the firm as an hourly employee in the operations cage in 1980. He grew up in France and was a college educated engineer who fell in love with a young woman and followed her back to America. Upon arrival, he spoke little English but quickly learned the language by watching TV soap operas. We became friends early in his career, and he often mispronounced words intentionally to make sure that I was listening and to keep me on my toes.

Patrick is one of the brightest and most detail oriented people I have ever known, and in 2000, we offered him the opportunity to work with a small group as our first local institutional consulting research analyst. He enthusiastically accepted the job on the spot.

Laura graduated from the University of Georgia in 2001. I secretly hoped that she would join the team. She had asked me to help her get a job in drug sales. I had no influential contacts and could not help. I instead offered her a job. She had interned at our office with another advisor the previous summer and told me that she hated it. I assumed she would graciously decline, but she accepted.

At first, I was flattered that she chose to work with me. After further reflection, I concluded that she took the job only because she had no other options and knew that she needed to work. Laura started on July 16, 2001, as a sales assistant.

Testing was a valuable tool. It enabled us to encourage and even lead people to the jobs that played to their strengths. People were happier and more successful working in roles that challenged their strengths. John Engle captured this wisdom when he said, "Follow your passion and you will never work a day in your life."

In 2000, 2001, and 2002, the financial markets were in turmoil. It seemed as if they went down every day. People were confused and sometimes angry. This stretch of results would surely be recognized as some of the worst in history. It was financially difficult for everyone, but I continued to look for good teammates.

Our office had an ongoing discussion about creating a super team, and in 2002, we formed a team that included four high profile financial advisors. It started out as an exciting endeavor, but eventually fizzled for reasons beyond the scope of this book. Had it succeeded, we would have leapfrogged the competition and dominated the market in scope and scale. Unfortunately, we were ahead of our time and mutually agreed to dissolve the team after a year.

I contributed much to the failure. I am determined, stubborn, and naturally curious. This was a blessing and a curse. The curse is that I am prone to make a lot of mistakes going full speed ahead. The blessing is that I learn from every mistake, and I try not to make the same mistake twice. I do not sit around on my hands in idle conversation. I am a doer and have to live with the fact that I am often wrong but never in doubt. I can recognize good ideas when I see them and aggressively use them to advance the ball. Although the super team did not survive, I learned several valuable lessons.

The first thing I learned was that in order to build a team, you had to clearly articulate in writing a mission, vision, and value statement, and it had to include clear personal and team expectations. We would also have to develop solid disciplined systematic processes to ensure quality control, good performance, functional scalability, and team harmony.

The second thing I learned was to place people in jobs that they enjoyed. From experience I discovered that if they enjoyed their work, they would develop a passion and come to work early and stay late. This revelation would become a game changer, because it practically eliminated undesired turnover and resulted in a happy, harmonious, and naturally more productive environment.

The third thing I learned was the need to take the time to plan and communicate broadly, both internally and externally. Communication was key, and we committed all job descriptions, duties, goals, and expectations to writing. We established the career path, a team vision, and a compensation and savings plan linked to performance. These discoveries would all be essential to a successful future.

My team building efforts seemed to always be taking two steps forward and one step backward. In 2004, Jan Pearlman retired to be a fulltime wife. Shortly thereafter, I helped Stacy Womble transition to her own investment advisory business. She left the team but remained with the firm. Today, Jan is happily married to Scott Pearlman, whom I shall never forgive for stealing her. Stacy is a highly successful financial advisor of whom I am very proud.

Laura, Harris, Patrick, and I remained. We hired another sales assistant, but he didn't last long because he couldn't get to work on time. Being late was something I did not tolerate under any circumstances. After a third strike, I permitted him to resign.

When I dismissed him, I decided to close to new clients, which meant we would no longer spend precious time marketing. It was a controversial strategy that few understood at the time. I concluded that the four of us were not equipped to serve more clients. We were already shorthanded, and the stress levels were dangerously high. I did not want to lose Harris or Laura. I hoped that they would learn to lead by example and grow into important leadership roles. I did not worry about Patrick because I knew that he was in for the duration.

We would focus our energy, time, and resources on providing better and broader services to our existing clients. I had no doubt that our reputation was our greatest asset and would be our most productive source of new business in the future. We could not afford to screw up. What I knew for sure was that we were at capacity and needed time to attract a few more good people, reduce stress levels, and provide some additional runway to develop our team, culture, and infrastructure. Although we were technically closed, we were not stupid, and we occasionally made strategic exceptions to admit qualified new clients who were referred to us.

Our managing director, Larry Radford, was not pleased when he learned what we had done. When we met, he made it crystal clear that he thought closing was a big time bad decision. Shame on me for not keeping him in the loop. Once he understood the plan and the client centered vision, Larry did everything in his power to support us. We built out the team, and over the next few years became the top advisor in the office.

As we grew, I became engaged with the Atlanta Mission and found that I was eager to learn exactly what Winston Churchill meant when he said, "We make a living by what we get, but we make a life by what we give."

Eleven

COMPASSION

Character is established by what you do, not by what you say.

—Edward B. Wile

As a family we were blessed far beyond our needs, and we wanted to do something meaningful during the Christmas holidays. We aspired to teach our children that it was much better to give than to receive. When they were nine or ten years old we asked Laura and Chip if they would be willing to donate their gently used clothing and toys to the less fortunate children in our community. They agreed, and on Christmas Eve, we personally delivered their gifts to children at a nearby homeless shelter. Until then, they had no idea that there were any homeless children in Atlanta, because it was not a visible part of their world.

Laura and Chip were smart kids and quickly embraced what turned out to be a new Christmas tradition. After the first trip, they asked a lot of questions, and their excitement and engagement grew. They knew that without their help, care, and prayers, the homeless would have a sad and skinny Christmas. Throughout the next year, they proactively selected their best stuff and put it in the gift closet. When the holidays came, they wrapped their gifts in our most colorful paper, and we delivered the presents on the day before Christmas.

During those trips, we visited with the children and their mothers. Laura and Chip handed out Christmas presents while Vickey and I talked with the mothers. We learned their personal stories. It was a gratifying experience. Participating in the gift of giving with Vickey and the children lifted the holiday spirit. This became a family tradition and went on for years. It was soup for the soul and was ultimately an unintentional Christmas gift to ourselves. Little did I know that giving away gently used clothing and toys would eventually lead us to the Atlanta Mission?

The Atlanta Union Mission was established in 1938 on Crew Street as a soup kitchen for homeless men during the Depression. The name was later shortened to the Atlanta Mission. Along the way, the services were expanded to include women and children. Today, the Atlanta Mission is the city's oldest and largest provider of services to the homeless. It provides warm meals, emergency shelter, temporary shelter, recovery programming, job attainment, and transitional housing to more than one thousand men, women, and children daily. Darryl Russ, who runs men's services, affectionately refers to the Atlanta Mission as "the miracle factory."

I was introduced to the Atlanta Mission by Tommy Flagler. Mr. Flagler was the father of my good friend Thorne Flagler and the founder and owner of the Flagler Construction Company. He was a respected leader in the community. When I learned that he was a tenured board member, I cornered him in the Capital City Club golf shop early one morning and asked him what he could tell me about the Atlanta Mission. He smiled and said, "They are an amazing organization and do more with less than anyone I know. If you are truly interested in helping the homeless, you should get involved. I have been on the board for a long time, and I have found the work extremely gratifying and worthwhile. You will be humbled, and I can promise that you will get more than you can ever give."

Mr. Flagler's passion and enthusiasm were contagious. The next week, I approached Lamar Oglesby, a well-respected senior executive at our firm. I had interviewed with Lamar when I joined the firm many years earlier. He was a short, fit, distinguished looking man with a firm, matter of fact personality. I knew that he was on the Atlanta Mission Board of Directors, and I asked him how I might get involved. He said he would think about it and get back to me. I patiently waited until he called and asked, "Would you like to join me on the finance committee as an advisory board member?" I immediately accepted without even knowing what might be involved.

Sometime later, I learned that Lamar's father, Dr. Stuart Oglesby, was a minister at the Central Presbyterian Church on Washington Street and that he and a handful of community leaders had helped found and support the Atlanta Mission. Lamar is a private man, and he had never mentioned his father's founding role. As I learned the organizational history, I discovered that without Dr. Oglesby's bold leadership, the Atlanta Mission would not exist.

After I served with Lamar on the finance committee for several years, he called one day and asked that I come to his office. From the tone of his voice, I thought that I might be in serious trouble. When I arrived, he asked me to take a seat. It was an intimidating, large corner office with nice furniture, plants, and pictures—quite different from mine. He asked a few questions about my experiences on the finance committee. He then smiled and said, "Atlanta Mission is going to ask you to join the board of directors." The board was a small group of business leaders— among the most powerful people in town.

When I arrived home, I shared the news with Vickey. I was interested in getting her reaction and approval. I made few decisions these days without her input. She is a wise woman, and her response was no surprise. "They will be lucky to have you, and I would suggest that you accept, roll up your sleeves, and get engaged," she said. "I think it will be good for you and may be a magnificent learning opportunity for our family." I listened and then took her advice.

Atlanta Mission announced it first capital campaign shortly after I joined the board at a lunch meeting at the 755 Club at the Braves Stadium. It was a well-orchestrated event, and everyone who was anyone in Atlanta was in attendance. It was a big deal. I invited Laura to accompany me to the event. I recognized most of the people on the program, but I also noticed a tall, attractive woman about Laura's age seated at one of the shelter guest tables who looked familiar but out of place.

As folks got up to speak, I was still perplexed by the identity of the young woman. The curiosity was killing me, and I wondered why she was here. When she got up to speak, it all came together, and I realized why she looked so familiar. She had played basketball against Laura in high school and had been a star player at another private high school. Still, I did not understand why she was here to speak.

When she reached the podium, she confidently looked over the crowd and began her story. After she graduated from high school, she went to college on a full basketball scholarship, got hooked on drugs, and dropped out. She followed a boy to the West Coast, got pregnant, had a baby, and moved back to Atlanta. She was white, the baby was black, and the father was gone. She was fortunate to discover My Sister's House, our shelter for homeless women and children. They welcomed her and the baby with open arms. When she finished her powerful story, I could hear people around me crying. When the message finally registered with me, it was like being blindsided by a 300 pound lineman. She was clear in her message. Under the right circumstance, this could happen to anyone, even my precious daughter, Laura.

During my tenure on the board, I was fortunate to have served on many committees. Eventually, I found myself on the verge of a two year term as the vice chairman, which would be followed by a two year term as chairman of the board, a position that made me uncomfortable.

The organization was going through a rough patch. The chairman of the board, Pitts Carr, terminated the president and asked me to chair a search committee to find a new one. I had never served on or led a search committee, but I agreed to do it. We assembled a small committee of board members, interviewed several prominent national search firms, and hired Boardwalk, a local firm that specialized in finding senior executives for nonprofit organizations. They helped us identify potential candidates, and it took us several months of interviews to find the right group of finalists.

We were down to three. As I did research, I discovered that one of the candidates was Mr. Key's longtime pastor. I decided to call Mr. Key to see what I might learn, a sort of character reference check.

After twenty-five years of irreconcilable differences, bad feelings, and radio silence, I picked up the phone and called him. We met for dinner that same night; discussed the candidate, whom we did not hire; and patched up our differences.

We finally settled on a business guy with broad management experience in the private sector, including service as the CEO of a New York Stock Exchange company. The only downside was that he did not have a single day of nonprofit experience. We offered him the job, and he accepted. His name was Jim Reese, and I would later learn that the Atlanta Mission was a calling for him.

Jim and his wife, Dina, have three girls. They are strong Christians and people of character. As I got to know Jim better, he inspired me in many uncomfortable ways. When I took over as chairman of the board, Jim had just finished his first year on the job. He had already made many difficult but necessary organizational changes, and he had done it with grace and dignity. He was a pro! I was still unsure how to best fulfill the duties as chairman.

Jim was the leader, and I wanted to be careful not to get in the way. When I took over, we agreed to meet in my office on Monday mornings twice a month. That worked quite well and gave us a chance to get to know each other in a casual, private setting. After several months, we decided to change to a monthly breakfast. We eventually decided to include the vice chairman. The benefits were immediate, and the chairman's breakfast became a game changer.

The lessons and experiences of compassion and stewardship at the Atlanta Mission were precious gifts. I was fortunate to have been afforded the opportunity to serve with people who unselfishly shared their time, treasures, and talents—people who were committed to ending the dreaded perils of homelessness. People who boldly led by example. People who truly cared about changing lives, even knowing that it could only be done one friend at a time.

Jim Reese and I were participating in a UBS sponsored children's back to school event held annually at My Sister's House, our facility for mothers and children. I knew that most of the kids in the room had arrived there with their mothers carrying everything they owned in a brown paper bag. When you are a child without a home, from a broken family, life is hard enough. Trying to keep up was sometimes more difficult for them, so at the beginning of each school year, UBS employees made it their responsibility to provide each child with new clothes and a backpack complete with school supplies. We wanted to make sure they were just as prepared and equipped as their classmates and hoped this would ensure that they received the same opportunities as the other children.

During the event, Jim turned to me with tears in his eyes and said, "You know that many of the children who come through these doors have never known a father or had a positive male influence in their lives. They have never had a role model, and as a result they do not know how to act, what to do, or even what will be expected of them as they grow up and become parents. They need our love, attention, guidance, and care if they are to have a chance to make a better life. The time spent here may be their one and only chance. This is an important job, and we cannot afford to screw it up."

I slowly looked around the room and saw a gathering of children, many of whom had been abandoned by their fathers. Most were confused and already suffered from a lack of self-esteem. I knew from experience that, over time, they would eventually feel discarded and worthless. Even with a hand up from My Sister's House and the Atlanta Mission, they would have little chance of survival and happiness, let alone success. Jim was right: without a hand up and the outside influence of role models, they would repeat the cycle because it was all that they knew. Most of the mothers, who were their children's primary caretakers were here because they had made a bad decision or had taken a wrong turn. It may have been the death of a spouse, drug addiction, spousal abuse, or just simply bad luck. No matter the reason, they were in bad places in their lives. I could imagine mom and grandmother being in this same place absent some good and maybe lucky choices.

Jim and I had grown up with very similar challenges, and I strongly suspected that was one of the reasons he had taken this job. Once I fully digested the significance of his message, I turned to him and said, "Jim, these children, in many ways, are just like you and me." I smiled. "You are correct, and I agree. This is important work, and we cannot afford to screw it up."

Over the years, Jim has transformed the organization. He brought an authentic passion, unlimited energy, and creative curiosity. He proactively made many uncomfortable changes. He replaced ineffective people, updated old programs, added Tuesday morning Bible studies, implemented performance measurement systems, and updated facilities, which led to dramatic cultural changes. It was amazing to watch him at work. He genuinely loves and cares for the people, both guests and employees. He worked tirelessly and did what was required to advance the institution. He was harder on himself than anyone I have ever known, and I often felt his pain. Jim was a good influence, and I learned much from him, which included a few things about business and many important things about life. As a team, we were able to leverage each other's gifts and ultimately developed a uniquely close friendship.

During my time on the board, the Atlanta Mission had two capital campaigns. The first was $4.5 million. I was a young board member, and I wanted to make a difference. Vickey and I discussed the needs of the mission and made what we thought was a stretch pledge. We gave enough to get our names on the major donor list, which was nice, but when I wrote the check, it hurt. I would soon discover why from my good friend and mentor Walt Sessoms.

Walter W. Sessoms was a native of Darlington, South Carolina, a sleepy southern farm community. He earned a bachelor's degree in economics and business administration in 1956 from Wofford College. He was a strong farm boy and talented baseball player and attended Wofford College as a student athlete on a scholarship. He was so gifted that he was invited to spend his summers catching for a semipro team. Had he not joined Southern Bell after college, he would have surely played professional baseball.

Walt and I often talked about the impact of Wofford College on our lives. The first time we met, we joked about which of us was the poorest. "I was so poor that I arrived with my belongings in a secondhand cardboard suitcase," Walt said.

I was not impressed and responded, "I did not own a suitcase, nor did I have enough stuff to fill one. I packed everything I owned in an old, worn out duffel bag."

"I hitchhiked to school from Florence," he said.

"I had a friend bring me here from Ohio, and it took twelve hours," I responded.

Growing up poor was something Walt and I had in common that bonded us. We were both student athletes from humble beginnings. We were just trying to do our best to get a college education. What we both knew for sure was that without athletics we had no chance of attending college. Our relationship matured over several decades, and Walt became a most valued mentor.

Walt joined Southern Bell in 1956 after graduating from college and retired as a group president in 1997 after a forty-two year career. His successful management style, peppered with Dizzy Dean and Yogi Berra wisdom, did not change as he climbed the corporate ladder. He said, "It's not work unless you'd rather be doing something else." It was obvious that he lived his life that way. He served on the boards of Wofford College, the Atlanta University Center, the Robert W. Woodruff Library, the Georgia Chamber of Commerce, and the State Board of Education, to name just a few. Walt had a great sense of social justice and was a deep thinker. His knowledge of baseball and its history made him an advocate for the Negro Baseball League and its players. He successfully fought for the recognition that he thought the players were entitled to but were denied. I am told that, behind the scenes, he purchased uniforms, jackets, and equipment for the teams.

Walt selected me to serve on a local Wofford College alumni board in the early eighties. I respected him and appreciated the opportunity to be included. In 1985, he educated, inspired, and then engaged a group of alumni to establish an endowed scholarship fund known today as the Witan Fund. It was seeded with $100,000 that came from a broad group of Atlanta alumni.

He continued to promote me as the face of the Atlanta alumni association. As a result, in 1989 I was asked to serve a two year term as the president of the Wofford College National Alumni Association which I humbly accepted.

In 1999 we were attending a Wofford College alumni social gathering in Atlanta, and Walt asked me if I wanted to be involved in the yet to be announced $100 million plus capital campaign. I was born at night, but not last night, and I knew that if I agreed, I would get the opportunity to write a big check and, if I was really lucky, a large multi-year pledge. I was flattered that Walt wanted me, but I still had mixed emotions. He was aware that I was a smaller donor and that I had made regular gifts to the college.

We discussed the purpose of the Wofford campaign, and I confidentially shared my philanthropic experience with the Atlanta Mission. I knew that another large pledge was going to be painful and stretch our limited cash resources, but I was open to the idea.

I shared with Walt, "We are currently giving until it hurts."

He laughed and said, "Well, that is a problem."

"A problem? What do you mean?"

"You should not give until it hurts. You should give until it feels good," he laughed.

"I am confused. What exactly do you mean?"

Walt paused, leaned forward, and whispered, "Here's the secret to the joy of giving. You and Vickey will want to support organizations where you are engaged and have a passion. You will want to give generously to them, and you should expect it to feel good—in the spirit of full disclosure, it will oftentimes cost more, but you will discover that it is almost always worth it. If it does not feel good, that's a warning sign that you probably should have given more." He then stepped back, looked into my eyes, and smiled.

We decided to make a substantial five year pledge to the campaign. It was our largest gift ever to Wofford, and I agreed to serve on the capital campaign's committee. I learned that Walt was right: it does cost more to feel good, and it really is worth it.

Walt Sessoms was a generous man, and his unselfish mentoring and wise advice enriched the lives of everyone he touched. In 2004, after years of watching him lead by example, Vickey and I established and endowed two Wofford College football scholarships. The first was to memorialize Vera Parsons, and the second was to honor Jack Peterson. They are awarded to young men of good character and are designated for student athletes who might not be able to attend college without their existence.

Walt passed away on July 2, 2006, at the age of seventy two. Shortly after his death, the Wofford College Atlanta Invitational Golf Committee established the Georgia Alumni Endowed Baseball Scholarship Fund to honor and memorialize Walt and his lifetime friend, fellow trustee, and Wofford teammate, Russell King.

Jim Reese and Walt Sessoms are extraordinary people, and I found their kind, unselfish and humble demeanor unique. I viewed them both as inspirational leaders and teachers.

Without them Vickey and I would have never discovered that *you can have almost anything in the world that you want, as long as you are willing to help everyone along the way get what they want first,* nor would we have ever experienced the many joys of the Atlanta Mission where we learned that Tommy Flagler was right when he told me that *we would always get more than we could ever give.*

Twelve

EMPOWERED

Example is not the main thing in influencing others.
It is the only thing.

—Albert Schweitzer

Laura was the nearly perfect child with few issues. She was competent, driven, smart, sociable and competitive. She had it all and came with little baggage. Chip, on the other hand, had severe learning difficulties and this chapter chronicles his challenges. Those who have dealt with children's learning issues will truly appreciate this part of the journey.

It all started when Vickey received an urgent telephone call from his first grade teacher insisting that we come to school for a meeting the next day.

"I am concerned by Chip's erratic behavior. He is a very disruptive child, and it is not fair to the other children in class," she said. "I would strongly suggest that you have him tested."

I was confused and asked, "Tested for what?"

"For ADD," she said.

"Is that a disease?" I asked.

"No, sir. ADD stands for attention deficit disorder, a relatively new discovery. Many young boys are being diagnosed with the disorder. The good news is that it can be treated and managed with medications," she said, as she looked down her nose at me.

We agreed to get him tested, and Vickey took him to the recommended psychologist the next day and ultimately had him tested three times. On the third trip, I accompanied Vickey, and we had the good sense to finally ask the clinician if there was a problem with the test.

"Yes, we think there definitely is," she said.

"Why do you think there is a problem?" I asked.

"Because Chip's scores are off the charts," she said. "In fact, we have never seen scores like his."

"Will he be all right?" Vickey asked.

"Yes, he will be fine, but we are certain that he has a severe case of attention deficit disorder, more commonly known as ADD," she said.

I felt bad for Chip as I watched him struggle in school. The work was difficult, and he had trouble focusing his energies and staying on task. Still, his social skills did not suffer, and he was popular.

Vickey quietly struggled, but she made sure that Chip was in the best schools available. Over the years, he attended more than his share of the private schools in Atlanta. We both strongly believed that an education was something that we could provide that no one could ever take away. You might remember that mom shared that wisdom with me when I headed off to college. The expensive private schools forced us to make a financial sacrifice, one that we could only hope and pray would pay off.

Chip did better at some schools than others, but the work was a constant struggle, and stressed an already fragile and confrontational mother son relationship. Out of love, Vickey was always on his case for something. Much of the success that he enjoyed at school was a result of the teachers, and we were pleased that he had so many good ones. He attended the Schenck School, Woodward Academy, and Saint Francis Academy. I noticed that as he matured, he seemed to do better.

We assumed that he would graduate from Saint Francis Academy, but after the ninth grade he shocked us when he asked, "Can I go to Pace Academy with Laura?"

"Are you serious? No way! It is not possible," I said.

Mean to Meaningful

"Why not?"

"You would not be happy at Pace Academy," I said. "It is a far more rigorous academic environment for which you are not equipped."

This was a negative message with destructive overtones being communicated to a fragile, highly impressionable teenager. I was glad I thought to ask the next question. "Why do you want to leave Saint Francis, where you are doing so well, to go Pace Academy?"

Chip thought for a minute and then said, and I quote, "I am tired of being the dumbass in our family, and I want to go to college. I think that Pace Academy will give me a better chance to get into a good college, one of my choice."

I was shocked by his straightforward answer. "Let me think about it. I will speak with your mother tonight and get back to you."

Vickey talked with David Wood, the upper school principal at Pace Academy, and I made a few phone calls. Even though he was far less qualified than his sister on paper our history made the process and hurdles much easier the second time around. Chip entered Pace Academy as a sophomore. He did well, thrived socially, and even played basketball. He graduated and was accepted into several colleges.

He concluded that the College of Charleston was his best chance for success. They had an outstanding curriculum that included a program track designed specifically for students with attention deficit disorder. Vickey and I were pleased when Chip earned a 2.9 GPA his freshman year. We were so delighted with his early success that we agreed to allow him to transfer to the University of Georgia the next year. Chip's girlfriend attended UGA, and I am pretty sure that was his primary motivation. I could not understand how he could leave all those girls at the College of Charleston. At the time, the ratio was eight to one. He did tell me some time later that he felt like he had to transfer because he knew that with all those beautiful girls and abundant parties, he would have never made it to graduation.

Over the Christmas holidays Chip worked as an intern for the Peach Bowl all through high school and college. Charlie Cobb, a former football player and team captain at North Carolina State University, recruited him. Charlie is a close family friend who is now the athletic director at Georgia State University. We know Charlie from many family ski trips together. He recognized something special in Chip and offered him an internship. I think Chip enjoyed the job because there was always something to do. There was never an idle moment. Vickey and I owe Charlie an enormous debt of gratitude for giving Chip this unique opportunity. The experience had a major influence on the shaping of his future.

It was Christmas of Chip's junior year at UGA. It was business as usual for Chip, but we were concerned about his survival. He was very social, and college, to Chip, was one big fraternity party. Making good grades and learning were the last things on his mind. He was majoring in fun. He was a smart kid, but we had difficulty communicating to him the importance of attending class, earning good grades, finishing college, and earning a degree. He had reached the age where he knew everything about everything.

It was December 18 when Chip's grades arrived. The envelope ended up on the kitchen counter, but it seemed that I was the only one who noticed it. I knew it was his grades, but as Christmas approached, it simply sat there unopened. I said nothing, not wanting to ruin the holidays.

As soon as Christmas was over, Chip left for the Peach Bowl. He enjoyed this week of living at the Marriott Marquis with the teams. His assignment was gofer, and he loved it. One thing you must know about Chip is that no job is ever too big or too small for him; he just loves the excitement of being part of the deal. Over Chip's seven years, under Charlie's leadership, the Peach Bowl grew in popularity. Chick-Fil-A had become the title sponsor, and the intern program had grown dramatically. Chip was now the senior intern and led a team of eight.

When he left, we opened the envelope and the results were no surprise. We found three Cs and a D. Chip had made one other D a year earlier. He was skilled at just skimming by. If he made a 2.1 or 2.2 GPA for the quarter, he would seem disappointed because he only needed a 2.0 to graduate—he seemed to think he could have attended another party or two and still passed. We were both disappointed, and the second D was a death sentence.

Mean to Meaningful

We felt that it was important for us to clearly establish our expectations after the first D, so we established what we called the D rule. We mutually agreed on the terms and hoped that this would eliminate underperformance in the future. We spent much time discussing and developing the terms of the agreement. The language was specific, and the consequences were the following: (1) we would cease making monthly deposits into his checking account, (2) we would no longer pay for any college tuition, (3) he would immediately return the Jeep to us, and (4) he would be welcome in our home by invitation only.

These were intentionally harsh consequences. Even though we mutually agreed on the terms, I felt that if we were ever required to enforce the punishment, Chip would happily withdraw from college, move out west, and begin a career as a ski bum with no college degree. Don't get me wrong—I see nothing wrong with living in the beautiful outdoors and doing what you love, and Chip really loved to ski—but on the other hand, I felt that as parents we would be letting Chip down if we did not aggressively encourage him to successfully finish college. We were frustrated because we stressed to both Chip and Laura the importance of doing your best. *You must do your best to be your best.* We constantly reinforced this message, just like Grandma did for me.

That year, the week of the Peach Bowl was difficult as enforcement weighed heavy on my mind. I am a disciple of having a clear plan of action and executing the plan. I believed that discipline was one of the most critical components of success. I am a just do it guy, and I was not looking forward to Chip's return home.

I read the terms of the agreement repeatedly from front to back, trying to find a way out. There were no loopholes, and the language was simple, crisp, and clear. By design, there was no discretionary latitude. It was black and white, no gray. We were trapped with no obvious way out. I wanted Chip to succeed and be happy in life, and I knew that a college degree was an important part of the equation. I had hoped for a different outcome.

We lived in Derby Hills, a wonderful neighborhood in Atlanta. We had made great memories there for almost twenty years and had a strong neighborhood support system. We were very close, and many of our neighbors were our best friends. During a Derby Hills Christmas party in 1981, several of the men formed a neighborhood poker club. We started meeting every other Monday night, and we rotated the host honors among houses. There were seven original members. We have a special bond that has endured for over thirty-five years. Only a few of the guys are actually good card players. It is a dime quarter game, so no real money has ever changed hands. We get together primarily for the camaraderie and the chance to solve the problems of the world.

It was Monday night, and I went to the poker club as usual. Chip's dilemma was tearing me apart. I knew he would return home from the Peach Bowl festivities on Wednesday night. Time was running out. Tonight, Ben Jones was the host. The games had become more somber during the last year due to the health conditions of one of our members, Thorne Flagler, who suffered from terminal cancer. Thorne lived a couple houses down the street from Ben, and we both arrived early that evening. Thorne had an engaging personality and was one of the most positive people I have ever known. He handled this difficult battle with courage and grace, and from his upbeat attitude, you would never even have known he was sick. He and his wife, Becky, had three children. He never complained and always had a smile on his face and an encouraging comment for everyone. The doctors had given him only a few months to live.

Thorne always joked that he was never a good student. After graduating from West Georgia College, he went to work with his father and eventually took over the family construction business. Thorne was a happy go lucky guy who never missed a party. He was like Chip in many ways.

Everyone in the group was there that night. Charlie Hawthorne, a successful real estate guy; Walter McClelland, an attorney and a senior partner of a very successful law firm; Buzz White, an engineer and Georgia Tech graduate who owned and operated a successful home inspection business and was a real estate investor; Joe Lombardi, who was retired from a long and successful sales career; and Ben Jones, who retired after thirty years as a senior government executive. It was a full house.

Mean to Meaningful

I was in a miserable state of mind and arrived early to talk with Ben and get a beer or two before the game started. It was around eight o'clock when they all arrived. As the group sat down at the poker table, I realized that these good friends might be able to help me solve the D rule dilemma. They all knew Chip and had watched him grow up in the neighborhood, so I decided to ask for their help. I shared the details and carefully described the background and terms of the agreement. When I finished, I asked for their advice, and I got more than I could have ever imagined.

Thorne was first to speak. "All that for a D. Isn't a D still passing? It was when I was in college. I am pretty sure that it still is. I think you are being too harsh, and the punishment certainly does not fit the crime."

Joe offered some additional thoughts but said that he agreed with Thorne and believed that the punishment was probably too severe.

Buzz said, "You know you can still graduate from college with some D's, and an occasional D will keep you humble and honest." From a Georgia Tech guy, that came as a surprise.

Charlie's wife was a minister, and he naturally suggested that I seek solutions from the Bible. I was not a biblical scholar, and I told Charlie that I needed him to be more specific. He was quick to recite a familiar verse from the New Testament: "Do unto others as you would have them do unto you."

Walter was up next, and as my next door neighbor for twenty years, he knew that I had not been a good student at Wofford College, and he warned me that this one would hit close to home. He smiled and blasted: "Ye who is without sin cast the first stone."

Ben then added, "People in glass houses should not throw stones."

The productive dialogue continued and lasted for over an hour. I heard many new colorful stories. Everyone shared at least one private self-deprecating story that offered valuable content or perspective.

I was desperate for voices of reason, and I got just what I needed. I came to the game thinking Chip was an unmotivated failure, but they helped me understand that he instead was a rare gem. They helped me see that the true beauty lies in the eye of the beholder. I must have been visually impaired, because until that night I failed to see that I was blessed with a healthy son, a bright young man who struggled in school, but who possessed unlimited potential. He was a diamond in the rough, and I concluded that with a little more time and polishing that Chip would turn into a precious jewel.

On Wednesday night when Chip arrived home, we sat down and talked for an hour, which was a very long time to keep Chip's attention. We agreed on a compromise. Chip understood the severity of the situation and it was a good talk. I think that he appreciated the compassion. I asked for him to draft a new agreement that he thought was fair and that he could honor. He left for school early the next morning and left a thoughtful note with a signed copy of a new agreement on the kitchen counter, exactly where the grades had resided. His word was good, and he never made another D.

We were heading into Chip's final semester. The family was gathered for Christmas dinner and gift exchanges. I did not give many gifts because I was a bad shopper, but this year I had decided to give Chip a revered white envelope. White envelopes were a long standing tradition in our home. The family was sitting around the Christmas tree in front of the fireplace, and the fire was well stoked and glowing. We were approaching the end of the gift openings when I presented Chip with his white envelope. When he opened it, he was reminded of the one that he received as a freshman in high school with one significant enhancement.

The new envelope stated that if he earned a 3.0 GPA or better, he would earn a new car. This idea was something we had come up with for our children when they earned their driver's licenses. We thought it was important to do your best in school, and we put our money where our mouths were and reinforced that belief with the reward of a new car, a bribe for academic performance. In all these years, Chip had yet to accomplish that feat. This white envelope was his final reminder that this generous challenge was about to expire. Laura earned her new car in high school the first semester it was offered. Chip was driving his mother's black Jeep, a loaner that he would have to return to us at the end of the school year. Although it was in a nice car in good shape, it had 150,000 miles on the odometer, and the end of its useful life was in sight.

The new enhancement included a feature that, although attractive, I believed was technically riskless. A 3.5 GPA or better would entitle Chip to an upgrade. He laughed and indicated that even a 3.0 was impossible because he was taking eighteen hours in order to graduate on time. We had a gentleman's understanding that we would pay for only four years of college. There would be no fifth year of football games and UGA parties on us. Christmas that year ended on a positive note, and I wondered if Chip would take me up on this generous final offer.

As the semester progressed, I asked Vickey if she had heard anything from Chip. She said that she had not talked with him in over a month. That was not like Chip. He was always calling to reassure his mother that he was doing well. He talked a big game but seldom delivered. I was concerned that he was struggling with the heavy class load and that he would not graduate.

It was a hot afternoon, and I was on my way to a client meeting in Arkansas. I flew into Fayetteville early that morning. It had been a long week, and I was tired. My cell phone rang. Only my family members had my private cell phone number, and it was only to be used for emergencies. I saw that it was Chip. I assumed that he was calling to inform me that he would not be graduating. I had been programmed from childhood to expect only bad news. I did not feel good about the call. I thought that if he was not going to graduate, this was a coward's way out. I felt like he should handle that conversation face to face. That would be the man's way to do it. I was overwhelmed with negative thoughts and feelings, and I almost let the call ring through to voice mail, but I didn't.

I answered the call, putting the negative feelings behind me. He asked where I was and what was I doing, and I told him. Then he said, "I have completed my final exams."

Hearing that, I immediately got a large knot in my stomach. "Oh, really?"

"Yes, I am done. I took the last exam yesterday afternoon," he said calmly and then continued. "I have all of my final grades."

"Final grades. What exactly does that mean? You mean you *think* you know your final grades?"

"No, I know and have confirmed them."

"How did you get them so quickly?"

"I got them off the Internet."

"Well, how did we do?" I asked with great trepidation.

"I made five A's and one B, and if it is OK with you, I would like a gray Tahoe," he said, with what I imagined was a huge grin.

"That is great news! I am proud of you, and a gray Tahoe works for me," I said and then continued. "So you are really going to graduate. Who'da ever thunk it? You know, you really had me worried when I saw your number come up on my phone; I just assumed that you were calling with bad news," I added. "Hey, will you do me a huge favor?" "Sure, you name it. Anything!" he said.

"Please call your mother and share the exciting news with her. She would really enjoy hearing from you," I said.

"Yes sir, I will! She is next on my list," he said.

As his message aged, I was overwhelmed with emotions and was unable to continue, and had to abruptly end the call. His new gray Tahoe was waiting for him when he arrived home later that week.

When Chip was six years old, as a surprise, I took him to Walker's Cay, a fishing island in the Bahamas. The main purpose of the trip was to bond. I had been an absentee dad due to my rigorous work schedule, and I felt guilty. The trip helped alleviate some of my self-imposed pain. We flew into Fort Lauderdale, walked across the tarmac, and boarded a seaplane to get to Walker's Cay. Chip sat in the copilot's seat, which was undoubtedly the highlight of the trip for him. When we landed at Walker's, we walked to the modest hotel and registered. We then took the five minute tour of the island. After that, we went to the marina to find our boat captain and scope out the boat. We found Captain Black, a legend at Walker's, with his beautiful girlfriend, who was much younger than him, at the bar. On the way back to our room, I told Chip that he was probably the greatest fishing captain in the world.

Mean to Meaningful

The next morning, we met Captain Black at the marina, boarded his forty-five foot fishing boat, and made our way out to the Gulf Stream, which was only a couple of miles off the island. It was deep sea fishing at its best. We had a world class day, catching a small blue marlin, an eighty pound sailfish, a sixty pound tuna, and a forty-two pound mahi-mahi, which Chip landed all by himself after an intense forty minute battle.

Captain Black's girlfriend accompanied us on the trip. They lived together on the boat. She was a beautiful young woman, and after she prepared our lunch, Chip discovered her sunbathing topless on the front deck of the boat. During the afternoon, I noticed that he went up there several times and talked with her. I never asked, but I am confident those were treasured educational experiences.

As a surprise, I planned that exact same trip for Chip's college graduation. We flew into Fort Lauderdale, and we were walking that same tarmac to the seaplane when I realized that Chip had stopped. I looked back and saw that he was visibly upset. I was concerned and went back and asked, "What is wrong?"

He could hardly talk. Once he gathered his composure, he said, "I screwed up. I am so sorry. I had no idea."

"No idea about what?"

"I owe you and Mom a huge apology."

"What do you mean?"

"You and Mom ask very little of me. You supported me and always encouraged me to do my best. You told me that doing my best was one of the most important things in life. I really thought that I was until this last semester, when I discovered that I could do better, much better. I am so sorry. Will you tell Mom?"

I smiled and said, "I think that it would be better for you to tell her. She is proud of you and loves you very much. You are her favorite son, and it would be more meaningful for you to tell her, in person."

It was gratifying to know that Chip had learned that the only person he was cheating by not doing his best was himself—a significant life changing *God wink*.

Thirteen

The two most important days of your life are the
day you are born and the day you find out why.

—Mark Twain

The children were gone. They were now two college educated adults who were happy and gainfully employed. Thank you, Jesus! Since they would not return home, I believed our parenting duties were complete.

In the past twenty years, I had achieved modest success, sometimes in spite of myself. I broadly searched for the next big challenge, and I eventually discovered it in plain sight. It was the significance of developing a boutique team at UBS. This was something I had struggled with for years, but up until now it was still a big guns, no bullets idea. I realized that over the past decade, I had failed to make much notable progress, but that was about to change!

With a renewed commitment and a few more good ideas, I decided to aggressively market our institutional consulting services to other financial advisors in the firm. This innovative strategy would allow us to leverage our resources and experience to attract nontraditional fiduciary clients who, until now, had not even been on our radar screen. A successful launch would create a steady flow of new business. To win, we needed only a few eager partners.

We ventured out full speed ahead. Over the next year, Harris and I traveled every week, offering to partner with other financial advisors. By partnering with us, they could win complicated new business. We were experienced and had a prominent client list, which provided enormous credibility and leverage. The requirements, needs, liability, and investment processes for these client relationships were complicated, and many financial advisors were uncomfortable asking for an opportunity to compete for the larger company assets. We needed only the introduction, and we would do the rest. We were asking the advisors only to help us help them. However, even with our great sales abilities and brilliant presentations, we generated little interest.

After a while, we realized that we were fighting an insurmountable headwind. We were early to the game, but slowly the value of teams and partnering began to be acknowledged, and eventually we would partner with financial advisors across the country.

I discovered there was more to lasting significance and legacies than just attracting new business. That was easy and just sales success. I felt as though I would have to do more, much more, to have any lasting impact on others. I wondered if there was a meaningful way to share the basic secrets of business success with others. The answer was yes, and I returned to my coaching days and crafted a simple plan to systematically educate, inspire, and engage people whom I cared about—those people on the team.

As we served our precious clients with care and passion, I reached a mountaintop. After a twenty year climb, I moved into a large corner office. A short time later, we tore down the adjoining wall and added a conference room with a flat screen TV and a large conference table, and we used the space as a classroom.

I began the coaching process by implementing the "learning plan." The simple personal development plan made our people think intentionally about what they could do to make themselves more valuable. The formal process required a simple written plan with measurable goals submitted to me in writing each year. Initially, many of the plans were simply thoughts written on the back of a napkin. That changed dramatically when I introduced the bonus plan.

We paid competitive salaries, but the good people were always in high demand. If we were not willing to supplement base salaries, we ran the risk of losing our best people. This was an important issue that commanded more attention. To address this risk, I created an attractive bonus plan that rewarded savings, learning plan achievements, team growth, and personal job performance. The plan directly linked bonuses and total compensation to behavior and performance. The expectations were well articulated, and the best people were generously compensated.

Justin Patteson, an athletic, clean cut, good looking University of North Carolina graduate, joined the team in 2006. He had been with UBS for a year working with another advisor and proactively lobbied for the open position. He knew the team, job, systems, and technology, and we would naturally expect more from him. As with most others, he initially struggled with the *reach higher* environment. Fortunately, Justin had the opportunity to work on many research projects with Patrick.

Patrick took him under his wing and unselfishly taught him everything he needed to know and a whole lot more. They clicked, and I watched Patrick work his magic with Justin and others over the years. Frenchie is one of a kind, and I know that there is no one else like him anywhere on the planet. Absent his talent, inspiration, and determination, the team would have been challenged to accomplish any level of significance. With the skillful training of Patrick and the team, Justin would become our senior research analyst.

In 2006, we branded our business as the Wile Consulting Group. Shortly thereafter, we established a business advisory council, an exclusive group of eight that functioned as an advisory board. We sought out smart, demanding people who we knew would aggressively push us to be better. They were commonly known as the BAC. It was a great opportunity for us to share our process, ideas, and results in ways that would make them insiders.

We had regularly scheduled quarterly meetings, and at the conclusion of each meeting, we would go around the table for questions, ideas, and suggestions. The meeting format was structured so we could ask questions, report our results, and enjoy a nice dinner. The BAC turned out to be a fertile source of ideas but was also a brutal exercise in self-evaluation. We quickly learned exactly what we had to do to get better, and the ideas were more valuable than we could have imagined.

Mean to Meaningful

The Family Forum, a one day educational symposium for families, originated from the BAC. The first year took an enormous amount of work to originate, but it was worth it. The event was so popular that the next year we added the Fiduciary Forum, a one day educational symposium for fiduciaries. We now offer and conduct these events annually and they are the centerpiece of our educational programs.

In 2007, we started a paid internship program to help us with account administration, research, and various other back office duties. It was another brilliant idea from our BAC. We needed the help but could not afford more full time employees. It worked well, and we eventually added research to intern responsibilities. It was a great way for the interns to build résumés and permitted us to maximize our resources. We were hopeful that new talent might emerge from the program. That has not been the case to date, but I recently learned that Harris hosts a dinner for former interns each year and communicates with them regularly. It is my guess that his care for those talented young people will yield some interesting outcomes in the future.

That same year, I took dramatic action to make the business planning process more collaborative. I would no longer write the plan and distribute it to everyone for review. The dictatorship had run its course. The new process would involve the entire team. We divided the plan into three parts and assigned a small group to work on each component separately. We planned to go on a business trip to collaborate and finalize the team plan.

Similar to our anniversary trips, I decided to keep the location a surprise until the last minute. In early December, when it was freezing in Atlanta, we went to the international airport and boarded a Delta jet headed for the warmer weather, clear blue waters, and white sandy beaches in the Bahamas. We would work, visit, and relax together. We had a simple agenda but few other expectations. We worked hard, bonded, and enjoyed the luxurious resort amenities. That first business trip was so productive that it would become an annual tradition.

In 2008, the markets were more difficult than the 2000–2002 period. It was one of the worst performing periods since the Depression, but we were still hiring. In hindsight, our effort to hire good people during the darkest of times looked brilliant, but honestly, the purpose was to provide better client care and results. We continued expanding our team and service capabilities. Our efforts focused on performance results and communications, and the results ultimately showed up in our client retention and business success.

After research, study and endless discussions, we decided to formalize our financial planning and asset management process. This turned out to be a major relationship enhancement. The procedure required clients to complete a comprehensive financial planning or fiduciary risk questionnaire that yielded written, quantifiable financial goals, including specific needs, wants, and restrictions. It was mandatory to open an account. Quantifying expectations was another significant game changer for the team. With specific goals and risk parameters in place, we comfortably accepted control and full responsibility. We selected the best investment managers and made quarterly performance reporting mandatory.

In 2009, we hired Elizabeth Foster, another University of North Carolina graduate. She joined the team as a client service associate. She was smart and asked a lot of good questions. It did not take long to see she was not the prototypical client service associate. She thrived on challenges, and I liked her aggressive confident attitude.

When she had been with us for a year in the wrong job, I asked her to accept a newly created position. After a brief discussion of the vision, she accepted the new challenge. She would be responsible for printed materials, advertising budgets, and educational events. She took over the responsibilities for the Fiduciary Forum and the Family Forum. The quality of the events improved and the attendance exploded under her leadership. She would eventually redefine and manage the internship program too.

Shortly after accepting the new job, Liz came into my office and asked if she could have a few minutes to discuss some ideas. I was pleased with her ambition and invited her have a seat. She wasted no time, got right down to business and advised that she had researched and learned that our team could qualify for several national industry awards and recognitions. She was aware that in the past, I never wanted to seek public recognition, and in her opinion, I had been too private. She said, "I know these industry recognitions and awards are hard to get, but I am absolutely sure that they will validate credibility, enhance value, and make clients feel good. This is simply Marketing 101, and I can promise you that the publicity will be good for relationships and good for business."

In the first year, we were recognized by *Barron's* and *PLANSPONSOR*. The next year, we received more recognitions and awards, and it has continued. Liz proved that proper recognition was good for UBS and good for our business. Many clients told me that they enjoyed seeing us recognized for outstanding achievements. It made them feel good. Liz taught me a valuable marketing lesson: *it ain't bragging if it is true.*

Over the next few years, I continued to talk with peers and evaluate creative growth options—those that might help us take advantage of new scalable opportunities. I knew there were several wild cards in the deck that could have a dramatic impact on the future. The most significant were: strengthening fiduciary oversight, regulatory changes, or formalized changes within the firm. Any of these would provide hurricane force tailwinds, and I often wondered if we would we be ready.

The fear that we might miss that once in a lifetime opportunity triggered many sleepless nights and required me to travel down a lot of promising dead end roads. I aspired for us to be the leaders and did whatever was necessary for us to be better. It always caused me great discomfort when I heard people say, "That's the way it has always been done." Many large companies went down that path and resisted change. Kodak is a perfect example. In 1996, they had 140,000 employees, controlled 85 percent of camera sales, and was one of the largest companies in America. Sixteen years later, Kodak filed for bankruptcy. Their failure to innovate and capitalize on their dominant market position, and competitive advantages contributed to the demise.

This is a stretch comparison, but I did not want us to suffer the same fate. I aspired to be more like Apple as innovators and opportunists. As stewards, our first responsibility was providing clients with our best investment work. Our care for them was critical to our mission and ultimate success. That said, I challenged everyone to always be on the prowl for opportunities to serve, improve, and grow.

In 2010, we started the book club. I constantly looked for new ideas that would inspire our team. I believed that if we could educate, inspire, and engage the entire team, they would dream bigger. I wanted to inspire bold goals that would make them uncomfortable and cause them to *reach higher*. I saw this as an excellent exercise to teach team leadership, and I believed that if successful, we would discover how to win big together. William Arthur Ward said, "The mediocre teacher tells. The good teacher explains. The superior teacher demonstrates. The great teacher inspires." Our first book was "Good to Great" by Jim Collins. It taught us the importance of focus and inspired us. It was a wonderful start and eventually led us to John Maxwell, Winston Churchill, George Patton, and even Peter Drucker, who said, "Management is doing things right; leadership is doing the right things." We started every Monday morning with a one hour inspirational lesson in leadership. We took turns leading the sessions. The simple objectives were to challenge one another, stimulate new ideas, and learn the differences between being a leader and being the boss.

I had assembled a formidable team of talented people. They were handpicked, and I was confident they would mature nicely over time, like fine wines! I continued to creatively paint clear visions, provide learning opportunities, establish bold goals, and encourage character building moments. It took me almost three decades to finally get it right.

Today, it looks and feels like this: Everyone serves meaningful a role for which they are well suited, and they understand it is their duty to lead by example as people of character. We have a culture of respect, and it is satisfying to know that everyone is excited about their work and are proud to be on the team. We are approaching one heartbeat and it feels like we may have finally cracked the secret code.

Fourteen

GRATEFUL

*The hardest arithmetic to master is that
which enables us to count our blessings.*

—Eric Hoffer

In July 2010, Vickey and I were on a trip to Lake Como and Venice followed by a twelve day cruise on the Black Sea. It was our thirty sixth anniversary trip. Vickey had planned this trip, and as with all of her others, every detail was perfect: big corner hotel rooms, king sized beds, perfect weather conditions, private verandas, exciting guest lecturers, educational excursions, and quiet romantic dinners.

Toward the end of the trip, Vickey shared something over a quiet dinner that caught me completely off guard. "I visited the doctor last month, and they discovered a suspicious lump on my thyroid gland. When we get home, I am going in for a biopsy. They tell me there is a chance that it might be cancerous."

"There is a chance that it might be cancer. What exactly does that mean?" I asked.

"The doctor said it is a small lump, and he is pretty sure that it was not present during my last exam. All things considered, he said there was only a slight chance that it was cancerous, but they will not know for sure until they do the biopsy."

"You seem pretty calm considering your Mother died of cancer at the age of sixty."

"I will be fine," she said without hesitation.

Her calm demeanor went a long way in easing my concerns. Nothing else was said that night. The next day on the sundeck, as the ship approached Istanbul, Turkey, we were reliving the past few days and the memories of our many wonderful anniversary trips. I asked, "What do you think are the secret sauces?"

Vickey thought for a moment. "I believe it is because we are doing something special for a loved one. We plan a unique experience that we know will make them happy. The ingredients, such as destination, timing, accommodations, trip agenda, other invitees, and especially the surprise factor, are all just parts of the recipe. When they are mixed together, they create a magical experience."

"I never thought about it that way. The magic emanates from the love and the care. In looking back, this tradition has taken us around the world with our friends and family to some wonderful places."

As we relived some of those rich memories, our conversation somehow shifted to bucket lists. We each had one, but there was no formal plan for execution. They were just wish lists, so I asked, "Is there a way to formalize the bucket list and its execution process?" At the time, I was just using the bucket list discussion as a distraction to avoid talking about cancer.

We kicked the idea around for a few minutes and decided to proceed. During the afternoon, we crafted some simple disciplines and guidelines around what would ultimately become another Wile tradition. Vickey said, "I think we should combine our individual bucket lists and limit the choices. That way, we can collaborate and focus on the most treasured experiences."

"I agree, but in the spirit of full disclosure, I believe that we should thoroughly discuss the full list, in detail. That way we will not miss anything."

"OK, but then how do we decide which ones to do?"

"That's easy. We will limit the list to seven choices and simply prioritize the list. We will secretly rank each experience from one to seven, and the cumulative scores will determine the rank order. Once we have them prioritized, we can focus all of our time and energy on completing the top choice. Nothing else."

"What do we do after we complete the top experience? Can we then just rinse and repeat the process?" Vickey asked.

"Exactly, but I would suggest that we start from scratch each time because the joy is in the collaboration. We just repeat the process: new list, new priority ranking, and new experience."

"I like it. Let's do it."

We sat in the sun and dreamed about places we wanted to go and things we wanted to do. Together, we crafted our first list on the back of a Crystal Cruise cocktail napkin, and it looked something like this:

1. Skydiving
2. European River Cruise
3. Mustang across America
4. A trip to explore Normandy
5. African safari
6. Climb Mount Kilimanjaro
7. A trip to Australia and New Zealand

We felt like this was a good first list, and we were pleased with our creation. When we got home, we committed the formal process and list to paper.

We completed the last few days of the cruise and spent a whirlwind day exploring Rome. When we returned to Atlanta, Vickey went in for the biopsy. The test results were inconclusive, but most signs indicated that the growth was new and cancerous. We thought, better safe than sorry, and we met with a surgeon the next week. He assured us that he could remove the thyroid and the cancer, and we prepared for surgery. We had the best surgeon in town, so we had to wait several months for our turn on the operating table.

As we waited, I planned the first bucket list experience. I found an airport in Cartersville, Georgia, that offered skydiving. I checked them out and made a reservation for the next weekend. I was so proud of my proactive efforts. After dinner, I gave Vickey the good news. "I made us a reservation to skydive this weekend."

"What do you mean?"

"We are going to the Cartersville Airport this weekend. They have a skydiving operation, and we are going to complete the first item on our bucket list."

"I have had a lot on my mind with this operation. I am talking to the nurses and trying to secure an earlier date for the surgery. Please remind me again, what was number one on our bucket list?" "It is skydiving," I answered.

"That is not funny. What did we decide was number one?"

"It really is skydiving. It will be great fun. You'll see."

Unfortunately, the first reservation did not work out due to bad weather, which included both rain and low hanging clouds. We hung around the airport awhile, and when it was obvious that it was not going to happen, we went home. I know that Vickey was somewhat relieved. On the way home, she said, "I still do not fully understand how skydiving made it to the top of the bucket list. It was certainly not my top choice."

"It was my top choice, and it was number three on your list. That made it cumulatively our number one choice. The river cruise was number two."

On Monday, after checking the weather forecasts, I canceled a business trip to New York and made us a reservation for Tuesday. When I informed Vickey of the new date, she thought that I was kidding because she knew that I had planned to be in New York that day, but when I did not leave that morning, she became suspicious and asked, "When are you leaving for New York?"

"I decided to cancel the trip so we could go skydiving. The weather today is supposed to be perfect."

We arrived several hours early, which in hindsight was not a great idea. Upon arrival, I lined up at the payment window. When it was my turn, the clerk asked, "Are you jumping from ten thousand feet today?"

"What are the choices?" I asked.

"Either ten thousand or fourteen thousand feet."

Vickey butted in front of me and blurted out, "Ten thousand feet."

The clerk looked to me as I pushed Vickey aside. "We would like to jump from fourteen thousand feet, if at all possible," I responded.

"Fourteen thousand feet it is. Do you want a videographer?" the clerk asked.

"No, absolutely not," Vickey snapped.

"Please do not pay any attention to her. She is my wife, and is nervous, but I am paying, so yes, I want a videographer. I want to see the looks on our faces when we jump. The video will document for our children and grandchildren that we really jumped, and it will provide unquestionable documentation for the lawsuit in the event that the parachutes do not open," I joked.

Vickey paced around the hangar like a cat on a hot tin roof, talking with anyone who would listen. She said I was forcing her to skydive and called me names, some of which were not kind. She said, "I just want to get out of here and go home." I ignored her erratic behavior, and for the next few hours, I watched a group of scantily clothed hot babes fold and pack parachutes.

Once we were signed in and paid, we were assigned our jumping partners. I talked with my guy, who was a retired military man who had jumped more than four thousand times. He briefed me, and we went our separate ways. When our turn came, we went to the tarmac and boarded an old single engine plane. There were four paying skydivers with experienced tandem partners, two videographers, and one crazy looking, skinny redheaded kid who was just freeloading for the jump. The door on the side of the plane was a rough fit and rolled up like a garage door, which seemed to make Vickey even more nervous. I knew from her erratic behavior in the hangar that she was probably not going to jump.

As we got into our seats, I quietly asked my partner, "How many of the skydivers that go up actually jump out of the plane?"

"All of them."

As we reached five thousand feet, I asked the question again, and he responded the same. As we approached six thousand feet, Vickey asked for them to close the garage door, and I could see that she was as white as a ghost. When we reached ten thousand feet, I decided to try my question one more time. "I do not think that you understand the question. One more time: How many of the skydivers who go up in the plane actually parachute down?"

"All of them."

"I find it hard to believe that they all jump. How can that be?"

"It is quite simple. When it is your turn to jump and you get to the door, 'No, no, no' sounds the same as 'Go, go, go!' Like I said, they all jump one way or another."

When it was time, they opened the garage door, and we jumped one right after the other. Thank goodness, there was little time to think. The skinny redheaded kid went first, the first videographer went next, and when it was Vickey's turn, she never hesitated. Out she went. The videographer got it all on tape. Her facial expressions said it all. At fourteen thousand feet, on a clear day, you can see forever. I discovered when it was my turn that it was not all that easy. It took a bold act of courage to leap out of that perfectly good airplane into thin air, but when I did, it was exhilarating.

I arrived on the ground first and was able to see and hear the last minute or so of Vickey's descent. I couldn't believe my ears. She was laughing as she came in for her landing. She jumped up and wanted to go again. For me, skydiving was a thrilling experience. I am glad to have done it, but I have no desire to do it again. On the other hand, Vickey, who was scared to death, loved the experience, and we have the video to prove it.

Fortunately, there was a cancelation, and our appointment for the cancer surgery got moved up to September 7, 2010, which was our anniversary. Miff Cone, Vickey's sister who was living in Mount Pleasant, South Carolina, came to Atlanta and stayed with us. I welcomed the help; I was not exactly clear how this journey would unfold. I just did what I was told.

Miff and I rose early that morning and took Vickey to the Emory University Hospital for the seven o'clock surgery. We met with the doctor, and he said, "We will remove the damaged thyroid and send it across the hall to the lab to have it tested to see if it is cancerous. If everything goes well, she should be done and out of surgery by nine o'clock at the latest. We will call for you when the surgery is completed."

Miff and I went to the waiting room and waited. At ten o'clock, we still had no news. I called down to the operating room, and the nurse said they were still in surgery. I wondered what might be wrong. After all, this was a hospital, and she had been put to sleep so they could slit her throat. It was a very bad visual. At eleven o'clock, the doctor finally called. "We completed the surgery, and it was worse than anticipated. The tumor tested positive, so we decided to go back in and remove the entire thyroid as a precaution. The good news is that we believe the cancer is contained. Vickey is in the recovery room. She should be in her hospital room within the hour, and you can see her then. I want to assure you that she is doing well and everything is going to be fine."

Vickey remained in the hospital for a couple of days. Miff stayed with us and served as the maid, cook, and head nurse. When Vickey came home, Miff attended to her every need. Unfortunately, after a few days, she had to go back to South Carolina to take care of her family. I was left alone with limited nursing skills and little insight into what had just happened. I believed and hoped that everything would soon return to normal.

After the surgery, Vickey resumed her life as though nothing had ever happened. She did not slow down one bit, and we had a lot of things going on during the fall that she believed commanded her attention.

On September 14, 2010, a week after the surgery, our twin grandsons were born in High Point, North Carolina. We went for a short visit and left a baby nurse behind to help our sweet daughter in law, Catherine. At the time, it was all that we could offer. The next week, we went to the Wofford College board meeting, and Vickey participated in the daily spousal activities and trustee dinners.

In October, she organized and directed a big event for my 1970 Wofford College football team. We were celebrating our fortieth anniversary with a weekend team reunion. Later that month, I was inducted into the Wofford College Football Hall of Fame, and Vickey personally handled the many details, including getting mom to the ceremony.

In November, she helped orchestrate the Agape Dinner, the annual fund raising event for the Atlanta Mission, where I served as the chairman of the board. Later that month, she returned to the hospital for a single radioactive treatment. A subsequent scan indicated the treatment was successful. She was naturally excited to be cancer free, and we went on with our fast paced lives. We decided to spend Thanksgiving at our home on Kiawah Island.

In December, there were some changes going on that were not immediately obvious to the outside world. Vickey developed a ringing in her ears, which led to insomnia. Almost overnight, she added anxiety and depression to the list. These were the first real signs of trouble. We celebrated New Year's Eve alone at the beach but returned to Atlanta as the symptoms worsened. We discussed these new developments with the doctors, but they offered no solutions or remedies. Absent answers, we felt compelled to craft a plan.

Vickey felt like we should first deal with the ringing in the ears, which we would learn was tinnitus. She believed that if we could address the tinnitus symptoms, everything else would get better too. We sought out the top audiologist in the South, who fortunately was located just outside of Atlanta, and went to see her for an exam and assessment. We ultimately set up a series of appointments, and Vickey met with her every other week. We purchased a sound machine and a special program to treat the symptoms. We felt good about the plan, but the progress was slow. We prayed that she was on the road to recovery, which we would soon discover was not the case.

I did not immediately realize the severity of the anxiety and depression. In hindsight, I had no idea that their impact could be life threatening. I marginalized her misery and incorrectly assumed that these symptoms were a result of the tinnitus or in some way self-induced. I suggested that she go see our local physician, who had been our trusted doctor and friend for many years, and she did. She shielded me from the severity of the changes until I discovered that she was going to the doctor two or three times a week and taking medications for sleep deprivation, anxiety, and depression, which she thought were helping. I had no idea what she was going through. I was fully engaged at work and was oblivious to the devastating symptoms and dramatic changes.

In January, I brought home several good books on attitude and gave them to Vickey to read. I included in the collection *They Call Me Coach* by John Wooden. I directed her to my favorite chapter, which had the list that Coach Wooden's father gave him upon graduating from elementary school. One item on the list was "Make every day your masterpiece." In my simple mind, I hoped that this type of inspirational reading would cure her, only because it had always helped me. It was all I knew. I did not realize that this would be very devastating for her because it would make her feel as though I was disregarding her screams for help. I believe the mind is a powerful tool, and I thought she could read her way out of this terrible situation, which was already far beyond our control.

In February, our family doctor—I believe as a last resort—referred Vickey to a psychiatrist. I think that he had gone the extra mile and had done all that he could for her. Vickey confused the referral with progress. One night after a late dinner, she proudly reported, "I am seeing a new doctor."

"What kind of doctor?"

"A psychiatrist."

"Are you kidding me? A psychiatrist? Do you think he is helping?" I cautiously asked, disguising a preconceived suspicions of psychiatrists.

"I am not sure, but I think so," she said.

"How often are you seeing him?"

"Once a week."

This was not what I wanted to hear. At the time, I believed that psychiatrists preyed on the weak. Vickey was a lot of things, but she was not weak. She was sweet but among the strongest women I've ever known. Something was not adding up as the situation continued to deteriorate. It was obvious that she was on a downward spiral, but death still never entered my mind as a possible outcome.

A few weeks later, Vickey thought it would be a good idea to add a psychologist to her list of medical advisors. I went with her to several sessions with this new psychologist. I liked her. She seemed to be a bright and caring person, and some of her psychological gibberish and gobbledygook even made sense.

In March, I went to Deer Valley, skiing with a group of friends. I should have stayed home, but I had agreed to go on this trip a year earlier, prior to the cancer. Chip joined us for the trip, and after skiing, we met his wife, Catherine, in Las Vegas for a NASCAR race. He was working. I was looking forward to spending some time with them, and I used this time to share the details of Vickey's evolving medical challenges.

While I was gone, Merry Jeanne Millner and Elizabeth Reid, Vickey's two younger sisters, came to Atlanta to stay with her. They were all close, and they yearned to help. Even though Vickey tried to act like everything was fine, they could sense the desperation. They cooked, cleaned, and listened, but they eventually had to go home.

In April, we were at the beach and planned to drive to Spartanburg to attend the Wofford College donor dinner, an annual function that honored the endowed scholarship donors. This had always been one of Vickey's favorite events. We looked forward to having dinner with our student athletes and seeing Coach Peterson and his wife, Marge, hosting their student athlete.

At the last minute, Vickey decided that she did not want to go. "I am not feeling well. I'm not going to the donor dinner," she said.

"Excuse me?" I responded, thinking that I had misunderstood her.

"I am too anxious to be around a lot of people tonight. I just want to get back to Atlanta and see my doctors."

"But I thought you were looking forward to this event. You have always enjoyed meeting your scholarship students and asking questions, and you love the festivities around the dinner," I said sympathetically.

"I just want to get back to Atlanta. If you want to go, you can go alone."

I thought for a moment and decided that the best course of action was to dictate, something I had learned to avoid in our marriage at almost all costs. The activities of this event were important to her, so I decided to help her help herself.

I responded in a cautious but bold tone of voice. "I will not allow you to miss this event, your favorite of the year. It is not fair to you. The boys are looking forward to seeing you. You are not thinking straight right now, so I will make this call. We are going! There will be no further discussion. Now, go and get ready. You can thank me later."

She was frustrated and upset, but she knew this was no time to argue. In the spirit of full disclosure, it was not without payback. I got the dreaded cold shouldered silent treatment. She was unresponsive for the entire four hour drive from Kiawah Island to Spartanburg. I talked to her, but she never talked back. When we arrived, she changed her clothes, popped a few pills, and endured dinner. She relied on her abundant supply of drugs to get through the event. When we returned to the car, she again shut down for the three hour drive from Spartanburg to Atlanta. It was complete radio silence. There were some harsh feelings, but they were short lived because we both knew that we had other monstrous demons to battle.

In May, I began attending her sessions with the psychiatrist. I did not want to go, but somehow I knew that I should. I guess that I could sense Vickey's quiet screams for help. During those appointments, I found that there were no answers, just more questions and more drugs. Every week, we tried something different. The abundance of drugs concerned me, but I rationalized that it was a critical part of the therapy and recovery process. Still, nothing worked, and as time passed and her mental health deteriorated. I was afraid to leave her alone. I started coming home for lunch, working shorter days, and even taking days off, something that I had never done. I was concerned about her safety and well-being and frustrated that I could not take away her pain.

There were still lots of questions but no answers. Vickey's personality changes were dramatic. The anxiety and depression had progressed to the danger zone and were now life threatening. She withdrew from everyday life and became reclusive. The sweet, thoughtful woman I married no longer existed. My precious brown eyed girl was gone. I wondered, was this temporary, or was she lost forever?

I learned more than I wanted to know about the power of the thyroid, the quarterback of the body. Her condition continued to worsen, and the many medications provided little relief, but with no other answers in sight, we continued with them. She was addicted and relied on the drugs to get her through the day, and she could not leave home without them. They were probably not helping, but she believed in them, and they were her salvation and security blanket. She threatened suicide and tried to leave several times. It was a miserable existence.

In June, Laura and Chip joined me for an appointment with the psychiatrist. I explained to the doctor that our family was concerned, and he reluctantly agreed to allow Laura, Chip, and me to sit in on the session. We gathered in the room and spread out around the doctor. He reviewed Vickey's history and treatment plans with us and then asked what else we wanted to know. His demeanor was cautious, and he was anxious about having our whole family present for the session. "What are the long term prognosis and your treatment plan for Mom?" Laura asked.

"That is a good question. Your mother is suffering from severe anxiety and depression. I have been seeing her regularly for several months. We have tried many of the generally useful corrective drugs, but we have yet to discover anything that has made a significant difference. She is not responding, and I believe that I have done all that I can for her," he said.

Chip blurted out, "No kidding. No disrespect intended, but this plan is not working. In the last few months, she has gotten a lot worse. She has become addicted to the drugs, and it is time for us to make a change." He was emotionally charged, and visibly upset with his mother's condition.

"Do you have any further suggestions that you think can help her?" Laura asked.

"Yes. I would suggest that you find a reputable treatment center. There are several that I can confidently recommend, or I can set up a visit with one of the local treatment facilities," he said. The psychiatrist went into his office and brought out several brochures for spa like facilities in Arizona and California and gave them to us. He again offered to set up an interview at one of the local treatment centers in Atlanta. We declined any further assistance.

It was an emotional morning for the four of us. Chip and Laura could not wait to get out of the office. They were visibly upset. As we left the parking lot, it dawned on me that we were running out of options.

In desperation, we eventually got an appointment with the head of psychiatric medicine at Emory University Hospital. We were referred to him by a friend. Even with a good connection, we still waited several weeks for an appointment. It seemed like several years. This doctor was different. He methodically analyzed Vickey's lengthy records of prescribed medications and discussed the purpose, effects, and impact of each drug. He asked many questions and listened. After going to great lengths to understand Vickey's plight, history, and circumstances, he suggested that we discontinue all but one of the drugs and then suggested that we find a treatment center for care and drug addiction.

This was the first medical advice in months that made any sense. To be sure that I understood his suggestions, I asked, "What would you do if Vickey was your wife?"

He repeated his advice and added, "At this point, I know that Vickey would benefit from around the clock care, so I would seek a good drug treatment facility immediately."

"In what ways will a treatment center help her?"

"They will get her off the addictive medications, clean her up, and do some simple mental rehab. Right now, she is confused and a mental wreck from all the drugs. It will be tough on both of you, but if nothing else, the detox will significantly speed up the recovery process."

"Will she get better and return to her old self?"

"It is possible, but that is a question I cannot answer with any certainty." We were both comforted by the doctor's authentic demeanor and gentle kindness.

We had discovered a treatment facility outside of Knoxville, Tennessee. Vickey liked it because it was all women. I called and made an appointment, and we made the five hour drive that weekend to visit the property and tour the facility. I could tell on the short tour that Vickey was comfortable with the environment, which was important, and we agreed it was a reasonable plan. We had run out of options, and the clock was ticking. When we got back to Atlanta, I immediately called and reserved her a place. We returned the following weekend for admittance to the month long program.

I checked her into the facility on Sunday, July 17, 2011. She was suffering from tinnitus, drug addiction, severe anxiety, and depression. The check in process was surprisingly quick, efficient, and painless. I learned during the check in that I would not be permitted to talk with or see Vickey for three weeks. I could write, but no visits or calls. I did not care; I just wanted her to get well. I left her and drove home alone.

Although I was a man of few words who struggled with writing, I composed and sent a short love letter to Vickey every morning. With little experience, I was surprised at how easily the delicate words about those deepest feelings flowed seamlessly together. While Vickey was gone, I reflected on our storybook life together. I thought about what life would have been like without her...how it would have been different. Those were sobering thoughts. We had been married for thirty-six years, and it seemed like we had grown up together—in many ways, we had. We had married when she was only twenty years old. From our first introduction, she had been my most treasured teacher. I concluded that without her, I would likely have been dead or in jail. She educated and inspired me. She led by example, showing me how to be a good man, a good father, a good friend, a good husband, and a good leader...and most of all how to love out loud!

Mean to Meaningful

This caused me to think about the many things I would want to do for Vickey if we survived this journey. I continued to go to work every day, but my heart wasn't in it. I sat at my desk and tried to work, but Vickey was always on my mind. I knew there was a good chance that I was going to lose her forever. I was an emotional wreck, and I noticed that everyone started cutting me a wide berth. I had always been able to bury myself in work, but this time was different. I could only think about Vickey and the wonderful life that we shared. I was deeply troubled, because I knew that I could have done more and that I could have been a better husband. I decided that if she recovered, I would retire early to focus on making her happy—very happy.

When I returned for the first visit three weeks later, I discovered that nothing had changed. If anything, she was worse. She was a stranger—unengaged and distant. We had dinner and I spent the night at a local hotel. I returned early the next morning and we had breakfast. It was an extremely uncomfortable experience, and I stayed the minimum amount of time. It was depressing, and the return trip to Atlanta was one of the worst times of my life.

When I arrived home, I went straight to our bedroom. I unpacked my bag, got down on my knees at the foot of our bed, and prayed. "Dear Lord, I know that I am a challenging work in progress for you. I have hurt people and have done many bad things, but I am working hard to recover. I want you to know that I am always trying to do better. I know that I do not deserve any special favors, but you already know that I have exhausted all the worldly options to help my precious Vickey. I am coming to you, as a last resort, only because I have nowhere else to go. Vickey is on a journey and has lost her way. She is in a bad place both mentally and physically. On her behalf, I would like to point out that she is a loyal and faithful servant. She is a kind and humble person, like none I have ever known. I have to believe that she is among your best work. I was with her this morning, and it appears as though she will not recover. Without your help, she may not find her way back and will be lost forever. My prayer request is simple: please bring her back to me. If you cannot see your way clear to do it for me, please do it for her. Thank you for listening. Amen." When I finished, I crawled into the bed and cried myself to sleep. It was four o'clock on Sunday afternoon.

I returned the following week to bring Vickey home. It had been exactly thirty days. It was a long and lonesome drive, and I was fully prepared for the worst. I felt helpless and believed the situation was hopeless.

I'd had dinner with Laura and her family the previous Saturday, and I went shopping afterward with our beautiful granddaughters, Parks and Tyler. I wanted to get Laura a couple of nice birthday presents. Vickey always did our shopping, so I was at a loss, but our granddaughters stepped up and helped me pick out several nice presents for their mother. They knew that their "meme" was coming home but had no idea what was going on, and they believed Meme would bring the presents to their mother's birthday party. I said nothing.

It took several hours to get through the exit interviews, medical releases, and detailed checkout process. As I observed her, it was obvious that nothing had changed. She was quiet, emotionless, and unresponsive.

As we prepared to leave the facility, I was genuinely concerned about her well-being and wondered what was next. I was certainly not prepared or capable to become her full time caregiver—nor did I want to. As we drove through the gate and departed the property, she took a deep breath and seemed somewhat relieved, but she remained silent.

As we continued on the two lane road toward the interstate highway, I reminded Vickey that it was Laura's birthday. It was Monday, August 15, 2011. We had always celebrated Laura's birthday at a Japanese hibachi restaurant. It was a tradition for Laura that Vickey had begun at an early age. I tried to engage her in a conversation. "I went to dinner with Laura and her family on Saturday night and took Parks and Tyler shopping after dinner. They helped me select several nice presents for Laura's birthday, from us." She looked at me but sat silent, so I continued. "When we get home, we can do whatever pleases you. There are no expectations or plans. As I see it, we have many options. We could go home and relax, or we could go to Laura's for a short visit with her and the grandchildren and give her the birthday presents, or we could go to the restaurant and join them for the traditional birthday dinner celebration. We can do none, some, or all. It is completely up to you."

She made limited eye contact but still said nothing. She sat quietly in her seat for over an hour and startled me when she spoke. "I want you to know that I love you, and I know that you love me," she said in a whisper. I thought we were making some progress, but then she went silent again. After a long pause, apparently contemplating her choices and searching for the right words, she continued. "I think that I want to go to Laura's house and see the grandchildren. Then I want to try to go to the birthday dinner."

She looked at me and smiled for the first time in what seemed like forever. It was that same precious smile that she flashed me on the drive to Savannah on our first surprise anniversary trip. I wondered if this might be an early sign that she was on her way back to me. Were my prayers being answered? She slowly opened up and began to share the details of her hospital journey and described in great detail the other women and their horrible addictions. She shared her many personal experiences at the treatment center. I think that she needed to share them with me. I listened intently and noticed that the farther we got from the hospital and the closer we got to home, the more she opened up.

We met Laura and her family at their home and, after a brief visit, proceeded to the restaurant for Laura's birthday celebration. The grandchildren were happy to see their grandmother, Meme, and it was a nice birthday present for Laura to have her mom back.

As the weeks progressed, Vickey continued to improve. She got stronger and began to walk and work out again. The anxiety and depression were gone. They disappeared as quickly as they had appeared. She still had the ringing in the ears but learned to manage the symptoms. Over the next year, she made a miraculous recovery. I had my precious brown eyed girl back, and I got to be with her every day and sleep with her every night. God heard me and answered my prayers. Now it was up to me.

In the fall of 2013, I advised Laura and Harris that I would be retiring early and leaving in the spring. We had a brief discussion about the whys. They both knew the story well, and it was a short conversation. I asked them to keep the news confidential. I promised to tell the team in December at our business planning meeting in Mexico.

Later in 2013, Robert Tamarkin joined our office as the branch manager. Robert was a young man and well respected. He had a great reputation and was someone you liked being around because he listened and did what he said. I did not want him to be blindsided in his new role. We had become acquainted that fall during a weekend golf outing that I hosted at our home on Kiawah Island. On his first visit to the office, he made it a point to come see me. I invited him into my office and asked him to take a seat and make himself comfortable. We talked about business awhile, and then I got up from my desk and closed the door.

I looked him in the eye and said, "I hate surprises, so I always proactively address any and all possible surprise situations. That being said, I want you to know that I plan to retire next spring. I believe that Laura and Harris are ready. They lead by example, are well trained, and have surrounded themselves with a capable group of people. It is their time, and I hope that you will support them."

"Are you kidding me? This is a joke, right? Is this being recorded? Where are the cameras?" he asked as he looked around the room.

"This is no joke. I am going to retire in May 2014, and I am sharing this with you only because I do not want it to be a surprise. Only you, Laura, and Harris know. I have told no one else."

Robert looked at me in disbelief, and the confusion in his voice became more pronounced with every question. It was clear that he did not know me well. I was a quiet guy who worked hard and generally kept to myself, so it wasn't his fault. He was looking for answers, and he continued with his questioning. "Why would you retire? You have a great team and are a leader in the office. It just doesn't make sense to me. Please help me understand why."

I humbly responded, "I have been here for over thirty-one years. It has been a wonderful career working with great people, but I now have other things that I need and want to do. You probably do not know, but in 2010, Vickey was diagnosed with cancer. It was supposed to be no big deal, according to the doctors. She underwent surgery, and the prognosis was excellent, but she developed tinnitus. And then, almost overnight, depression and anxiety showed up. The doctors prescribed medication after medication in a seemingly futile effort to provide relief. The severe depression and anxiety became so overwhelming that I worried about leaving her home alone. The situation went from bad to worse to desperate and was more challenging than anything I have ever had to deal with in business. It was terrible, and I thought on many occasions that I was going to lose her. I spent a lot of time at home on my knees praying and thinking about what I would want the future to look like if she survived. After much soul searching and serious deliberation, I have to tell you that eighty hours a week at my UBS desk was never a consideration. I will retire in the spring with three simple goals: make Vickey the happiest woman in the world, climb Mount Kilimanjaro with her, and finish writing my book."

"Is there anything that we can do or say to change your mind?"

Robert is a great leader and I hated that I was not going to get the opportunity to work with him.

Fifteen

PURPOSEFUL

Try not to become a person of success,
but rather try to become a person of value.

—Albert Einstein

It was the end of the year and we were enjoying our annual learning plan dinner. We were seated at a large round table in a quiet, cozy corner of the restaurant. We were finishing a wonderful dinner and the time had come to present the learning plans. Over the years, this exercise had evolved into an important part of building a successful team culture. I intentionally waited to be last, which was in itself suspicious, because in the past I had always gone first to set the tone. When everyone else had made their presentations, the team turned to me.

I looked around the table and saw a successful group of professionals—a uniquely gifted team. As I sat there quietly searching for the right words, tears began to roll down my cheeks. When I was able to regain my composure, I shared a story and then formally announced the details of my retirement.

I began the transition to retirement in May 2014. Systematically disconnecting myself from work was far easier than anticipated, and I began to casually train for the Mount Kilimanjaro climb, our next bucket list experience. We were scheduled to leave the United States on July 10.

As I reflect back on my career, I want to share some important life lessons, many of which I learned in the school of hard knocks. Harris once referred to this private collection as "Wileisms."

You can be young without money, but you cannot be old without it.

—*Tennessee William*

The savings plan was important to building a stable team. I wanted the people who worked with me to get to a better place in life and have something to show for their efforts. I aspired for them to establish personal wealth as a gift to themselves.

My objective was to teach the right people to act responsibly. I believed this gift would help reduce turnover and keep good people in their seats. What I knew for sure was that there was no such thing as a free lunch, and I believed that it was irresponsible to depend on the lottery, the government, a rich relative, an inheritance, or even social security for our well-being or retirement.

I knew from personal experience that the only person that was going to take care of them was them. I often said, "You have to take care of yourself first. You cannot count on others to do it for you." I regularly preached the importance, purpose, and benefits of saving.

I strongly encouraged and, when necessary, gently dictated. When that did not work, I boldly dictated. To reinforce the importance, I provided matching funds. I felt that it was my responsibility to encourage people to do the right thing—even when they disagreed or resisted.

The savings plan eventually evolved into a powerful retention tool and taught me a valuable leadership lesson. If you really care about someone, you should help them do what is right, even when it is unpopular.

The growth and development of people is
the highest calling of leadership.

—*Harvey S. Firestone*

We required everyone on the team to submit a written learning plan each year. I hoped that it would help them uncover all of the things they could do to improve their future selves. I often said, "It is hard to see today if you cannot see tomorrow." The requirement was simple. At first, the only guidance I provided was to include at least one business and one personal goal. The standards and instructions were purposefully vague, and some took the exercise more seriously than others. Some plans were short lists on cocktail napkins, and some were essays.

As the team matured, Harris said, "I like the idea and agree with the intent, but we should provide more guidance on the specific goals, and we must tighten up the process and the discipline. The goals must intentionally make each person more valuable to both themselves and to the team. What would you think about allowing us to submit our written plans to the team at the annual business plan meeting? It might be fun to allow each person to formally present his or her plan. It would definitely create more intentionality and accountability. You might even consider the idea of a critique, but if we decide to do this, we must eventually require unanimous approval for each plan. There should be no more lightweight plans. It is not fair to them or to us. We must help all team members to *reach higher* to be the best they can be even if we have to push them harder and be the bad guys."

I was intrigued by Harris's suggestions. His ideas were well thought out, and my initial reaction was "Wow! What a great improvement." We continued the discussions and then implemented these valuable changes.

By failing to prepare, you are preparing to fail.

—Benjamin Franklin

As an exercise in Life 101, I have always had a business plan with goals. The first plans were simple, but I've discovered that when you formally commit plans to writing, the goals are more likely to get accomplished.

I was a stubborn and determined leader. As a dictator, I was modestly successful and proud of the fact that it was my way or the highway. That is, until I read something Helen Keller said that opened my eyes. It was a simple quote. "Alone we can do so little. Together we can do so much."

This amazing revelation caused me to make some drastic changes to our planning process. What resulted was an engaging team exercise that promoted shared governance, accountability and ownership.

During our annual business planning meetings, we seemed to always rediscover how important we were to one another and how essential each member's work was to the team's success. This exercise and process promoted a free flow of ideas. It was so effective that it often seemed like we were dreaming out loud.

At the conclusion of each meeting, we shared a common vision and were fully invested in one another's achievements and careers. It was an efficacious experience that afforded each of us a rare opportunity to get more than we gave.

Your talent is God's gift to you.
What you do with it is your gift back to God.

—Leo Buscaglia

A reputation takes a lifetime to establish, but it can be destroyed in just a few seconds. That does not seem right, but it is true. I believe that our reputations are more treasured than gold and silver. They are arguably among our most precious assets. With forty plus years of business experience, I know this to be true 110 percent of the time.

During our lifetimes, we are not judged by the cards we are dealt, but instead by how we play the hand. My sister Diana is a perfect example. She has led a bountiful life and did not grow up with a chip on her shoulder as I did. We were dealt the same losing cards, but she played her winning hand like a professional. I was not so lucky. I had to lose a lot of hands before I finally started winning.

Wrong choices and bad decisions can change a life, influence outcomes, and often inflict irreparable personal damage. I made lots of mistakes and learned through trial and error that whenever in doubt, it is best to defer to the golden rule. You will never have regrets for doing what is right, even when it causes substantial losses and personal pain.

If you don't know where you are going, any road will take you there.

—Lewis Carroll

Our learning plan exercise helped people advance their careers. We encouraged everyone to *reach higher* because, as Michelangelo said, "The greater danger for most of us lies not in setting our aim too high and falling short, but in setting our aim too low and achieving our mark."

We worked diligently to get people into the right positions, which were almost always those that capitalized on their strengths. We did it in a timely fashion because we did not want to waste anyone's time. Through testing, we knew where in the organization they were most qualified and would enjoy doing their best.

We aspired for people to have the opportunity to dream big and succeed beyond their expectations. This is important because success breeds success which ultimately produces large quantities of passion. When this occurs, it creates an exciting win-win environment where people feel more significance and achieve higher levels of success. It is a game changer, and witnessing those big life changing achievements is a gratifying experience.

Encourage, never criticize.

—Ron Baus

I looked for the good in everyone and operated from a deck of simple principles. If I hired you, it was clear from the very beginning that I expected you to do well. Encouragement was a part of my daily routine and found it exhilarating to recognize people for good work.

I often walked around the office and asked, "What are you doing today to make yourself more valuable?" It was important for them to know I was watching and cared. I seldom criticized unless someone really earned it.

As the coach, it was my responsibility to share the exciting visions of tomorrow. They say that a picture is worth a thousand words. That is incorrect! The talent of painting vivid pictures with words is a rare skill that is vastly underutilized and is actually worth more—much more. You could make the argument that it is priceless. I aspired for everyone to see where they fit into the bigger picture and understand how their work impacted their future and the futures of others. That was just one of the ways we inspired people to become better players.

The true test of a man's character is
what he does when no one is watching.

—John Wooden

You have to be a person of good character to lead. Growing up, I lacked character, unless you counted bad and very bad. Without a formal role model, I had to start from scratch. The voyage was a slow, arduous process for which I was unequipped.

Once Vickey arrived on the scene, I began to slowly emerge from the ruthless character coma. Over time, she gently corrected the fatal flaws while showing me how to lead by example with an abundant attitude. I worked much harder to be a role model, both at home and at work.

At first it was unnatural, but I quickly learned to talk the talk and walk the walk. When I began to lead by example putting other people's interests ahead of my own, I discovered how gratifying it was to see others *reach higher* and succeed.

I make a conscious effort every day to be the poster child for the sign that hangs in Chip's kitchen that reads, "There is never a right time to do the wrong thing." The team inspires me when I see them leading by example or serving as a role model.

Edward B. Wile

Weakness of attitude becomes weakness of character.

—Albert Einstein

There are two types of attitudes: scarcity and abundance. Attitude influences motivation, inspiration, happiness, and success. Life is too short to spend precious time around people with bad attitudes. Their glass is always half empty, and they spend all their time complaining. They are losers and live in a world of scarcity. They lack serious motivation and are always looking to build their reputations on the backs of others or on the promise of what they are going to do instead of what they actually do.

It is better to surrounded yourself with people of character who possessed good attitudes. Their glasses are always half full, and think in terms of abundance. They are good for morale, work harder, have more fun, and are almost always successful. They do not let the things they cannot do interfere with the things they can do. They see opportunities in every problem instead of problems in every opportunity.

They are better partners, and are much more likely to achieve greatness when greatness is expected of them. Lou Holtz summed it up well: "Ability is what you are capable of doing. Motivation determines what you do. Attitude determines how well you do it."

You have to do your best to be your best.

—Laura E. Little

In that final lecture in graduate school, Dr. Mike Mescon hammered home the fact that an important part of success is simply showing up. That is true, but I have watched many very intelligent, talented people fall on their swords. They were not on time and did not come dressed to play. Stephen King was referring them when he said, "Talent is a wonderful thing, but it won't carry a quitter."

You can determine an employee's talent and character during their first week on the job. It is simple: you only have to observe when one arrives at and departs from work. It is true that the early bird catches the worm, and you should choose to be in the trenches with people who show up early and stay late. It is amazing how far good people, hard work, direct communications, honesty, and clear vision can take you.

Whether it was at home or work, there was never any doubt about the expectations. I have been told that I am hard to please, even by the best. I expect people to always *reach higher*, so I find those comments gratifying.

I am blessed that Grandma planted the "you have to do your best to be your best" seeds in my consciousness as a child. She was a precious lady and somehow made it a part of every conversation. Even though she was in heaven when the seeds finally sprouted, I know she is smiling.

There is nothing on this earth more to be prized than true friendship.

—Thomas Aquinas

This is not a Wileism, but it should be. Over my lifetime, I have found true friendships to be extremely underrated. In 1995, I initiated a small golf event that would become fondly known as the Kiawah Cup. It would be an event hosted for and with good friends. It turned into a wonderful event that took on a life of its own.

The twenty five trips have now taken us to some of the world's most prominent golf venues. As a fiercely competitive small gang, the group shared a unique camaraderie. We partied together, and I discovered that you did not really know someone until you played a round of golf and drank dirty vodka martinis on the rocks at Kiawah, expensive red wines at Pebble Beach, a yard of beer at the Broadmoor's Golden Bee, or Texas margaritas at Whistling Straits or Bandon Dunes with them. Those friendships, memories, crazy experiences, and the resulting drunk bet stories kept us all coming back for more.

You often do not appreciate how important something is until you believe you are going to lose it. Friendships are that way. The men of the Kiawah Cup became the brothers I never had. When John Mansfield, Bill Ervin, and Albert Harris each suffered life threatening events and illnesses, Mackie Horton, Tommy Millner, Allen Wright, Walter

McClelland, Joey Wright, and I were present. Those health scares showed me that true friendships are fragile, and are among life's most precious gifts. They should never be marginalized or taken for granted because when they are gone they are lost forever. I am grateful to the Kiawah Cup brotherhood for teaching me how to be a true friend.

Although the Wileisms seem to be focused mostly on advancing careers and developing business, those simple lessons came home with me every night. They would become me, and I would become them, and they provided valuable context for family issues and opportunities. I used them to teach at home, but with little parental training, it was not always an easy task. Thank goodness Vickey was present to ensure that we got the messages right.

I found parenting to be a challenging job, and I always questioned how we were doing. One day, with great trepidation, I asked, "Vickey, when will we receive our final parenting grades?"

"They have yet to be issued," she quickly answered.

"When do you think we might know something?" I asked.

"Never, silly. We will never receive an earthly evaluation or grade. We will not know anything for sure until we get to heaven, so stop holding your breath unless you are ready to go now. If you must know, just look at them. From my vantage point, they appear to be good citizens of the world, and as professionals and parents, they are doing well. I think that we are passing with flying colors. Why do you think we have been blessed with seven healthy grandchildren?" she answered with a big smile and continued. "There is a reason! They are the precious rewards for a job well done, but our parent and grandparent work is never finished. There is still much to do, so just sit back, relax, and enjoy the ride."

Neither of our children moved back home after college. That should be no surprise, because Vickey made the children her life's work. First and foremost, they knew right from wrong. They knew what to do and what was expected. She is an amazing woman and has done a marvelous job of providing our grandchildren with capable caring parents.

Laura graduated from the University of Georgia in 2001 with honors and joined UBS Financial Services Inc. in Atlanta, Georgia, where she has worked her entire career. I hired her, and she accepted the job out of desperation. She proved to be invaluable, and I was blessed to have the opportunity to work with her every day for thirteen years.

Today, Laura is a senior vice president at UBS. In 2015, she was recognized by *Barron's* as one of the top one hundred women financial advisors in the United States. She ranked forty-nine and is among the youngest in the group. In 2017, *Forbes* named her as one of America's top two hundred women financial advisors. She leads the team at the Wile Consulting Group responsible for wealth management duties.

She has a big heart and is charitably minded, serving on the boards of the Fellowship of Christian Athletes and Children's Healthcare of Atlanta. It is gratifying to see how she gracefully manages her life, never allowing business to trump family. Laura married Robert Wellon in 2001, and they have four children.

Chip graduated from the University of Georgia in 2002 and followed his passion in sports management. He moved to High Point, North Carolina, to join a company in an entry level position. His job was to set up and manage the Viagra tent for Mark Martin's NASCAR team. We were concerned about the longer term career prospects, but it was his choice. It was a small job, but he used the opportunity to prove himself and forged many meaningful NASCAR relationships.

During his career, he has been fortunate to have connected with some great mentors—people like Roger Bayer, Bill Davis, Roger Penske, Tommy Millner, Steve Turner, and David Hyatt. They helped him see the world through their eyes, in ways that made him different. When we talked at night, it was interesting to hear how he was resolving problems and capitalizing on opportunities. He seemed wise beyond his years.

On August 22, 2013, Chip was named the ninth president of Darlington Raceway, a historic NASCAR track in Darlington, South Carolina. At thirty-three years old, he was the youngest president of a NASCAR track ever. In three years, he helped Darlington regain its historical significance, glory, and prominence as "The Track Too Tough to Tame." On April 25, 2016, Chip was promoted and assumed the role of president of Daytona International Speedway, NASCAR's center stage. In 2017, the *SportsBusiness Journal* named Chip as a "40 under 40" honoree and in 2018 the University of Georgia named him as "40 under 40" honoree.

As I watch him grow, I am humbled by his balanced drive for success and his care for others, but I am most gratified by his behavior as a father and husband. Chip married Catherine Rigsby in 2003, and they have three children.

Sixteen

UNDERSTANDING

You can have almost anything in the world that you want, as long as you are willing to help everyone along the way get what they want first.

—Edward B. Wile

When the day came, I was anxious, but as promised, I followed Vickey up the mountain's Whiskey Route. Neither of us knew what to expect. We were unsure if we were going to enjoy the thrill of victory or suffer the agony of defeat. All we knew for sure was that we would have to trust our leaders to show us the way.

The trip did not start out well. Two hours into the climb, Vickey was looking for a bathroom. The guides informed us that there was a new outhouse on the trail just ahead. When we arrived, Vickey grabbed my backpack, which contained the toilet paper, and rushed into the ladies' room. When she pulled out the role of toilet paper, my BlackBerry jumped out and skidded across the floor into a small hole that served as the outhouse toilet.

We were going to be out of the country for a month, and the BlackBerry was our only means of communication with the children, who were concerned that we were going to die on the climb. I immediately rushed into the ladies' room and got down on my hands and knees to examine the hole and discovered that it was far too deep and nasty to recover the phone. I was frustrated with her apparent carelessness and exploded. I was livid at what I considered absolute stupidity. I stomped around in anger and said many bad words. When I regained my composure, I concluded that this must have happened for a reason, and apologized to Vickey and the crew.

That evening, when we got to our first camp, she sincerely apologized for her carelessness but then laughed. "You should have seen it. It was like a perfect putt. Once it popped out of your backpack, there was never a doubt about its destination as it rolled twenty feet across the smooth, wet tile floor, making its way directly into the center of the hole. Tiger Woods would have been proud."

Day One—Machame Camp, Elevation 9,350 Feet

The first day, we hiked for seven miles, and it took over six hours to reach the first camp. The experience was nothing like I had expected. The climbing process was formal, with strict rules and regulations. We could not climb without a permit, and we were required to sign in with our guide each night at the ranger station, without fail. We were permitted to camp only in designated areas, which were limited. The various climbing routes came together each day into common camps, which accommodated two hundred or so campers.

I had visualized the trip as a slow walk in the park, because that was how my friend Steve Isaf had described it. The first day we hiked through the thick rain forests. It was cloudy with a light mist, the temperatures were pleasant, the terrain was lush, and the trails were steep and muddy. We saw some small monkeys and other wildlife. It was more difficult than I had anticipated, but it in no way prepared us for what was ahead.

When we got to camp, we spent time visiting with the crew. They spoke some English and were able to teach us just enough Swahili to communicate with them. We were exhausted, and after dinner, we made our way to our small two person pup tent, climbed into our sleeping bags, and retired for the night.

Day Two—Shira Camp, Elevation 12,500 Feet

The next morning we were up in time to see the first rays of sunshine. After breakfast, we hiked for six hours, with short hydration breaks every hour. We stopped at noon for a lunch break. This day's hike was relatively steep with more large boulders, and the difficulty seemed to increase as the day progressed.

Day two confirmed that this was not going to be a walk in the park. The weather turned colder, and the vegetation gradually disappeared. The conditions worsened, but the views were majestic. As we waited for dinner that evening, the guides told us all about Lava Tower to prepare us for the next day's climb.

We walked around the camp that evening admiring the beauty of our surroundings. We appeared to be the only people from the United States in the camp. After dinner, we joined the crew to watch the sun go down.

That day, we had experienced the sunrise and sunset and were totally exhausted. We retired to our tent for what would be a more difficult night of sleep. The thinning air was beginning to wreak havoc on our bodies. Temperatures were dropping, our appetites were slowly disappearing, and the uncertainty of our final destination weighed heavily on my mind.

Day Three—Barranco Camp, Elevation 13,044 Feet

The next morning, we got up, had breakfast, and hiked through the Garden of the Senecios up to Lava Tower and the Shark's Tooth rock, elevation 15,190 feet, and back down the southern circuit to our camp. The day was long, and we covered more than seven miles. It was cloudy in the morning—one of those soupy days. Without the sun, it was obviously much cooler, and this was the first time I noticed any significant chill in the air. It became uncomfortable, and during the second hydration break, we added another layer of clothing. We were told that it would get much colder as the trip progressed.

When we reached Lava Tower, we had a casual lunch. We took some time to look around and take pictures before we hiked on to our next camp. We had hiked all day, and we were told that it was arguably one of the most important climbing days of the trip because it gave us the opportunity to climb high and sleep low, which was important for proper acclimatization. From camp, we could see the Barranco Wall in the distance, across the scrub brushed valley. It was a daunting sight: a sheer granite face that appeared to rise straight up into the sky. The sun finally came out late in the afternoon and warmed things up. We had a quick dinner, and the guides encouraged us to stay up for the sunset. As the sun disappeared on the horizon, the rays reflected uniquely on the face of the mountain and the beautiful colorful sunset was well worth the wait.

At the time, I was unaware that we would have to climb that intimidating mountain face first thing the next morning. Had I known what was in store for us, I would have been up all night.

Day Four—Karanga Camp, Elevation 13,106 Feet

We had a small breakfast and then hiked through the valley and crossed a small stream, which led directly to base of the Barranco Wall. For the next two hours, we climbed straight up, across, and around the face of the wall. We were required to navigate the large rocks, traverse the narrow ledges, and hike the steep cliffs. We did a lot of what the guides and marketing brochures simply referred to as "rock scrambling."

Vickey had no trouble and seemed to enjoy the experience. For me, it was a different story. Those exercises without harnesses or safety ropes on the edge of the mountain were near death experiences. I knew that one slip, miss, or stumble, and I was done.

After scaling the Barranco Wall we hiked another four hours to the next camp. When we arrived, our guide Francis pointed to a peak in the distance and suggested that we hike to that peak and back. He said it would take two hours, and was essential to building our altitude acclimatization and stamina.

When we finally returned to camp, I noticed that giant black and white ravens had joined the party. They seemed to appear out of nowhere. We learned that they inhabited the higher altitudes and served as the mountain's garbage collectors. They were enormous birds with wingspans of more than three feet. When they flew, we could hear and feel the whooshing of their wings, and they looked like baby dinosaurs in the sky.

I was exhausted, and when we sat down to dinner, I had no appetite and I noticed that Vickey did not eat much either. We were discovering the altitude's dramatic effect on our appetites.

Day Five—Barafu Camp, Elevation 15,331 Feet

We could now see the snowcapped mountain in the distance, and it was daunting. We got up early the next morning, had a cup of coffee and headed for the next base camp. We arrived around two o'clock in the afternoon, and Vendelin suggested another training exercise. I quickly pointed out that I had trained enough and that I was done for the day. I did not disclose that I was suffering severe hip pains, because I did not want Vickey to know because she would worry.

We had a light midafternoon meal and then met with our guides for final instructions. We learned that we would start the ascent that night at half past eleven. We had come a long way and were excited but anxious about the ascent challenges. There were many questions but none more important than the obvious. Would we be able to complete the grueling climb to the top?

Day Six—Millennium Camp, Elevation 12,590 Feet

We took a short nap and were up, packed, and ready to go at eleven o'clock. We enjoyed a breakfast that included a hot cup of tea and biscuit, and left Barafu Camp on time. As we started on our journey, the guides warned us to keep our water bottles in our coats to prevent them from freezing.

We knew it would take approximately eight hours to get to Stella Point, elevation 18,885 feet. It was pitch black dark, and we required headlights to see the narrow trails and to avoid the eminent dangers of falling off the mountain.

We left the camp and hiked across the sandy plains to the trail leading up the mountain. We would follow that trail and make our way up and over the boulders and through the heavy scree as we systematically zigzagged our way up the mountain. We were a couple of hours into the hike when I remembered a conversation that Steve Isaf and I had during one of our preparation dinners in Atlanta.

When I learned that Steve and his family had successfully ascended the previous year, I invited him and his wife, Cindy, to dinner. Over the next year, they helped equip and prepare us for the trip. During our first dinner, we talked about the experience. Steve was quick to share his Lebanese humor and said, "On the final night, under no circumstances do you want to look up the mountain for the people ahead of you." "Look up? Why would you want to look up?" I asked.

"You will be curious to see how far you have traveled and wonder how much farther you have to go. It is a natural reaction, but you should avoid the temptation, at all costs."

I was still unclear exactly what he meant and asked, "Steve, please tell me why."

"Because it will cause you to become terribly discouraged."
"Discouraged? Terribly discouraged? Why?"

"Because at that moment, you will discover that the mountain is gigantic, bigger and taller than you ever imagined. When you look up in the darkness of night, all you can see are the headlights of the climbers ahead of you. They will be straight up, almost vertical into the sky, and nearly out of sight. Some will be so far ahead of you that their lights will be dim and hard to see. That sight will overwhelm you, and you will begin to question if it is even possible to get from you to them," he said in a very serious tone, but after a few seconds, he broke out laughing.

"All kidding aside, the day you go to the top is grueling. The ascent to the top will challenge you both physically and mentally, in ways that you never imagined. You will be oxygen deprived, which will take an unexpected toll on your mind and your body." "I will not look up," I promised.

Mean to Meaningful

"Yes, you will. There is actually no way to avoid it. I was warned, and I knew the consequences, and I still looked up," he said with a smile.

Steve was right. I tried my best, but the curiosity was just too great.

During the trip, Vendelin shared many stories about climbers who did not make it to the top. Many of them got within spitting distance. His assessment was that they could see the finish line but did not have the stamina or the heart to make the final charge.

I found the stories of failure sad, but then he offered an inspiring tale about an older lady who was climbing with her children. "She was the poster child for *pole pole* [pronounced *polay,* this is a Swahili expression that means going slowly]. She was by far my slowest climber ever. She was the first hiker to leave in the morning, and she was the last hiker into camp at night. After a few days, *pole pole* made it necessary for me to become her personal guide. She worked hard, and I was committed to helping her finish well. She struggled and many times along the way, I thought she was done, but she never quit. She continued with sheer unadulterated determination and fought her way to the top. She was an amazing lady whom I came to really admire."

After reflecting on the many stories, I started to question how our climb might end. I had always assumed we would make it to the top, but now I started to think about the other possible outcomes. It was dawn, and we still had an hour or so until we reached Stella Point. We were running a little behind schedule due to *pole pole*. When the sun came up we could see our base camp. We had climbed almost four thousand feet in elevation and hiked over five miles, and Stella Point was now in sight.

The air was thin and I was nearly out of gas, but I continued to follow Vickey and the guides up the mountain. I was physically exhausted to the point that I had to rest every few minutes. During each stop, I thought to myself, "Am I going to make it?" I glanced down at my watch and saw that we had been hiking for eight hours.

My body suffered from the physical stress and was fatigued by the lack of oxygen. I continued in spite of the physical pain and sheer exhaustion until we finally reached Stella Point. Once we arrived, we sat down, rested, and enjoyed a gourmet lunch: a frozen peanut butter sandwich, a banana, and a hard-boiled egg. After we took pictures and celebrated, we continued the quest to Uhuru Peak. It was clearly visible in the distance—but still another one mile hike and 453 feet of elevation away.

As we started up the trail, I suddenly stopped in my tracks and fell to my knees. I was exhausted. I thought about what it would take to complete the journey and realized that our hiking day was only half over. We still had to make the trip back down the mountain. I motioned for Vickey, and she came over and hugged me.

"Are you all right?" she asked.

"No, I am done. I cannot make it to Uhuru. I have to save what energy I have left for the hike down. At this point, I am not sure I can even make it back to the base camp. I want you to go to Uhuru. I can wait here for you and rest."

"No way! We promised to do this together or not at all," she said. "We have summited Stella Point, so if you are unable to continue, I believe it is best that we start down. You are right. The day is only half over, and it is going to be a long and grueling descent."

She turned and started her descent. Vendelin, who had watched me struggle for the past few hours, walked over to check on me. He knew what was happening because he had seen it many times before. He kneeled down, smiled and put his hands on my shoulders, and looked directly into my eyes. He waited for quite some time before he spoke. I knew what he was going to say was important, because it was one of those slow motion moments. "Ed, you know that Vickey wants to go to the top." He paused. "And so do you!" He leaned back to check that his words were connecting. I must have been blurry eyed, because he allowed plenty of time for the message to be absorbed by my oxygen deprived brain, and then he delivered the final punch. "If both of you do not go to Uhuru today, you will regret it for the rest of your life. I know that you are no quitter. When we met and started this journey, you asked me to show you the way. No, you *told* me to just show you the way. I promised you that I would, so I want to be sure that you know the way, right now," he said as he slowly raised his arm and pointed to Uhuru.

I digested Vendelin's shrewd advice. I knew what he meant, and that he was right. If we did not go to Uhuru today, it would haunt me for the rest of my life.

I called out to Vickey, "Stop! Please come back! Vendelin says that we must go to the top. He says there will be no quitting today." Vickey turned around, smiled, and immediately started back up the mountain. Vendelin was right. She wanted to go all the way. I followed her, step by excruciating step, to the top. It was a long tough hike, but we finally and safely reached the very top of Mount Kilimanjaro at nine o'clock in the morning on Monday, July 21, 2014.

It was exhilarating. We wished we could have stayed longer, but the guides insisted that we begin our descent. We had to sleep below 15,000 feet, and at our pace we would be challenged to get to our new base camp before dark. The views from the top of the world were astounding as we viewed the sky and the clouds over a glacier on one side and the volcano's deep crater on the other. We took our pictures and expeditiously started our descent.

It was a five hour hike to Barafu Camp, where we planned to get a quick snack. Since we could not sleep at that elevation, we planned to hike another couple of hours to the Millennium Camp, elevation 12,590 feet, where we would spend the night.

For me, it was a difficult trek down. The hip pains worsened, and I was slow. We decided after several hours that it might be better and quicker if we split up, so we each took a guide. Vickey took Vendelin, and I took Francis. They arrived back at the Barafu Camp more than an hour before us.

I struggled with the rocks and the scree, but continued. My hip worsened from the downward forces, and the pain became almost unbearable. Every step was a job. When I got to the Barafu Camp, I collapsed on the ground and crawled into a small tent to join Vickey.

I was in excruciating pain, and she knew it was serious when I said, "I need a helicopter." She laughed out loud, and I told her that I was not being funny. I was serious. We briefly discussed the excruciating hip pains. She gave me some miracle drugs and left the tent to talk with the guides. She briefed Francis and Vendelin on the situation.

At that point, she became my personal caretaker, and she was large and in charge. I could hear their discussion just ten feet away. "Ed says that he wants a helicopter," Vickey laughed.

Vendelin frowned and said, "That is not an option. Nothing with a motor is permitted on the mountain. It is against park rules."

Francis weighed in and said, "Just so you know, he is really struggling. He is relying heavily on the hiking poles and is very slow. I doubt that he can continue. I believe it will be a miracle if he can even make it to the next camp."

Vickey thought for a moment. "You may be right. The pain must be really bad, because Ed never complains."

"We can get a gurney if he really wants one, and we can carry him out, but if he does not leave under his own power, I know that he will not be happy," Vendelin said.

"I will give Ed his choices and let him decide how he wants to proceed," Vickey said.

She crawled back into the tent, sat down beside me, and held my hand. "There will be no helicopter. You heard the conversation and you know your options. What do you want to do? Do you want me to ask them to get a stretcher? Are you going to quit? Is that how you really want this journey to end? Talk to me. I need to know your thoughts."

"No stretcher. I plan to finish what we started, if that is all right with you. I will walk off this mountain under my own power. That is how I want this journey to end," I said with a smile.

Vickey chuckled and said, "Then you'd better get up off that fat ass and start hiking if you want to make it to our next camp before dark."

I slowly crawled out of the tent, struggled to my feet, and gasped out the words that had served as my compass for a lifetime: "Just show me the way." Vendelin smiled and again pointed me in the right direction.

With a renewed attitude and some miracle drugs, I had no problem keeping up. We hiked down the mountain to the Millennium Camp, elevation 12,590 feet, had a bowl of noodle soup, and went to bed.

Day Seven—Mweka Gate, Elevation 5,380 Feet

We were up early, enjoyed a small breakfast, and hiked off the mountain through the Mweka Gate without incident. When we checked out of the park we received our official Mount Kilimanjaro gold certificates, documenting the achievement. We then proceeded to a surprise celebratory lunch. I was never so excited to see a box lunch and real Coca Colas.

After lunch, we participated in a celebration hosted by the crew. It was quite an event with native songs and dances. Vickey was enjoying the last hour with her guides and was in the middle of the gala. She was happy to have completed the climb but sad to be leaving the men who had been so kind and attentive to her.

To my surprise, Vickey had a white T-shirt and a black Sharpie in her backpack. As the colorful celebration was concluding, she got the shirt out of her backpack and showed it to the men and said, "I would like for each of you to sign this shirt. It will allow me to always remain close to you, the special men who took me to the 'Roof of Africa' and back."

We gathered for the final act. I was in charge of giving the men their tips, which was a significant portion of their compensation. We had two tables set up on opposite ends of the yard. One table was for the men to sign for and receive their money, and the other was for the men to sign Vickey's T-shirt. We had twenty-three porters on the trip. When the tables were set and the men lined up, there were twenty-one in Vickey's line waiting to sign her shirt and only two in the money line.

We then boarded the bus and headed back to the Dik Dik Lodge. We celebrated together, but we went our own ways at the end of the day. Some of the men got off the bus in their villages, and others left us shortly after we arrived at the lodge. The trip ended as it had begun.

We spent that night at the Dik Dik Lodge and thoroughly enjoyed the many creature comforts that had been missing on the mountain—things like a solid roof over our heads, heat, fresh food, soft pillows, a real bed, fresh linens, clean blankets, and a real bathroom, but especially the long, warm, soapy showers and clean, fresh bath towels. Together we had lost more than forty pounds, but this was not a weight loss program that I would personally recommend.

Kilimanjaro was a challenging and an exhilarating experience. The climb was very different from what I had imagined. It was more physical and mental than I had ever expected—but the pain was worth the gain. Thank goodness Vendelin and Francis were there to guide us. I am certain that absent their gentle encouragement and skillful prodding we would have never made it to the "Roof of Africa" and back.

The next day on the drive to the airport, I could not help but think about the climb to the top. In so many ways, it seemed to mirror another familiar journey.

As we started up the mountain, I recalled childhood memories of being angry and confused, just trying to find the way with no idea of what would be expected or whom to turn for advice and guidance. It was a dark time, but the lights began to flicker when I chose to go to college.

As we progressed up the mountain to the famous Lava Rock, I was reminded of the early business successes. It was a happy time, but as the climb became more difficult I was painfully reminded of the feelings of failure when I was fired.

On the final days of the climb, I reflected back on my UBS career and concluded that the most impactful discoveries had occurred after I already knew everything. For example, I now know that the best leaders lead by example. It is how they earn success, respect, and power, because there is no other honorable way to get it. I know that people want to know how much you care before they care how much you know; that my word is my bond, and more valuable than gold and silver; that a major part of success is just showing up; that looking the part is important, and you will never get a second chance to make a first impression; that without a process everything is harder than it needs to be; that discipline often trumps intelligence; that saving and establishing wealth are more important than having the nicest clothes, the newest car, or the biggest house; that attitude is a personal choice every day, and that an attitude of abundance is more powerful than one of scarcity. I know that it is important to give more than you get; that the sharing of our time, treasures, and talents is good stewardship; that helping people help themselves, as difficult as it may be at times, is just part of the job; that character is born out of actions; that accountability and trust come from doing what you say you are going to do; that there is no such thing as entitlement; that uncommon wisdom is priceless; that it is far less important to get it right than it is to get it wrong; and that the golden rule should be the foundation of every decision in life.

I am not that smart, and had to learn a good bit of this stuff in the school of hard knocks, but as I sit here today, finishing this book, it all seems so simple.

In closing, I would like to thank those who took a personal interest in the journey and were willing to share their precious time, treasures and talents. Why, I do not know, but I do know that their care, guidance and generosity allowed me to grow up with dignity and have the opportunity to participate in the great American dream. Those people include Joan Jewell, Laura Little, Diana Montgomery, Virgil Nelson, Ron Baus, Milo Messmore, Don Sigler, Don Morrison, Jack Peterson, Fisher DeBerry, Vera Parsons, Jerry Richardson, Ernest Key, Dan Maultsby, Barbara Jeanne Key, Joe Lesesne, Walt Sessoms, Lewis Holland, Jim Reese, Harold Chandler, Tom Bower, and, of course, Vickey Wile. I am eternally grateful to each of them for providing a hand up.

If you have any questions or comments about the journey or discover that I can help you in any way please feel free to email me at edward.wile@gmail.com. Thank you.

The End

Epilogue

I still have an important piece of unfinished business that goes back to the summer of 2006. We were completing a $105 million Wofford College capital campaign that was chaired by Jerry Richardson, the founder of the Carolina Panthers. We completed the campaign two years ahead of schedule, and it was a special night for the college.

After the grand celebration, Harold Chandler asked if I would like to help him with an athletic fund raising project. Harold was a former football teammate, and I was honored that he would consider me a worthy partner. Harold was a Phi Beta Kappa, valedictorian, and Rhodes Scholar finalist, and I had barely graduated. I eagerly accepted Harold's offer without much thought.

I would soon discover that Harold's project was a bold vision. He suggested that we begin a quest to fully endow all the athletic programs. We had both attended Wofford College on athletic scholarships that were provided by generous local donors. We could not have attended college without them.

When I got around to doing the math, I realized that it would take over $200 million of new endowment. Back then, the athletic endowment was almost nonexistent.

Harold's vision was an institution changing strategy. It would provide a valuable opportunity to educate, inspire, and engage alumni and friends to strengthen an aspiring culture of appreciation and promote an emerging pay it forward legacy.

It was clear that we would have to lead by example and encourage others to get involved and be generous until it felt good. As Walt said, "It costs more to feel good, a lot more." After considerable discussion, we decided to go to Charlotte, North Carolina, and share the vision with our friend Jerry Richardson and get his thoughts.

Jerry is among the most influential alumni of the college. We arrived early in the morning and spent the day talking, brainstorming, and visiting with him. He is a humble, quietly generous man known for his straightforward common sense. At the end of the meeting Jerry encouraged us to "just do it."

He then wished us the best of luck, offered his support, endowed the first scholarship, and then called a friend who would endow a second football scholarship to honor our friend Corry Oakes. We were off to a good start, and with his guidance, support, and encouragement, we embarked on the journey full speed ahead.

We have made excellent progress over the past decade. With the support of Richard Johnson and many others we are now approaching $50 million. This is a good beginning, but there is still much work to be done.

Our family is committed to this project and therefore, all book royalties from *Mean to Meaningful* will be donated to the athletic endowment fund at Wofford College to assist student athletes who might need a hand up.

Acknowledgements

I want to first thank our children Laura Wellon and Chip Wile for giving us permission to candidly share our family journey. Without their colorful stories there would be no book. I want them both to know what an unexpected delight it was for their mom and dad to discuss and relive those many rich childhood experiences. It was a nice walk down memory lane.

I am grateful to my friend Greg Vistica, who for over a decade, provided the necessary inspiration, guidance and advice to keep me going. His priceless experience as a successful author and celebrated skills as an investigative reporter with *The Washington Post* were invaluable. Absent his encouragement and friendship this book project would have surely died.

Completing this book is a tribute to Vickey Wile, my precious brown eyed girl. She is a remarkable person, and I am blessed to have her as my wife and best friend. The love and care that she exhibited throughout this seemingly endless project was incredible. I am certain that without her constant encouragement and brilliant coaching I would have never made it to the goal line.

Made in the USA
Middletown, DE
15 February 2020